# THE SENSE
# OF REALITY

# THE SENSE
# OF REALITY

*Studies in Ideas and their History*

ISAIAH BERLIN

Edited by Henry Hardy
With an introduction by Patrick Gardiner

Chatto & Windus
London

First published in 1996

1 3 5 7 9 10 8 6 4 2

Copyright © Isaiah Berlin 1996
Selection and editorial matter © Henry Hardy 1996
Introduction © Patrick Gardiner 1996

Isaiah Berlin has asserted his right under the Copyright,
Designs and Patents Act, 1988, to be identified as the author
of this work, Henry Hardy as its editor

First published in Great Britain in 1996 by
Chatto & Windus Limited
Random House, 20 Vauxhall Bridge Road,
London SW1V 2SA

Random House Australia (Pty) Limited
20 Alfred Street, Milsons Point, Sydney
New South Wales 2061, Australia

Random House New Zealand Limited
18 Poland Road, Glenfield
Auckland 10, New Zealand

Random House South Africa (Pty) Limited
PO Box 337, Bergvlei, South Africa

Random House UK Limited Reg. No 954009

Papers used by Random House UK Limited are natural, recyclable
products made from wood grown in sustainable forests. The
manufacturing processes conform to the environmental
regulations of the country of origin

A CIP catalogue record for this book
is available from the British Library

ISBN 0 7011 6579 0

Typeset by Deltatype Ltd, Birkenhead, Merseyside
Printed in Great Britain by
Mackays of Chatham, Chatham, Kent

For Alfred and Irene Brendel

# CONTENTS

# EDITOR'S PREFACE

DURING the last six years I have had the privilege of assembling and editing Isaiah Berlin's extensive unpublished work: essays, addresses, lectures, broadcasts and discussions (categories that are of course not mutually exclusive) spanning the last sixty years and more. My sometimes elusive sources have included manuscripts and typescripts, recordings (often unscripted),[1] and transcripts – very various in accuracy – of recordings that no longer exist. The edited typescripts I have accumulated are approximately equal in extent (at some one million words) to Berlin's hitherto published work.

Two long studies drawn from this corpus of material, on Joseph de Maistre and J. G. Hamann,[2] have already been published, and the nine pieces selected for inclusion in the present volume are from the same source. They and their harbingers have three properties in common. First, they existed as more or less finished scripts, most if not all of which had been thought of by Berlin at the time of composition as potentially publishable, though for one reason or another they had escaped being printed. Secondly, they seem to me, and to others who have read them, fully to deserve addition to Berlin's published *oeuvre* – to put it no less modestly. Finally, they are linked thematically, in that they all exemplify his central concern with ideas and their history, as my subtitle indicates. My hope is that more of the unpublished material will in due course see the light, and that more of Berlin's published but hitherto uncollected writings will be brought together; but with a

[1] I have deposited copies of the recordings at the National Sound Archive in London.

[2] 'Joseph de Maistre and the Origins of Fascism', in *The Crooked Timber of Humanity: Chapters in the History of Ideas* (London, 1990; New York, 1991); and *The Magus of the North: J. G. Hamann and the Origins of Modern Irrationalism* (London, 1993; New York, 1994).

few exceptions – chiefly his pieces on Soviet Russia and on Zionism – the present volume, added to its predecessors,[1] completes the collective publication of Berlin's more finished longer essays.

I turn now to the origins of the pieces. 'The Sense of Reality' was the basis for the first Elizabeth Cutter Morrow Lecture, delivered on 9 October 1953 at Smith College, Northampton, Massachusetts, under the title 'Realism in History'; some of the matters it deals with have been touched on by Berlin in other essays, for example 'The Hedgehog and the Fox' and 'The Concept of Scientific History', but this is his most sustained treatment, and clearly merits a place in this collection. 'Political Judgement', which also has points of contact with 'The Sense of Reality', but from a distinctively political angle, was a talk (the sixth in a series of seven entitled 'Thinking about Politics') first broadcast on 19 June 1957 on the Third Programme of the BBC: the text is jointly based on a prepared script and on a recording of the broadcast. 'Philosophy and Government Repression' was a lecture prepared for a series entitled 'Man's Right to Freedom of Thought and Expression', which was part of the bicentennial celebrations at Columbia University, New York; the lecture was scheduled for 24 March 1954, but in the event Berlin was unable to attend. 'Socialism and Socialist Theories' differs from the other pieces by having appeared in print at the time it was written: it was first published in *Chambers's Encyclopaedia* (London, 1950: Newnes; New York, 1950: Oxford University Press), and in a revised form in a subsequent edition of the same work (Oxford, New York etc., 1966: Pergamon); the present version incorporates further revisions intended for a new edition of the encyclopaedia which never appeared, and is included partly for that reason, partly because it has not previously been collected, and partly because of its appropriate subject-matter. 'Marxism and the International in the Nineteenth Century' was the basis of a lecture given at Stanford University in 1964 at a conference held to mark the centenary of the First International Working Men's Association. 'The Romantic Revolution' was written for a conference in Rome in March 1960, where it was delivered in an Italian translation: during the long gestation of this book the Italian text has appeared in Isaiah Berlin, *Tra la filosofia e la storia delle idee: intervista autobiografica*, ed.

---

[1] Listed opposite the title page.

Steven Lukes (Florence, 1994: Ponte alle Grazie), and Dutch and German translations of the original English text in, respectively, *Nexus* and *Lettre international*. 'Artistic Commitment' is a revised version of a talk first given in the United States in the early 1960s. 'Kant as an Unfamiliar Source of Nationalism' was the First Humayun Kabir Memorial Lecture, delivered in New Delhi in 1972. 'Rabindranath Tagore and the Consciousness of Nationality' was also delivered in New Delhi, on 13 November 1961, at a conference held to mark the centenary of Tagore's birth.

As in the case of previous volumes, I have received generous and indispensable help from a number of scholars, to whom I offer my very grateful thanks. Patrick Gardiner (to whom I am also indebted for his excellent introduction) and Roger Hausheer read all the essays that I chose, as well as a number that I didn't, and helped me both to make the selection and to solve a number of specific textual problems. Professor G. A. Cohen read and commented on the pieces on socialism and Marxism, helping me to convince Berlin, who is irremediably sceptical about his work, that they should be included; and Professor Terrell Carver, among other acts of intellectual largesse, has enabled me to add references to the latter essay. Dr Gunnar Beck helped invaluably with Fichte, Andrew Robinson with Tagore, Professor Frank Seeley with Turgenev, Dr Ralph Walker with Kant, Helen McCurdy with several Russian problems. Dr Derek Offord put his expert knowledge of Belinsky and other Russian authors at my disposal with a truly heroic generosity, patience and effectiveness that leave me especially deeply in his debt. I also profited, not for the first time, from the prodigious learning of Dr Leofranc Holford-Strevens. Isaiah Berlin himself with considerable forbearance read and approved my edited text of all the pieces, making a number of revisions in the process. Without his secretary, Pat Utechin, nothing would be possible; and the same has been true since 1990 of the most generous benefactors who have financed my Fellowship at Wolfson College, and of Lord Bullock, at whose instigation the post was created for me. Finally, I should like to thank my editors at Chatto and Windus, Will Sulkin and Jenny Uglow, for their help and support; and Elisabeth Sifton of Farrar, Straus and Giroux for a careful reading of the typescript that yielded numerous refinements.

April 1996                                      HENRY HARDY
Wolfson College, Oxford

# INTRODUCTION

*Patrick Gardiner*

ISAIAH BERLIN's writings have impinged upon so many distinct spheres of thought and enquiry, and have ramified in such different and at times unexpected directions, that a question may be raised as to what leading conceptions have ultimately guided or held together his varied excursions into these apparently disparate intellectual domains. This is not as straightforward a question as it might look; indeed, in the eyes of some of his admirers it may seem to be quite inapposite, missing the essential point. For they might claim that much of the distinctive value of his achievement lies precisely in the notable absence it displays of any unitary ambitions or systematic pretensions; the range and sheer diversity of what he has written, involving amongst other things a constant readiness to consider on their own terms both sharply conflicting beliefs and the points of view of those holding them, have played a key role in enlarging the horizons of his readers and in loosening the grip of obstructive prejudices or dogmas. Berlin himself has characterised as 'doctrinaire' a person who is 'liable to suppress what he may, if he comes across it, suspect to be true', and it is certainly the case that his own outlook stands in complete contrast to this. Even so, and notwithstanding the openness and objectivity of approach he has consistently shown, it seems possible to discern in his work the outlines of particular preoccupations and themes that give it an inner coherence not the less impressive for being relatively unobtrusive and unemphatic. What at first sight may appear to be stray or unrelated strands in his thinking frequently turn out on closer examination to be threads in a wider pattern, forming parts of a more inclusive whole. They can be seen, in other words, as contributing to an intricate complex of subtly interconnected ideas rather than as belonging to the framework of some rigid theoretical system. Furthermore, the complex in question can itself be said to reflect the presence of certain overarching concerns whose pervasive influence has manifested itself in various ways throughout Berlin's intellectual career.

One of these recurrent concerns is with the nature and significance of history, a subject which is central to the title essay of the present collection. Berlin has often denied that he is or ever has been a historian, and it may be that there is some accepted if restrictive sense of the term in which this is so. The fact remains, however, that he has made a unique and celebrated contribution to the history of ideas and hence possesses an intimate working knowledge of issues and problems of the kind to which this branch of enquiry into the human past gives rise. Moreover, in pursuing his studies in eighteenth- and nineteenth-century thought he has inevitably been confronted by widely varying theories concerning both the character of the historical process and our cognisance of it. Thus when writing his first book, on Karl Marx, he was obliged not only to come to grips with Marx's own highly influential accounts of the forces governing historical change and development, but also to read the works of such important predecessors as Helvétius, Condorcet, Saint-Simon and Comte. In one way or another these writers shared the conviction, widely current among thinkers of the French Enlightenment, that scientific methods and categories of the type that had proved so successful in advancing our knowledge of the natural world should be extended to the study of humanity and its history. Berlin has described elsewhere how, in the course of investigating the sources of these and allied claims, he sought to understand from within the problems that obsessed those who had propounded them; the ideas of the past (he felt) could only be brought to life by 'entering into' the minds and viewpoints of the persons who held them and the social or cultural contexts to which they belonged. In following this procedure, however, he was aware of engaging in a kind of thinking that seemed far removed from what was proposed by the writers he was immediately concerned with, imaginative and empathetic understanding of the sort in question having no apparent parallels or analogues within the natural sciences. Where, on the other hand, he did discern a responsive echo was in the works of two eighteenth-century thinkers of quite a different cast of mind. Vico and Herder were in various respects conspicuously at odds with the prevailing temper of their time, and not least in their attitude to what they held to be the distinctive character of the historian's subject-matter.

This, in their view, made attempts to assimilate historical methodology to that of the sciences misconceived in principle. For
whereas in the case of the latter we could never obtain more than a
purely 'external' knowledge of the phenomena with which they
dealt, the cognitive relation in which we stood to the phenomena
specific to history was of a wholly dissimilar order. Here it was
possible to achieve a direct or inward grasp of the mental processes
that found expression in the doings and creations of historical
agents; the underlying humanity historians shared with those they
sought to comprehend enabled them to ascertain from the inside
what it was that moved and activated the subjects of their
enquiries, even when – as was frequently the case – this was a
matter of recapturing through imaginative effort the interior life of
other periods or cultures whose pervasive outlooks and preconceptions differed profoundly from their own. Both Vico and Herder,
albeit in varying ways, implied that such an approach was fundamental to any meaningful pursuit of the human studies, and it is a
conception of historical practice whose cardinal importance Berlin
– in common here with their twentieth-century admirer and
follower Collingwood – has likewise insisted upon.

The influence of such contentions, involving an emphasis on the
essential autonomy of historical thought and understanding, may
be said to lie behind some of the theses advanced in 'The Sense of
Reality', where the contrast drawn between history and other
disciplines recalls the attention Berlin has accorded to various
aspects of this complex topic in a number of notable essays.
Nevertheless, in the present instance he approaches it from a
direction that diverges in significant respects from ones taken in
some of his other discussions, his perspective here having more
general implications and encompassing practical as well as academic
issues. The title given to the piece is indeed indicative of this, and
partly reflects his characteristic suspicion of attempts to simplify,
or reduce to artificially abstract terms, the 'dark mass of factors'
that constitutes human existence, whether these are undertaken for
purely theoretical purposes or whether with a view to implementing comprehensive plans of a political or social nature. He has
always shown himself to be acutely aware of the perennial
fascination exercised by the prospect of discovering some infallible
formula or universal prescription capable of resolving the multifar-
ious problems presented by the human condition in a way that
would leave no loose ends or dangling uncertainties. And in this

connection he has also stressed the extent to which in the modern period – that is, roughly since the end of the seventeenth century – such an aspiration has often found expression in efforts to demonstrate that the historical process conforms to ineluctable laws or uniformities which can be understood to hold for the future as well as the past, thus possessing predictive as well as explanatory potential. But he considers none the less that the fascination alluded to represents a temptation which should be resisted, and that the difficulties underlying some of the projects it has given rise to are rooted in misunderstandings that extend beyond the bounds of historical interpretation and methodology, ultimately reaching into the depths and texture of all human life and experience.

As Berlin points out, historical theorising of the type he has in mind by no means conforms to a single pattern, representative accounts ranging from ones founded on mechanically-conceived regularities to others that invoke 'organic' or evolutionary laws of development. In the present context, however, his concern is not with distinguishing and commenting on different examples of the genre; rather it is that of questioning the whole notion of constructing a law-governed or systematic theory that would be capable of fitting into a unified scheme the multiplicity and variety of heterogeneous elements of which the historical process is composed. On the latter point he refers with approval to Tolstoy, and it is noteworthy that much that he says on this theme echoes the tone of the Russian writer's views on history as presented at the close of *War and Peace*. Not only did Tolstoy exhibit considerable scepticism with regard to the crude simplifications and bland generalities he attributed to the various philosophies of history and society that had so far been produced; he further implied that all projects involving the use of abstractions and schemata of the kind favoured by speculative theorists were bound in the end to founder, their being intrinsically unfitted to comprehend the continuum of 'infinitesimals' – the series of countless, minute and interrelated actions and events – that made up the life and story of humanity. In Berlin's own treatment of the subject one finds a similarly critical attitude taken up towards previous 'pseudo-scientific histories and theories of human behaviour', together with a comparable, though by no means identical, emphasis on the manner in which the dense material of history may be expected to resist the imposition of procedures originally adapted to radically different areas of concern and enquiry.

Such affinities are hardly surprising, Tolstoy's particular gifts as a creative writer making him in Berlin's eyes especially well equipped to appreciate the richness and diversity of human reality as it is lived and known: the endless variety and individuality of things and people, the subtle cross-currents of feeling involved in both social intercourse and personal relationships, the depths of self-regard and the confusions of aim lying beneath the surface of public life – these were amongst the myriad phenomena which his exceptional powers of observation and imagination captured and which led him to look through the smooth and regular outlines drawn by history's self-proclaimed interpreters to the uneven and often chaotic details of actual experience they concealed. As is well known, such aspects of Tolstoy's achievement are eloquently portrayed in Berlin's penetrating study, 'The Hedgehog and the Fox'. There, however, he was largely concerned to contrast Tolstoy's artistic insight and flair with another, quite opposite, side to his outlook and personality, one that hankered after some monistic or unitary truth which would altogether transcend the problems and distractions that plague our mundane existence. In the present context, on the other hand, he wishes to indicate the relevance of the novelist's specifically literary abilities to the essay's general theme, relating them not merely to the activities of historians engaged in reconstructing the past but also to those of politicians and so-called 'men of action' in their dealings with the world of practical affairs. Thus in 'Political Judgement', which follows 'The Sense of Reality' as a companion piece and elaborates on some of its points, Berlin suggests that qualities of mind analogous in certain respects to ones possessed by imaginative writers can be said to play a role both in the study of history and in the conduct of what he terms 'statecraft'. Like the trained historian, the effective politician needs a developed capacity for a 'non-generalising assessment of specific situations'; a finely attuned sensitivity to the shifting contours or levels of social existence, and, combined with this, an intuitive 'feel' for what is empirically feasible and for what hangs together with what in the intricate and frequently recalcitrant sphere of particular facts or circumstances, have perennially been amongst the distinctive characteristics of outstanding political leaders. Berlin notes that such 'practical

wisdom' or genius has tended to be treated by the great systemat-
isers of history as representing a haphazard 'pre-scientific'
approach which is no longer acceptable on theoretical grounds and
which stands in need of radical reform or replacement. But he also
points out that some of their proposed improvements can scarcely
be felt to have constituted an encouraging response to this alleged
requirement, the Utopian-style experiments they have inspired
resulting in unanticipated consequences of a kind with which –
ironically enough – history itself has made us only too familiar.

Taken together, these two articles have an ample sweep and
scope that exemplify their author's singular range and illuminating
breadth of vision. They were originally written in the 1950s, and
the various allusions they contain to speculative social theories and
blueprints may therefore partly be viewed as reflecting the preoccupations of a period acutely conscious of the totalitarian ideologies that continued to hold sway over much of the political
landscape. Even so, it would be a mistake to regard such references
as possessing no more than a limited or transient significance when
judged within the overall perspective of Berlin's thought. He was
almost from the first alert to the dangers inherent in a misplaced
'scientism' and the blurring of boundaries it is apt to engender, an
early resistance to reductionist trends in epistemology and the
philosophy of language prefiguring in some ways the objections he
was later to raise against influential doctrines in political and social
theory. He has never denied that it was proper and indeed
estimable to salute and seek to emulate methods that had promoted
the success of the natural sciences within their own domains; but it
was another thing entirely to advocate an uncritical extension of
these to alien fields of investigation or to quite separate levels of
experience. As we have seen, he has attributed misconceptions on
the latter score to certain eighteenth-century *philosophes* and their
followers in the approach they adopted to human affairs. That,
however, has not been the sole source of his dissatisfaction with the
views of such thinkers, the wider reservations he has from time to
time expressed in his writings raising questions about his attitude
to the Enlightenment as a whole. The nature of some of the
uncertainties that have been felt may be gleaned from other essays
included in the present volume.

In actual fact, and despite what is on occasions supposed, Berlin
has been far from reticent in characterising his own, admittedly
complex, position on the subject. Thus he has gone out of his way

to praise representatives of the Enlightenment for their courageous opposition to many of the evils of their time, including ignorance, oppression, cruelty and superstition, and for their support for ideals like reason, liberty and human happiness; as he succinctly remarked to an interlocutor,[1] this put him on their side. At the same time, though, and notwithstanding the attachment he feels to much that they stood for, he also considers that they were prone to give dogmatic credence to assumptions – often traditional in origin – which were by no means self-evident and whose validity their professed respect for empirical principles might have led them to query. These included specific conceptions of a uniform and basically unchanging human nature, together with closely related beliefs in the existence of universal values which were harmoniously realisable by human beings in the course of their lives. Some of the issues arising from such preconceptions are examined in 'The Romantic Revolution': here it is argued that the emergence of romanticism in the late eighteenth century constituted a dramatic change in the intellectual climate of the time, the objective status of accepted standards and norms being challenged by subjectivist doctrines in a fashion that had momentous repercussions within the spheres of ethics, aesthetics and politics. In concluding this arresting discussion Berlin suggests that one long-term effect of the resultant clash of outlooks has been that we find ourselves today to be the heirs of two traditions, with a tendency to 'shift uneasily from one foot to the other'. Equally, however, he maintains that the novel and subversive ideas introduced by the movement indisputably deepened and enriched the understanding of people and societies, both exposing limitations or lacunae discernible in the Enlightenment inheritance and simultaneously opening up fresh possibilities of thought and feeling which had hitherto lain beyond the bounds of the European imagination.

Berlin's treatment of the above tension between these different standpoints is consonant with the combination of acuity and empathetic insight that pervades his approach to the history of ideas as a whole. On the one hand, he has shown an exceptional ability to grasp from within, and appreciate the force of, intellectual and cultural outlooks that are often opposed to ones to which as a person he feels most sympathetic. On the other, he has been

---

[1] Ramin Jahanbegloo, *Conversations with Isaiah Berlin* (London and New York, 1992), p. 70.

quick to recognise and pinpoint the sinister implications latent in a number of the positions he has so vividly portrayed: not least the shapes of irrationalism and of aggressive forms of nationalism that lurk within some of the doctrines belonging to what he has called the Counter-Enlightenment. On the latter score, what he writes towards the end of his essay on Rabindranath Tagore is indicative of the line he wishes to draw between the beneficent and the destructively chauvinist guises in which nationalism can appear. Here as elsewhere, he comments, Tagore tried to tell the truth without over-simplification, and to that extent was perhaps listened to the less, for – as the American philosopher C. I. Lewis remarked – 'There is no a priori reason for thinking that, when we discover the truth, it will prove interesting.' Berlin quotes this observation with approval. In his own writings, however, it can truly be said that the truth invariably proves to be so.

# THE SENSE OF REALITY

WHEN MEN, as occasionally happens, develop a distaste for the age in which they live, and love and admire some past period with such uncritical devotion that it is clear that, if they had their choice, they would wish to be alive then and not now – and when, as the next step, they seek to introduce into their lives certain of the habits and practices of the idealised past, and criticise the present for falling short of, or for degeneration from, this past – we tend to accuse them of nostalgic 'escapism', romantic antiquarianism, lack of realism; we dismiss their efforts as attempts to 'turn the clock back', to 'ignore the forces of history', or 'fly in the face of the facts', at best touching and childish and pathetic, at worst 'retrograde', or 'obstructive', or insanely 'fanatical', and, although doomed to failure in the end, capable of creating gratuitous obstacles to progress in the immediate present and future.

This kind of charge is made, and apparently understood, easily. It goes with such notions as the 'logic of the facts', or the 'march of history', which, like the laws of nature (with which they are partly identified), are thought of as, in some sense, 'inexorable', likely to take their course whatever human beings may wish or pray for, an inevitable process to which individuals must adjust themselves, for if they defy it they will perish; which, like the Fates in the line by Seneca, 'ducunt volentem ... nolentem trahunt'.[1] And yet this way of thinking seems to presuppose a machinery in the universe which those who think in these terms do not necessarily accept, which indeed they may, if they are students of history rather than metaphysics, seek to refute by means of negative instances drawn from their own and others' experience. Nevertheless, even those who try to rebut this way of thinking find that they cannot

---

[1] 'draw those who are willing, drag those who are not'. *Letters*, 107. 11, adapting Cleanthes.

altogether abandon the concepts in question because they seem to correspond to something in their view of how things happen, although they do not, perhaps, believe in the machinery of determinism which is normally held to be the source of them.

Let me try to make this somewhat clearer. Everyone, no doubt, believes that there are factors that are largely or wholly beyond conscious human control. And when we describe this or that scheme as impractical or Utopian we often mean that it cannot be realised in the face of such uncontrollable facts or processes. These are of many kinds: regions of nature with which we cannot interfere, for example the solar system or the general realm dealt with by astronomy; there we can alter neither the state of the entities in question nor the laws which they obey. As for the rest of the physical world, dealt with by the various natural sciences, we conceive of the laws which govern them as unalterable by us, but claim to be able to intervene to some degree in altering the states of things and persons which obey these laws. Some believe such interventions are themselves subject to laws: that we ourselves are wholly determined by our past; that our behaviour is in principle wholly calculable; and that our 'freedom' in interfering with natural processes is therefore illusory. Others deny this in whole or in part, but that does not concern us here, since both sides are willing to grant that large portions of our universe, particularly its inanimate portion, is as it is and suffers what it does whether we will it or no.

When we examine the world of sentient beings, some portions of it are certainly thought to be governed by 'necessity'. There are, to begin with, the effects of the interplay of human beings with nature – their own bodies and what is external to them. The assumption is made that there are certain basic human needs, for food, for shelter, the minimum means by which life can be carried on, perhaps for certain forms of pleasure or self-expression, communication; that these are affected by such relatively fixed phenomena as climate, geographical formation and the products of a natural environment, which take the form of economic, social, religious institutions, and so on, each of which is the combined effect of physical, biological, psychological, geographical factors, and so forth, and in which certain uniformities can be discovered, in terms of which patterns are observable in the lives of both individuals and societies – cyclical patterns of the kind discussed by Plato or Polybius, or non-recurrent ones, as in the sacred works of the Jews, the Christians, and perhaps Pythagoreans and Orphics, the patterns and chains of being which are to be found in various Eastern religions and philosophies, and in modern days in the cosmologies of such writers as Vico, Hegel, Comte, Buckle, Marx, Pareto, and a good many contemporary social psychologists and anthropologists and philosophers of history. These tend to treat human institutions as not proceeding solely from conscious human purposes or desires; but having made due allowance for such conscious purposes, whether on the part of those who found or those who use and participate in institutions, they stress unconscious or semi-conscious causes on the part of both individuals and groups, and, even more, the by-products of the encounters of the uncoordinated purposes of various human beings, each acting as he does partly for coherent and articulate motives, partly for causes or reasons little known to himself or to others, and thereby causing states of affairs which nobody may have intended as such, but which in their turn condition the lives and characters and actions of men.

On this view, if we consider how much is independent of conscious human policies – the entire realm of insentient nature, the sciences of which take no heed of human issues; and such human sciences as psychology and sociology, which assume some kind of basic human reactions and uniformities of behaviour, both social and individual, as unlikely to be altered radically by the fiats of individuals – if all this is taken into account, a picture emerges of a universe the behaviour of which is in principle largely calculable. Naturally we tend to come under the influence of this picture, to think of history as growing in inevitable stages, in an irreversible direction, ideally, at least, describable as instances of the totality of the laws which between them describe and summarise the natural uniformities in terms of which we conceive of the behaviour of both things and persons. The life of the fourteenth century was as it was because it was a 'stage' reached by the interplay of human and non-human factors – its institutions were those which human needs, half consciously and half quite unawares, caused to come about or to survive, and because the individual and institutional life of the fourteenth century was as it was, the fifteenth and sixteenth centuries could not but be as they were, and could not resemble, say, the third or the ninth or the thirteenth century, because the fourteenth century had made that quite 'impossible'. We may not know what the laws are which social evolution obeys, nor the precise causal factors which function between the life of the individual and that of the 'social anthill' to which it belongs, but we may be sure that there are such laws and factors. We realise that this is so if we ask ourselves whether we think that history explains anything, that is, that any light is thrown upon the fifteenth century by what occurred in the fourteenth, in the sense that if we grasp the historical links we shall understand what made the fifteenth century what it was. To grasp this is to see what it is that makes it absurd to suggest that everything in the fifteenth century might have been an exact reproduction of what occurred in the thirteenth century – as if the fourteenth century had never been. And from this there appears to follow that cluster of concepts with which we began. There is a pattern and it has direction; it is not necessarily 'progressive', that is, we need not believe that we are gradually approaching some 'desirable' goal, however we define desirable; but we are pursuing a definite and irreversible direction; nostalgia for some past stage of it is *eo ipso* Utopian; for it is like asking for the reversal of the nexus of causes and effects. We may admire the past, but to try to reproduce it is to ignore this nexus. The oak cannot return to the condition of the acorn; an old man cannot, as it were, unlive what he has lived through and literally be young once more, with the body as well as the heart and mind of youth. Romantic hankerings after past ages are virtually a desire to undo the 'inexorable' logic of events. If it were possible to reproduce past conditions, historical causality would be broken, which, since we cannot help thinking in terms of it, is psychologically impossible as well as irrational and absurd.

We may be told that such expressions as 'anachronism' are surely themselves sufficient to convey this truth: to describe somebody or something as an anachronism is to say that he or it is not characteristic of the general pattern of the age. We do not need much argument to convince us that there is something gravely deficient in a historian who thinks that Richelieu could have done what he did just as well in the 1950s, or that Shakespeare could have written the plays which he wrote in Ancient Rome, or Outer Mongolia. And this sense of what belongs where, of what cannot have happened as against that which could, is said to imply the notion of an irreversible process, where everything belongs to the stage to which it does and is 'out of place' or 'out of time' if mistakenly inserted in the wrong context.

So far so good. We are committed to no more than that there are some criteria of reality – that we have some methods for distinguishing the real from the illusory, real mountain peaks from cloud formations, real palms and springs from mirages in the desert, real characteristics of an age or a culture from fanciful reconstructions, real alternatives which can be realised at a given time from alternatives realisable, it may be, in other places and at other times, but not in the society or period in question. It is in terms of some such principle that various historical theorists stake out their claims. Asked why Shakespeare could not have written *Hamlet* in Ancient Rome, Hegelians would speak of the Graeco-Roman spirit, with which such thoughts, feelings and words as Shakespeare's were not compatible. Marxists might refer to 'relationships' and 'forces' of production, which in Rome were such as to have 'inevitably' generated a cultural superstructure in which Virgil could function, and Shakespeare could not have functioned, as he did. Montesquieu would have spoken of geography, climates, the 'dominant spirit' of different social systems; Chateaubriand of the difference made by Christianity, Gobineau of race, Herder, the folk spirit; Taine – race, milieu, the moment; Spengler, the self-contained 'morphology' of mutually exclusive cultures and civilisations; and so forth. To be Utopian, to perpetrate anachronisms, to be unrealistic, 'escapist', not to understand history or life or the world, is to fail to grasp a particular set of laws and formulae which each school offers as the key to its explanation of why what happens must happen as it does and not in some other order. What is common to all the schools is a belief that there is an order and a key to its understanding, a plan – either a geometry or a geography of events. Those who understand it are wise, those who do not, wander in darkness.

And yet there is something peculiar about this, both in theory and in practice. In theory, because no attempt to provide such a 'key' in history has worked thus far. No doubt much valuable light has been thrown upon past conditions by emphasis on hitherto neglected factors: before Montesquieu and Vico, the importance of customs and institutions, of language, grammar, mythology, legal systems; of the influence of environmental and other undramatic, continuous causal factors in explaining why men behaved as they did, and indeed as an instrument for revealing how the world looked to men relatively remote in time or space, what they felt and said, and why and how, and for how long and with what effect – all this was largely unrecognised. Marx taught us to pay more attention to the influence of the economic and social condition of individuals; Herder and Hegel to the interrelations of apparently diverse cultural phenomena and to the life of institutions; Durkheim to unintended social patterns; Freud to the importance of irrational and unconscious factors in individual experience; Sorel and Jung to the importance of irrational myths and collective emotional attitudes in the behaviour of societies. We have learned a great deal; our perspective has altered; we see men and societies from new angles, in different lights. The discoveries which have led to this are genuine discoveries and historical writing has been transformed by them.

But the 'key' escapes us. We can neither, as in astronomy or even geology, given initial conditions, confidently reconstruct – calculate either the past or the future of a culture, of a society or class, of an individual or a group – save in instances so rare and abnormal, with such gaps, with the assistance of so many *ad hoc* hypotheses and epicycles, that direct observation is more economical and more informative than such attempts at scientific inference. If we ask ourselves how much we really can tell about a given period in a culture or a given pattern of human action – a war, a revolution, a renaissance of art or science – from knowledge of even its immediate antecedents or consequences, we must surely answer: scarcely anything at all. No historian, however steeped in sociology or psychology or some metaphysical theory, will attempt to write history in so a priori a fashion. When Hegel attempted this, with the courage of his anti-empirical prejudices, the result was seen as somewhat erroneous even by his followers; so too Spengler, when he insists that the streets of Greek cities were straight and crossed each other at right angles because of the geometrical spirit of the Greeks, is easily shown to be writing rubbish. The theorists of history certainly supposed that they were providing historians with wings enabling them to span great territories rapidly, as compared with the slow pedestrian rate of the empirical fact-gatherer; but although the wings have been with us now for more than a century, nobody has, as yet, flown; those who, as Henri Poincaré remarked in an analogous connection, tried to do so came to a sorry end. The attempts to substitute machines, methods of mass production, for the slow manual labour of antiquaries and historical researchers have all broken down; we still rely on those who spend their lives in painfully piecing together their knowledge from fragments of actual evidence, obeying this evidence wherever it leads them, however tortuous and unfamiliar the pattern, or with no consciousness of any pattern at all. Meanwhile the wings and the machinery are gathering dust on the shelves of museums, examples of overweening ambition and idle fantasy, not of intellectual achievement.

The great system-builders have in their works both expressed and influenced human attitudes towards the world – the light in which events are seen. Metaphysical, religious, scientific systems and attitudes have altered the distribution of emphasis, the sense of what is important or significant or admirable, or again of what is remote or barbarous or trivial – have profoundly affected human concepts and categories, the eyes with which men see or feel and understand the world, the spectacles through which they look – but they have not done the work of a science as they claimed, have not revealed new facts, increased the sum of our information, disclosed unsuspected events. Our belief that events and persons and things belong where they belong inevitably, inexorably, and *per contra* our sense of Utopia and anachronism, remain as strong as ever; but our belief in specific laws of history, of which we can formulate the science, is not too confident – if their behaviour whether as historians or as men of action is any evidence – even among the minority of those who pursue such topics. It is unlikely, therefore, that the first springs from the second; that our disbelief in the possibility of 'a return to the past' rests on a fear of contradicting some given law or laws of history. For while our attitude towards the existence of such laws is more than doubtful, our belief in the absurdity of romantic efforts at recapturing past glories is exceedingly strong. The latter cannot, therefore, depend upon the former. What, then, is the content of our notion of the inevitable 'march of history', of the folly of trying to resist what we call irresistible?

Impressed (and to some degree oppressed) by true considerations about the limits of free human action – the barriers imposed by unalterable and little alterable regularities in nature, in the functioning of human bodies and minds – the majority of eighteenth-century thinkers and, following them, enlightened opinion in the last century, and to some degree in our own, conceived the possibility of a true empirical science of history which, even if it never became sufficiently precise to enable us to make predictions or retrodictions in specific situations, nevertheless, by dealing with great numbers, and relying on comparisons of rich statistical data,

would indicate the general direction of, say, social and technological development, and enable us to rule out some plans, revolutionary and reformist, as demonstrably anachronistic and therefore
Utopian – as not conforming to the 'objective' direction of social
development. If anyone in the nineteenth century contemplated
seriously a return to pre-Raphaelite forms of life it was unnecessary
to discuss whether this was or was not desirable; it was surely
enough to say that the Renaissance and the Reformation and the
Industrial Revolution had in fact occurred, that factories could not
be dismantled and great mass industries turned back into small-
scale crafts, as if the discoveries and inventions and changes in
forms of life which these had brought about had never been, that
there had been advance in knowledge and civilisation, in the means
of production and distribution, and that whatever might occur
next, it was beyond the wit and strength of man to deflect a process
which was as uncontrollable as the great uniformities of nature.
Opinions might differ as to what the true laws of this process were,
but all were agreed that there were such laws, and that to try to
alter them or behave as if they were not decisive was an absurd
day-dream, a childish desire to substitute for the laws of science
those of some whimsical fairy-tale in which everything is possible.

It was true that the great men who had first achieved the triumph
of this new scientific attitude – the anti-clerical philosophers and
scientists of the late seventeenth century and the eighteenth century
– had over-simplified things. They evidently supposed that men
were to be analysed as material objects in space and that their lives
and thoughts were in principle deducible from the mechanical laws
which governed the behaviour of their bodies. This the nineteenth
century felt to be too crude a view, and it was condemned as
'mechanistic' by the German metaphysicians, as 'vulgar materialism' by the Marxists, as non-evolutionary and insufficiently
'organic' by Darwinians and positivists. Such mechanical laws
might account for that which is largely unaltered throughout
recorded human history – the permanent chemical, physical,
biological and physiological consequences of cause and effect, or
functional (or statistical) interrelations, or whatever was the central
category of these sciences. But history did not consist of mere
short-term repetitions: development occurred; a principle was
wanted to account for continuous change and not merely for
'static' difference. The thinkers of the eighteenth century had been
too deeply infatuated by Newton's mechanical model, which

explained the realm of nature but not that of history. Something was needed to discover historical laws, but as the laws of biology had differed from the laws of chemistry, not merely in applying to a different subject-matter but in being in principle other kinds of laws, so history – for Hegel the evolution of the spirit, for Saint-Simon or Marx the development of social relations, for Spengler or Toynbee (the last voices of the nineteenth century) the development of cultures, less or more isolable ways of life – obeyed laws of its own; laws which took account of the specific behaviour of nations or classes or social groups and of individuals which belonged to them, without reducing these (or believing that they should or could be reduced) to the behaviour of particles of matter in space, which was represented, justly or not, as the eighteenth-century – mechanistic – ideal of all explanation.

To understand how to live and act, whether in private or in public life, was to grasp these laws and use them for one's purposes. The Hegelians believed that this was achieved by a species of rational intuition; Marxists, Comtists and Darwinians, by scientific investigation; Schelling and his romantic followers, by inspired 'vitalistic' and 'mythopoeic' insight, by the illumination of artistic genius; and so on. All these schools believed that human society grew in a discoverable direction, governed by laws; that the borderline which divided science from Utopia, effectiveness from ineffectiveness in every sphere of life, was discoverable by reason and observation and could be plotted less or more precisely; that, in short, there was a clock, its movement followed discoverable rules, and it could not be put back.

These beliefs were rudely shaken by the evidence of the twentieth century. The notions, the ideas and forms of life which were considered to be inalienable from, 'organically' necessary to, the particular stage of historical evolution reached by mankind were broken or twisted out of recognition by new and violent leaders: Lenin, Stalin, Hitler. It is true that these acted as they did in the name of their own historical or pseudo-historical theories, the Communists in the name of dialectical materialism, Hitler in the name of racial hegemonism. But there was no doubt that they achieved what had hitherto been regarded as virtually impossible, contrary to the laws of advancing civilisation – a breach of the inexorable laws of human history. It became clear that men of sufficient energy and ruthlessness could collect a sufficient degree of material power to transform their worlds much more radically than had been thought possible before – that if one genuinely rejected those moral, political, legal concepts which were regarded as firm, as much elements of their own historical phase as its material arrangements, and if, moreover, one did not shrink from killing millions of human beings, against accepted beliefs as to what was feasible, against what was thought right by the majority in one's own time, then greater changes could be introduced than the 'laws' allowed for. Human beings and their institutions turned out to be much more malleable, far less resistant, the laws turned out to be far more elastic, than the earlier doctrinaires had taught us to believe. There was talk of a relapse into – a deliberate return to – barbarism, which according to the earlier revolutionary theories was not merely regrettable but wellnigh impossible.

It was a truth to the reception of which there was every kind of resistance. Thus when in Russia a regime openly and boldly exterminated many of the achievements of Western civilisation – both in the arts and, to some degree, in the sciences, certainly in politics and morals – on the ground that these belonged to the ideology of a minority condemned by history to destruction, this holocaust had to be represented, not as the reversal which it was, but as the continuation of a revolutionary leap forward of this very civilisation in the direction in which it had been proceeding previously, although in fact (unlike the great French Revolution) what occurred represented an almost total change of direction. This could not be stated, because the doctrines in the name of which the revolution was carried out – and which, ironically enough, the revolution did so much to expose and discredit – were too strongly ingrained as official radical shibboleths to which lip-service was still paid. Hitler, with a better understanding of what he was doing, proclaimed that he was indeed returning to an ancient past, and seeking to undo the effects of the Enlightenment and of 1789; and, although his plan was regarded as a mad dream, a sadistic neo-medieval fantasy which could not be realised in the twentieth century, and largely discounted accordingly by liberals, conservatives and Marxists alike, who shall now say that he totally failed? He ruled for only a dozen years, and in the course of them transformed the outlook and structure of life of his subjects beyond the expectations of the wildest historical and political thinkers of Western (and Eastern) Europe; if he lost in the end, he lost by so narrow a margin that it does not need an eccentric imagination to conceive that he might have won, and that the consequences of his victory would have finally reduced to nonsense the doctrines according to which his rise and his victories were demonstrably impossible.

In 1944 a plan was submitted at the Quebec Conference by Henry Morgenthau, US Secretary of the Treasury, whereby German industries were to be dismantled and the entire country turned back to pasture. It was a plan which could scarcely be taken seriously, although Roosevelt is said – I do not know how reliably – to have briefly inclined towards it. Nevertheless, those who were horrified by it and resisted it conceded that it was practicable. Yet the very notion that some such plan could be put into operation would have struck most historians, philosophers, statesmen, most intelligent men in the late nineteenth century – say at any time before 1914 – as wildly Utopian. To this degree Lenin, Hitler and Stalin and their minor followers elsewhere, by their acts rather than their precepts, demonstrated the truth, horrifying to some, comforting to others, that human beings are a good deal more plastic than was hitherto thought, that given enough will-power, fanaticism, determination – and no doubt a favourable conjunction of circumstances – almost anything, at any rate far more than was hitherto thought possible, can be altered.

The banisters upon which the system-builders of the nineteenth century have taught us to lean have proved unequal to the pressure that was put upon them. The techniques of modern civilisation, so far from guaranteeing us against lapses into the past or violent lunges in unpredictable directions, have proved the most effective weapons in the hands of those who wish to change human beings by playing on irrational impulses and defying the framework of civilised life according to some arbitrary pattern of their own. It became a question of where revolutionaries were prepared to stop – a moral more than a psychological question – since the resistance of habit, tradition, 'inexorable' technological progress collapses easily before sufficient and determined assaults. Efforts were made to prove that these assaults themselves followed a pattern, that whether they came from the right or the left, they too – the advances of totalitarianism – were inevitable, as progress towards individual liberty had once been proclaimed to be. But such analyses lacked the old superb conviction of those nineteenth-century prophets and seers who thought that they really had, at last, solved the riddle of history, and once and for all; it became all too clear that these were mere half-hearted, dispirited efforts to peer into a crystal ball, so suddenly once again covered with the mist of uncertainty after the lucid mirage of two centuries in which the rays of science were alleged to have pierced through the night of historical ignorance. Now, once more, it was only a movement of shadows, indeterminate and unsubstantial, describable only in terms of approximations, inspired guesswork, short-term conclusions from local phenomena, liable to be upset by too many unknown and apparently unknowable factors.

The obverse side of this was, of course, an increased belief in the efficacy of individual initiative – the notion that every situation was more fluid than had been supposed in more tranquil times – which pleased those who found the scientific and determinist picture or the Hegelian teleology too cut and dried, too stifling, too unpromising of novelty; too narrow for the assertion of revolutionary energies, for the testing of violent new sensations; and terrified those who seek order, tranquillity, dependable values, moral and physical security, a world in which the margin of error is calculable, the limits of change are discoverable, and cataclysms are due to natural causes only – and these in principle predictable with the advance of scientific knowledge. The social world certainly seems more disturbing, fuller of undiscovered perils, than hitherto; but then it would follow that there is a career more open to talents, provided they are audacious, powerful and ruthless enough.

Under these circumstances, it may be asked, why cannot we reproduce, let us say, the conditions of the fourteenth century, if we should wish to do so? True, it is not easy to upset the arrangements of the twentieth century and replace them by something so widely different; not easy, but surely not literally impossible? If Hitler, if Stalin, could transform their societies, and affect the world to so vast a degree in so short a time; if Germany could have been 'pastoralised'; if all the warning voices about how easy it would be to end human civilisation by this or that destructive weapon, how precarious the whole establishment is, are telling the truth; then surely there is a field for creative no less than for destructive capacities? If things are less fixed than they seemed, do not such terms as 'anachronism', the 'logic of the facts' and the rest begin to lose their force? If we can, given the opportunity, operate more freely than we once believed that we could, what *does* divide Utopian from realistic planning? If we really believe that the life of the fourteenth century is preferable to that of the twentieth, then, if we are resolute enough and have enough material resources, and there are enough of us, and we do not hesitate to commit all that resists us to the flames, why cannot we 'return to the past'? The laws of nature do not prevent us, for *they* have not altered in the last six centuries. What then is it that stops us – stops, say, neo-medieval fanatics from working their will? For there is no doubt that something does do so, that even the most extreme among them scarcely believe that they could literally reproduce some past golden age, Merrie England, the Old South, or the world of *le vert galant*, in the sense in which Communist or Fascist fanatics believe that they *can* cause the world to go through a transformation no less violent – to divert it, as it were, from its previous path by at least as sharp an angle.

Let us try to imagine what such a return to the past would entail. Supposing a man did get into his head to re-establish the conditions of his favourite time and place – to recreate them as closely as he could – what steps would he take? To begin with he would have to acquaint himself as minutely as he could with the former life which he wished to re-establish. He must suppose himself to know something about the form of life in question to have fallen so deeply in love with it. Whether his knowledge is real or delusive is for the moment not relevant. Let us assume that he is more than a sentimental enthusiast, that he is a profound student of history and the social sciences; he will then know that, in order to attain to a certain form of life, more must be done than to wear certain types of clothes, eat certain types of food, reorganise our social lives in accordance with certain sorts of patterns, or possess certain religious beliefs. We will not succeed in doing this, but merely go through our parts like actors on a stage, unless the bases of such life, economic, social, linguistic, perhaps geographical and ecological as well, are appropriate, that is, of such a kind as to make his ideal society possible and, indeed, natural and normal. Undaunted he sets about – let us assume him to be, if not omnipotent, at any rate in control of very powerful material resources, and to have to deal with singularly impressionable and docile human beings – he sets about to transform all the required natural and artificial conditions accordingly. If he is fanatical enough and isolates his society sufficiently from contact with the outer world (or, alternatively, if his experiment is world-wide in extent), he may at any rate in theory succeed to some degree. Human lives *are* radically alterable, human beings can be re-educated and conditioned and turned topsy-turvy – that is the principal lesson of the violent times in which we live. In addition to vast material resources and extraordinary skill in using these, he must also have an astonishing knowledge about the age which he is seeking to reproduce and the causes and factors which made it what it was. But let us assume that he has these too, and understands London in the fourteenth century, let us say, or Florence in the fifteenth, as no one has ever known it before. He will know it better certainly than its own inhabitants could have known it; for they took too much for granted, too much seemed so normal and habitual to them, so that they could not, however self-conscious the most analytical and critical of them may have been, notice the climate, the network of habits and thoughts and feelings in which they lived, in the way in which an outside observer, able to compare it with phenomena sufficiently unlike it to emphasise its peculiarities, can do. Nevertheless, it is clear that however skilful, minute, fanatically thorough such a reconstruction were, it would fail in its principal objective – the literal recreation of some past culture. And that not at all for the most obvious causes – because one's knowledge is liable to error, because one is looking at the golden age from some later vantage-point, different from that from which the Londoners in the fourteenth or Florentines in the fifteenth could possibly view themselves and others – for even if the creator of this world may himself be debarred from observing things from two points of view at once, yet he can skilfully and consciously, using the methods pilloried by Aldous Huxley and George Orwell, at any rate manufacture human beings whose viewpoint is transformed in the requisite fashion – nor, again, because of the many obvious practical difficulties in the realisation of so eccentric a scheme: all these could, at least in theory, be disposed of. Nevertheless, however triumphantly these are overcome, the result will always seem curiously artificial – a skilful forgery, a piece of synthetic antiquarianism grafted on inescapably contemporary foundations.

It seems clear that in trying to acquire knowledge about the world, external or internal, physical or mental, we inevitably notice and describe only certain characteristics of it – those which are, as it were, public, which attract attention to themselves because of some specific interest which we have in investigating them, because of our practical needs or theoretical interests: aspects of the world in terms of which communication between men takes place; characteristics which may be misunderstood or misdescribed, knowledge of which is in some degree important, that is, makes a difference to our activity, whether designed for use or pleasure; interested or disinterested objects of action or thought or feeling or contemplation. And we feel that we progress in knowledge as we discover unfamiliar facts and relationships, particularly when these turn out to be relevant to our principal purposes, to survival and all the means thereto, to our happiness or the satisfaction of the many diverse and conflicting needs for the sake of which human beings do what they do and are as they are.

What is left out of such investigations is what is too obvious to need mentioning. If we are anthropologists, and describe human habits or beliefs, we regard as worthy of notice and report those respects in which other tribes differ from us, or those in which they resemble us unexpectedly because their many differences might make us think otherwise. We do not record the obvious: for example the fact that the natives of Polynesia prefer being warm to being cold, or dislike hunger or physical pain; it is too tedious to record this. We take it for granted, quite naturally and justifiably, that if these natives are human beings, this will be true of them as it is of us, and of all the other human beings we have heard of – it is one of the components of normality. Neither do we report that the heads of these Polynesians are three-dimensional and that they have space behind and in front of them – this too almost follows from the definitions of these terms and must be taken for granted.

When one considers how many such facts – habits, beliefs – we take for granted in thinking or saying anything at all, how many notions, ethical, political, social, personal, go to the making of the outlook of a single person, however simple and unreflective, in any given environment, we begin to realise how very small a part of the total our sciences – not merely natural sciences, which work by generalising at a high level of abstraction, but the humane, 'impressionistic' studies, history, biography, sociology, introspective psychology, the methods of the novelists, of the writers of memoirs, of students of human affairs from every angle – are able to take in. And this is not a matter for surprise or regret: if we were aware of all that we could in principle be aware of we should swiftly be out of our minds. The most primitive act of observation or thought requires some fixed habits, a whole framework of things, persons, ideas, beliefs, attitudes to be taken for granted, uncriticised assumptions, unanalysed beliefs. Our language, or whatever symbolism we think with, is itself impregnated by these basic attitudes. We cannot, even in principle, enumerate all that we know and believe, for the words or symbols with which we do so themselves embody and express certain attitudes which are *ex hypothesi* 'encapsulated' in them, and not easily describable by them. We can make use of one set of symbols in order to uncover the assumptions which underlie another, and even as much as this is a most painful, difficult and crucially important task which only a very few, very subtle, very profound, very serious, penetrating and bold and clear-headed thinkers of genius have succeeded in performing to any degree at all; but we cannot examine the whole of our symbolism and yet employ for this purpose no symbols at all. There is no Archimedean point outside ourselves where we can stand in order to take up our critical viewpoint, in order to observe and analyse all that we think or believe by simply inspecting it, all that we can be said to take for granted because we behave as though we accepted it – the supposition is a self-evident absurdity.

The quality of depth in thinkers who are professional philosophers or novelists, or men of genius of other kinds, precisely consists in penetrating to one of these great assumptions, embedded in some widespread attitude, and isolating that and questioning it – wondering how it might be if it were otherwise. It is when one of these nerves is touched, nerves which lie so deep within us that it is in terms of them that we feel as we feel and think as we think, that we are conscious of those electric shocks which indicate that some genuinely profound insight has occurred. It is only when this unique, immediately recognisable, disturbing experience comes that we are aware that we are in the presence of this peculiar and very rare form of genius, possessed by those who make us conscious of the most pervasive, least observed categories, those which lie closest to us and which for that very reason escape description, however much our emotions, our curiosity, our industry, are mobilised to record the whole of what we know.

Everyone will know the quality I refer to. Newton dealt with problems which had long occupied the attention of philosophers and scientists, and proposed solutions to problems of a notorious difficulty, solutions characterised by a simplicity and a comprehensiveness which are marks of his particular kind of genius. But his results, if they were disturbing, were so only to specialists, other physicists or cosmologists. He altered many men's outlooks, no doubt, but nothing that he said directly touched their innermost private and quintessential thoughts and feelings. But Pascal questioned those categories, touched those half conscious, or altogether

unconscious, habits of thought, beliefs, attitudes in terms of which
the inner life, the basic components of their own private worlds,
presented themselves to the men of his time. He made great
discoveries in mathematics, but it is not for this that his thought is
credited with unique qualities of depth: in his *Pensées* there are no
formal discoveries, no solutions, not even clear statements of
problems with indications of how they are to be investigated. And
yet Locke, who did all these things, and was a thinker of
unparalleled influence, has never been regarded as an exceptionally
*profound* thinker; this despite his originality, his universality, his
massive contribution to philosophy and politics as compared with
the isolated fragments left by Pascal. It is so too with Kant. He laid
bare categories of a very pervasive, very basic kind – space, time,
number, thinghood, freedom, moral personality – and therefore,
for all that he was a systematic and often pedantic philosopher, a
difficult writer, an obscure logician, a routine professorial metaphysician and moralist, he was in his lifetime recognised to be what
he was, not merely a man of genius in many fields but one of the
few authentically profound and therefore revolutionary thinkers in
human history: one who discussed not merely what others were
discussing, saw not merely what others were describing, and
answered not merely what was generally being asked, but pierced
through a layer of suppositions and assumptions which language
itself embodies to habits of thought, basic frameworks in terms of
which we think and act, and touched these. Nothing can compare
with the experience of being made aware of the characteristics of
the most intimate instruments with which one thinks and feels –
not of the problems to which one seeks solutions, nor of the
solutions, but of the innermost terms, the most deeply ingrained
categories with which, and not about which, one thinks; of kinds
of ways in which one's experiences occur; not of the nature of the
experiences themselves, however remarkable, however instructive
an analysis of these last may be.

It seems clear that what is easiest for us to observe and describe
is the furniture of the external world – trees, rocks, houses, tables,
other human beings. Some people with a meditative cast of mind
are able to describe their own feelings and thoughts with sensitiveness and precision; some with keener and more analytical minds
can do much to distinguish and describe the main categories in
which we think – the differences between mathematical and
historical thought, or between the concept of a thing and of a

person, or between subject or object, or between acts and feelings, and so on. The concepts and categories involved in formal disciplines which have relatively clear rules – physics or mathematics or grammar or the language of international diplomacy – are comparatively easy to investigate. For those involved in less articulate activities – in the activities of the musician, in writing novels or poetry, in painting, composing, in the everyday intercourse of human beings and the 'common-sense' picture of the world – it is, for obvious reasons, far more difficult. We can construct sciences on the assumption of certain relative invariances; the behaviour of stones, or grass, or plants or butterflies, we assume to have been not so different in dim ages as to stultify the assumptions made today by chemistry or geology or physics or botany or zoology. And unless we believed human beings were sufficiently similar in certain basic and abstractable aspects throughout sufficiently long stretches of time, we should have no grounds for trusting those generalisations which, consciously or not, enter into not merely such proclaimed sciences as sociology, psychology and anthropology, but into history and biography and the art of the novelist, and political theory and every form of social observation.

Some of these generalisations lie too close to us and are too self-evident to be brought up into the light by any save those bold and original and independent men of genius. Pascal and Dostoevsky, Proust, St Augustine have succeeded, in such acts of deep-sea diving, in observing and reporting such basic structural attitudes and categories. Some of these apply to mankind over sufficiently long stretches of time to be regarded as virtually universal; some vary from age to age and culture to culture, and vary, doubtless, to some degree, between persons and groups of persons and at different times and in different circumstances. Provided the small differences are ignored, and what is treated is always some very large number, we can formulate laws which apply literally only to idealised entities, whose relationship to actual objects or persons is always a matter of doubt or intuitive skill on the part of the specialist dealing with the problem, like the application of the general laws of anatomy to an individual disease, only more so. The concept, for example, of a basic 'human' nature, which cannot be radically altered, and is that which makes most human beings human, is a vague effort to convey a notion of a complex of unvarying and unanalysed characteristics which we know by acquaintance, as it were, from the inside, but which is insusceptible to precise scientific formulation or manipulation. Such general terms – human nature, peace, war, stability, freedom, power, rise, decline – are convenient symbols which sum up, are a concentrate of, my observations; but however much the sciences bring under their sway, however detailed, scrupulous, verified, coherent are the accounts of our best historians, an immense amount is necessarily left out at both ends of the scale – both the deepest, the most pervasive categories which enter too much into all our experience to be easily detachable from it for observation, and at the other end those endlessly shifting, altering views, feelings, reactions, instincts, beliefs which constitute the uniqueness of each individual and of each of his acts and thoughts, and the uniqueness too, the individual flavour, the peculiar pattern of life, of a character, of an institution, a mood, and also of an artistic style, an entire culture, an age, a nation, a civilisation.

It is a truism to say that it is the differences and not the similarities that constitute the completeness of an act of recognition, of a historical description, of a personality – whether of an object or an individual or a culture. Vico and Herder, despite all their extravagances and obscurities, taught us once and for all that to be a Homeric Greek or an eighteenth-century German is to belong to a unique society, and that what it is to 'belong' cannot be analysed in terms of something which these persons have in common with other societies or entities in the universe, but only in terms of what each of them has in common with other Homeric Greeks or Germans – that there is a Greek or German way of talking, eating, concluding treaties, engaging in commerce, dancing, gesturing, tying shoelaces, building ships, explaining the past, worshipping God, permeated by some common quality which cannot be analysed in terms of instances of general laws or effects of discoverable causes, recurrent uniformities, repetitions which allow common elements to be abstracted and sometimes experimented upon. The unique pattern in terms of which all acts which are German are interlaced, or which enables us to attribute a painting or even a line of poetry or a witticism to one age rather than another and to one author rather than another – of that no science exists. We recognise these manifestations as we recognise the expressions on the faces of our friends. The interconnection of different activities which are seen to spring from, or constitute, a unique single character or style or historical situation is much more like the unity of an aesthetic whole, a symphony or a portrait; what we condemn as false or inappropriate is much more like what is rejected as false or inappropriate in a painting or a poem than in a deductive system or a scientific theory, or in the interlinked hypotheses of a natural science. How we perform such acts of identification and attribution it is almost impossible to say. Too many factors enter into the process; they are too evanescent, their links are often too subtle and invisible; the notion that they could be made the subject of a technique and taught to others systematically is plainly absurd, and yet they are among the most familiar experiences we have. They enter into the vast majority of our common-sense judgements and opinions and predictions of the behaviour of others, they are what we live by, our most ingrained methods, our habits of thought and feeling, they change and we hardly notice it, they change in others and we may not consciously notice that, but may react to it in a half conscious fashion. The investigation of such presuppositions – of what makes the unique outlook of an age or of a person – plainly needs far more sympathy, interest and imagination, as well as experience of life, than the more abstract and disciplined activities of natural scientists.

Every person and every age may thus be said to have at least two levels: an upper, public, illuminated, easily noticed, clearly describable surface from which similarities are capable of being profitably abstracted and condensed into laws; and below this a path into less and less obvious yet more and more intimate and pervasive characteristics, too closely mixed with feelings and activities to be easily distinguishable from them. With great patience, industry, assiduity we can delve beneath the surface – novelists do this better than trained 'social scientists' – but the consistency is that of some viscous substance: we encounter no stone wall, no insuperable obstacle, but each step is more difficult, each effort to advance robs us of the desire or ability to continue. Tolstoy, Shakespeare, Dostoevsky, Kafka, Nietzsche have penetrated more deeply than John Buchan or H. G. Wells, or Bertrand Russell; but what we know on this level of half-articulate habits, unexamined assumptions and ways of thought, semi-instinctive reactions, models of life so deeply embedded as not to be felt consciously at all – what we know of this is so little, and likely, because we do not have the time, the subtlety and the penetration, to remain so negligible, that to claim to be able to construct generalisations where at best we can only indulge the art of exquisite portrait-painting, to claim the possibility of some infallible scientific key where each unique entity demands a lifetime of minute, devoted observation, sympathy, insight, is one of the most grotesque claims ever made by human beings.

II

The ideal of all natural sciences is a system of propositions so general, so clear, so comprehensive, connected with each other by logical links so unambiguous and direct that the result resembles as closely as possible a deductive system, where one can travel along wholly reliable, logical routes from any point on the system to any other – wholly reliable because constructed a priori according to rules guaranteed as in a game, because they have been adopted, because it has been decided to keep and not break them. The usefulness of such a system – as opposed to its power or beauty – depends, of course, not on its logical scope and coherence, but on its applicability to matters of fact. This in its turn depends not merely on the skill with which we construct the system, but on the actual behaviour of things and persons in the world, to which the system is applied, or from which the system is generalised or idealised. For this reason it has always been the case that the more general and logically satisfactory a system was, the less useful it was in describing the specific course of the behaviour of a particular entity in the universe – the larger the number of entities, the more accurate the descriptive and predictive power of the system; the smaller the number of instances, the greater the margin of error, of deviation from the norm.

Historians, whose business it is to tell us what actually happened in the world, consequently fight shy of rigid theoretical patterns into which the facts may sometimes have to be fitted with a good deal of awkwardness and artificiality. And this instinct is a sound one. The proper aim of the sciences is to note the number of similarities in the behaviour of objects and to construct propositions of the greatest degree of generality from which the largest number of such uniformities can be logically deduced. In history our purpose is the opposite. When we wish to describe a particular revolution – what actually took place – the last thing we wish to do is to concentrate solely upon those characteristics of it which it has in common with as many other revolutions as we can discover, ignoring the differences as irrelevant to our study; and so what a historian wishes to bring out is what is specific, unique, in a given character or series of events or historical situation, so that the reader, presented with this account, should be able to grasp the situation in what is called its 'concreteness', that is, as it occurred at the particular time, in the particular place, as the result of the particular antecedents, in the framework of the particular events in which it and it alone occurred – the respects in which it differs from everything which has occurred before or is likely to occur after it. The historian is concerned to paint a portrait which conveys the unique pattern of experience, and not an X-ray photograph which is capable of acting as a general symbol for all structures of a similar type.

This truth was understood – and exaggerated – by those thinkers of the romantic movement who complained that previous historians had been too abstract or too pedestrian and mechanical with their lists of reigns and battles and irrelevant, disconnected chroniclers' tales, had failed to clothe these dry bones in the flesh of living reality, to paint either human character or society in such a way as to give the reader a sense of actuality, a sense of the kind of society or kind of character which he could imagine that he could have met or been himself in living relations with; and that historical novelists or painters or other men whose imagination was adequate to their knowledge did this more successfully.

This historical gift consists not merely in establishing facts by means of those recognised techniques, those ways of handling evidence, which specialists – palaeographers, epigraphists, archaeologists, anthropologists and so forth – have developed, which may well entail logical processes not altogether unlike those of the natural sciences, with their tendency to generality and abstraction, and the use of idealised models, but something at the opposite end of the scale, namely an eye for what is unique and unrepeated, for the particular concatenation of circumstances, unique combinations of attributes, which give a person, a situation, a culture, an age its peculiar character, in virtue of which it is possible to attribute this or that political decision, this or that painting or moral view or form of handwriting, to a given civilisation or phase of a civilisation, or even to individuals in it, with a high degree of plausibility.

How is it done? It is not at all easy to say. It requires scrupulous observation, accurate knowledge of facts, but is more than this: it is a form of understanding and not of knowledge of facts in the ordinary sense. When we say that we know someone's character well, that a given action could not have been performed by the man in question; or, alternatively, that we regard something as altogether characteristic of him, precisely the kind of thing which he and only he might do – a perception which at once depends on our knowledge of his style of life, his cast of mind or heart, and increases our understanding of them – what kind of knowledge is it that we are claiming? If we were pressed to set forth the general psychological laws from which we deduce or could have deduced this, and, moreover, the things upon which such generalisations are built, we should break down at once. Whether, theoretically, we could have arrived at our intimate understanding of our friend's (or our enemy's) unique personality by such scientific means I do not know – it seems evident that no one ever has, so far, arrived at this kind of knowledge by any such method. The sense in which the most learned and accurate psychologist, working purely on the basis of accumulated scientific data, and of hypotheses bolstered up by these, can describe and predict the behaviour of the human being in a concrete situation, from hour to hour and day to day, is very different from that in which someone who knows a man well, as friends and associates and relations do, can do so; it is far more general, far less accurate if applied to a particular situation. A medical chart or diagram is not the equivalent of a portrait such as a gifted novelist or human being endowed with adequate insight – understanding – could form; not equivalent not at all because it needs less skill or is less valuable for its own purposes, but because if it confines itself to publicly recordable facts and generalisations attested by them, it must necessarily leave out of account that vast number of small, constantly altering, evanescent colours, scents, sounds, and the psychical equivalents of these, the half noticed, half inferred, half gazed-at, half unconsciously absorbed minutiae of behaviour and thought and feeling which are at once too numerous, too complex, too fine and too indiscriminable from each other to be identified, named, ordered, recorded, set forth in neutral scientific language. And more than this, there are among them pattern qualities – what else are we to call them? – habits of thought and emotion, ways of looking at, reacting to, talking about experiences which lie too close to us to be discriminated and classified – of which we are not strictly aware as such, but which, nevertheless, we absorb into our picture of what goes on, and the more sensitively and sharply aware of them we are the more understanding and insight we are rightly said to possess.

This is what understanding human beings largely consists in. To try to analyse and clearly describe what goes on when we understand in this sense is impossible, not because the process in some way 'transcends' or is 'beyond' normal experience, is some special act of magical divination not describable in the language of ordinary experience; but for the opposite reason, that it enters too intimately into our most normal experience, and is a kind of automatic integration of a very large number of data too fugitive and various to be mounted on the pin of some scientific process, one by one, in a sense too obvious, too much taken for granted, to be enumerable. Our language is not meant to catch them; it is intended to communicate relatively stable characteristics, principally of the external world, in terms of which we deal with one another, which form the frontier of our common world, in the manipulation of which our lives largely consist. It is not intended to describe, either, those characteristics which are too permanent, too much with us, to be noticed, since they are always there – and therefore raise no specific problems, since they accompany all our perceptions (these are the categories which, with a singular effort of self-consciousness, philosophers reveal) – or, at the other end of the scale, those characteristics which are not constant enough, which are too ephemeral, which give its unique flavour to that which passes, which constitute the unique essence of a particular situation, a particular moment of history, which give it its irreplaceable character, the ebb and flow of differences which make each moment, each person, each significant act – and the pattern of each culture or human enterprise – be what it is in itself, uniquely different from everything else whatever. These fleeting properties in their turn presuppose those same constant characteristics, neither too omnipresent to be noticed nor too evanescent to be catalogued, with which the official disciplines deal – the sciences and the parasciences of mankind. And yet what makes men foolish or wise, understanding or blind, as opposed to knowledgeable or learned or well informed, is the perception of these unique flavours of each situation as it is, in its specific differences – of that in it wherein it differs from all other situations, that is, those aspects of it which make it insusceptible to scientific treatment, because it is that element in it which no generalisation, because it is a generalisation, can cover.

As I have said above, it is possible to say something about these unique differences – indeed historians and biographers attempt to do so. It is the ability to do this which makes some people profounder students of human beings than others, better advisers to them about their problems than others who are more learned, in possession of more facts and hypotheses. But in the end not everything can be set down, spoken or written: there is too much; it passes too swiftly; it infects the modes of expression themselves and we have no outside vantage-point from which dispassionately to observe and identify it all. What I am attempting to describe is, in short, that sensitive self-adjustment to what cannot be measured or weighed or fully described at all – that capacity called imaginative insight, at its highest point genius – which historians and novelists and dramatists and ordinary persons endowed with understanding of life (at its normal level called common sense) alike display. This is an essential factor in making us admire and trust some historians more than others. It is when a historian so describes the past that we are conscious of having brought before us not merely attested facts, but a revelation of a form of life, of a society presented in sufficiently rich and coherent detail, sufficiently similar to what we ourselves understand by human life or society or men's intercourse, that we can continue – extrapolate – for ourselves, go on by ourselves, understand why this man did this and that nation that, without having to have it explained in detail, because those of our faculties have been brought into play which operate similarly in our understanding of our own society, as opposed to some inductive or deductive conclusions – it is then that we recognise what we have been given as being history, and not the dry rattle of mechanical formulae or of a loose heap of historical bones.

This is what is called bringing a past age to life. The path is beset by treacherous traps: each age, each group of men, each individual has its own perspective, and these do not remain static, but alter, and this must be understood from such evidence as we have, and no final proof that we have understood, in the sense in which the sciences provide it, is here available. The tests of truth and falsehood, of honest methods and deception, of mere imaginative reconstruction and painfully gained, reliable insight, are what they are in ordinary life, where we do distinguish between wisdom and folly, men of genius and charlatans, without the employment of scientific criteria. Moreover, every past perspective itself differs in the perspective of all successive observers. There is the perspective – the unique pattern of attitudes – which is the Renaissance view of things or way of life (that which is common to its own inner variety of outlooks and characters, and so on); and there is, let us say, the eighteenth-century view, the spectacle of the Renaissance as it was viewed by, say, the French Enlightenment in the eighteenth century; and this will differ from its appearance to Victorian thinkers, or twentieth-century Communists or neo-Thomists. These perspectives and perspectives of perspectives are there, and it is just as idle to ask which are true and which false as it is to ask which view of the Alps is the true view and which false. But there is a sense in which 'facts', what can be demonstrated by the evidence, as opposed to interpretations, theories, hypotheses, perspectives, must remain the same for all these changing outlooks, otherwise we should have no historical truth at all. And blurred though the frontier may be between fact on the one hand and attitudes and interpretations on the other, yet it exists. Gibbon would not have rejected facts discovered by Ranke or Creighton or Pirenne because they were not what he considered to be facts (nor would Thucydides); he would have rejected them, if he had, only because he might have thought that they were false or trivial or not what he was looking for. Within Western culture there is sufficient agreement about what counts as fact and what is theory or interpretation (despite continual efforts to deny this by relativists and subjectivists of all kinds) to make doubts about the frontiers between them a pseudo-problem. Nevertheless a mere recital of facts is not history, not even if scientifically testable hypotheses are added to them; only the setting of them in the concrete, at times opaque, but continuous, rich, full texture of 'real life' – the intersubjective, directly recognisable continuum of experience – will do.

Yet so difficult are such insights to obtain, so subjective, too, does a succession of perspectives seem, that there is a natural temptation for historians who take their duty seriously to avoid them, or at least reduce them to a minimum. Hence the plea of those austere researchers who declare that to establish that the good King Dagobert or Emperor Leo the Isaurian died on this or that day of this or that year, however trivial and dreary this may seem, is to establish a firm fact, something which no future researchers will need to discover again, a solid brick in the temple of knowledge; whereas an attempt to analyse the 'medieval mind', to give so vivid an account of some portion of Frankish or Byzantine society as to make it possible for the reader to 'enter into it' imaginatively, is, in the end, only conjecture and journalism, a coherent fantasy, conceived, it may be, in impossible modern terms, likely to give way at some not too distant date to some other 'interpretation', no less arbitrary, reflecting all the interests and temperaments of the new interpreters; not history, not science, a piece of capricious self-expression, agreeable, even fascinating, but *nicht Wissenschaft, bloß Kunst.*

Our intellectual history is a succession of periods of inflation and deflation; when the imagination grows too luxuriant at the expense of careful observation and detail there is a salutary reaction towards austerity and the unadorned facts; when the accounts of these grow so colourless, bleak and pedantic that the public begins to wonder why so dreary an activity, so little connected with any possible human interest, is worth pursuing at all, a Macaulay, a Mommsen, a Michelet, a Pirenne restates the facts in some magnificent synthesis which restores the faith of the weary reader in history as an account of actual human beings, and not merely of some corner of their lives so isolated, so artificially abstracted from the rest as no longer to provide the answer to any possible question which anyone may reasonably be expected to wish to ask about the past. There is an oscillation between attempts to say as little as possible (to play safe – to take the least possible risks with the truth) and attempts to say as much as possible (not to say less than we can – to leave as little as possible out), a perpetual oscillation between horror of saying more than we know for certain, which leads one to say as little as possible, as nearly nothing at all (at any rate of interest) as we humanly can, and *per contra* the attempt to describe the past in real terms, to give it the look of life, something recognisably human, even at the inevitable risk of saying more than we can know by accredited 'scientific' methods, bringing into play those ways of assessing and analysing facts which are intrinsic to our normal daily experience as human beings in relation to each other – the whole intellectual, imaginative, moral, aesthetic, religious life of men – but which may not pass the scrutiny of a purely fact-establishing enquiry. And historians at a given time incline in favour of one or another of these poles as they react against some excessive earlier tendency towards too much exuberance or fantasy, or too puritanical a hatred of the imagination.

III

History is the account of the relations of humans to each other and to their environment; consequently what is true of history is likely to be true of political thought and action as well. The natural admiration for the triumphs of the sciences since Galileo and Newton has stimulated those forms of political theory which, on the assumption that human beings obeyed discoverable natural laws, and that their ills were due to ignorance or vice and could be cured, like those of their bodies, by the application of the right kind of social hygiene, formulated schemes whereby men could be made happy through, and virtuous by, some particular reorganisation of their lives. And indeed, if what men knew about themselves could be set forth in the same systematic form in which they formulate their knowledge of natural objects, they could perhaps count upon a similar degree of success in altering their lives. The triumphs of technology were rightly attributed to adequate knowledge of the laws of nature, which enabled men to predict the results of their own actions and experiments. They knew that they could not do everything, but they also could foretell, within a reasonable margin of error, how much, within the limits of what can be done, they would achieve. And yet, whenever this same method was applied to human affairs, notably in 1789 and 1792 and 1793, in 1848 and in 1917, the results seldom corresponded to the hopes of those human engineers who conducted the crucial social experiments. The great French Revolution failed to establish what its creators – impregnated with the human sciences of their time – had hoped and expected to create; liberty, equality, fraternity were not realised separately, much less together. What had gone wrong? Had there not been sufficient knowledge of facts? Had the Encyclopaedists offered mistaken hypotheses? Had there been a miscalculation in the mathematics involved?

Those who believed that the lives of human beings could be controlled and planned by scientists thought that they had found the error in insufficient attention to economic facts. This is what Babeuf had thought; this is what had inspired the abortive risings of June 1848 in Paris; but this last was a greater failure than its predecessor. What was responsible for failure on this occasion? Marxists were ready with an answer: the dominant principle of human development was the clash of economically determined classes; this had been forgotten or ignored by shallow-minded, unworldly politicians. Armed with this final insight the experimenters could not fail; and it was with supreme confidence that all the relevant knowledge was at their command – they knew what they were doing, they could calculate the result – that the Bolshevik Revolution of 1917 was launched and, in due course, failed to bring about what had been expected by its makers, failed on a more spectacular scale than any revolution hitherto.

Not that these revolutions were ineffective: 1789 and 1917 had each destroyed an old world, 'liquidated' entire classes, transformed the world very violently and permanently; but the positive element of the programme – the transformed human beings, the new moral world – conspicuously failed to materialise. Each revolution had been cursed and blessed, but the results seemed equally remote from the darkest forebodings of its victims and the brightest hopes of its leaders. Something had been miscalculated, something had proved recalcitrant to the social arithmetic employed. The makers of the revolution found themselves, in each case, swept on by the forces which they had released in a direction which they had scarcely anticipated. Some were destroyed by these forces, some attempted to control them but were plainly controlled by them, for all their efforts to dominate the elements. Observers of these great events were ready with *ad hoc* hypotheses to account for or explain away each failure, each frustration. Others fell into a kind of fatalism and gave up all effort to understand the unintelligible. Others again took refuge in generalisations so vast, patterns stretching over so many centuries and millennia, that minor bubbles upon the surface, wars and revolutions, were 'compensated for' in terms of the cosmic curve taken as a whole. The effort of imagination which went into this was grandiose, but its value in explaining specific events – the great revolutions of our time – was correspondingly small.

Plans for human improvement, from the most revolutionary and radical to the mildest reforms, assume some degree of understanding of the way in which social life occurs, together with some hypothesis as to what actions will be followed by what consequences. To the degree to which such views of society and hypotheses about the most efficient methods for transforming it take the form of explicitly held theories, they take into account, solely or principally, those facts of social life which are most noticeable, that is to say, neither – for the reasons we have given above – the most obvious nor the least obvious, but only those which obtrude themselves on our attention (for instance, those which have changed the most in the recent past, or which are the most prominent obstacles or aids to something which I or my class or my Church or my profession wish to promote). Moreover, the facts in question are those which lend themselves most easily to generalisations – and therefore fit most neatly into theories of society, history, political development and change. All theories involve a high degree of abstraction, and those, therefore, who base their actions upon such theories tend to take notice mostly of aspects of the situation that conform to such treatment. This is what we have called the upper level – outer, publicly inspectable social facts. Below them, at various levels of greater and greater complexity, is a complicated network of relationships involving every form of human intercourse, more and more insusceptible to tidy classification, more and more opaque to the theorist's vision as he attempts to unravel their texture, which becomes more and more complex, composed of smaller, more numerous and more elusive particles, as he attempts to analyse any given social unit, more or less arbitrarily defined, in its full individuality – as it actually occurs, uniquely different from every other unit. Nevertheless, it is evident that the distinction between the 'upper' and the 'lower' levels is artificial: each theorist abstracts as he does for his limited purposes, but the number of ways in which this can be done is literally infinite, the strands which connect the elements of social experience, the facets, interrelationships, interactions, are very numerous – certainly incapable of being exhaustively dredged up in any number, however great, of theoretical nets.

The political theory in terms of which, say, a revolution is made concentrates upon certain aspects of the upper, public level; with luck, energy, skill, resolution on the part of the revolutionaries, this level is radically altered; certain institutions are duly destroyed, others put in their place; human lives are altered, new ideas and policies imposed and acted upon. But this upheaval inevitably stirs up, if we may continue to use the metaphor, the lower levels of life. The texture of a society viewed vertically is continuous. Changes above cause tremors of violent force to run through the entire system. If the revolution at the top is very violent it penetrates to the lowest depths, the obscurest corners of the life of the society. The theorists of the revolution may suppose themselves able to predict the effects of their new model upon the portions of the social structure which they observe more or less clearly – that have a place in their theories – but they cannot discount the results of their acts upon the darker levels, and the way in which these will, in turn, affect the level with which they are familiar. Inevitably their acts affect more than they can possibly know. The less observable processes, which are insufficiently clear to be taken account of, naturally result in by-products which are largely incalculable; with the result that it is the regular history of all great revolutions – violent reversals initiated to create a new heaven and a new earth in obedience to a formula – that although they do indeed at times upset existing forms, and for good, they lead, more often than not, to totally new and unforetold situations equally remote from the expectations of the revolutionaries and of their opponents. The more abstract the formula, the less adapted to the tortuous, tangled lines of actual human relationships, the further the total effect from the cut and dried convictions of the theorists.

The prejudices of most men who regard themselves as practical against the solutions of social programmes urged by the theorists – the popular distrust of intellectuals and doctrinaires – rest upon a feeling that the schemata over-simplify the complex texture of human life, that instead of following their contours they try to alter them, to compel them to conform to the symmetry and simplicity of the schemata themselves, and that this does not pay sufficient heed to the shapeless living reality of human lives; and the less the application of such formulae yields the expected results, the more exasperated the theorists become, the more they try to force the facts into some preconceived mould – the more resistance they encounter, the more violent are the efforts to overcome it, the greater the reaction, confusion, suffering untold, the more the original ends are lost sight of, until the consequences of the experiments are beyond what anybody had wished or planned or expected, too often a bitter and purposeless struggle of planners and their victims in a situation which is too much for them, grown beyond the control of both.

Why should such terms as 'doctrinaire', 'fanatical ideologue', 'abstract theorist' be obvious terms of opprobrium if the doctrine, the ideas, the abstractions can be correct and true – if there is a science of society and we *can* foretell the results of radical acts with a fair degree of accuracy? Why should it not be proper to apply them to society? We do not blame physicists for believing in the doctrines of their science; we do not condemn astronomers for

unswerving devotion to mathematical methods; it is when economists or sociologists or political theorists obtain sufficient power to
alter our lives that men become suspicious or indignant or violently
upset. This may partly be due to natural conservatism, hatred of
change, unconscious adherence to 'common-sense' theories of their
own, no wit less stupid, unthinking faith in and loyalty to the old
establishment, however cruel, unjust, grotesque. But the whole of
this resistance to doctrine is not attributable to stupidity and
mediocrity and vested interests and prejudices and narrow egoism
and ignorance and superstition; in part it is due to beliefs about
what kind of behaviour does and what kind of behaviour does not
tend to produce successful results – to the memories of failed
revolutions, to the oceans of blood which have not led to the
Kingdom of Love but to further blood, more misery. And at the
back of this is a just feeling that statecraft – the art of governing
and altering societies – is unlike either the erudition of scholars or
scientific knowledge; that statesmen of genius, unlike the masters
of these disciplines, cannot communicate their knowledge directly,
cannot teach a specific set of rules, cannot set forth any propositions they have established in a form in which they can be learned
easily by others (so that no one need establish them again), or teach
a method which, after them, any competent specialist can practise
without needing the genius of the original inventor or discoverer.
What is called wisdom in statesmen, political skill, is understanding
rather than knowledge – some kind of acquaintance with relevant
facts of such a kind that it enables those who have it to tell what fits
with what: what can be done in given circumstances and what
cannot, what means will work in what situations and how far,
without necessarily being able to explain how they know this or
even what they know. What makes us distinguish Augustus Caesar
or Henry IV of France or Richelieu or Washington or Cavour
from such men as John of Leiden or the Emperor Joseph II of
Austria or Robespierre or Hitler or Stalin, in some sense certainly
no less remarkable? What is the 'secret' of the successes of the
former? How did they know what to do, when to do it? Why does
their work abide, while the work of men no less resolute,
knowledgeable, fearless has crumbled, and, as often as not, left
only untold human misery as its memorial?

Once we ask what the secret is, it becomes plain that there is and
can be none, that we are wondering what key these men had to the
mysteries of their own situations when, in fact, there is no key.

Botany is a science but gardening is not; action and the results of action in situations where only the surface is visible will be successful, partly, no doubt, as the result of luck, but partly owing to 'insight' on the part of the actors, that is, the kind of understanding of the relations of the 'upper' to the 'lower' levels, the kind of semi-instinctive integration of the unaccountable infinitesimals of which individual and social life is composed (of which Tolstoy spoke so well in the Epilogue to *War and Peace*), in which all kinds of skills are involved – powers of observation, knowledge of facts, above all experience – in connection with which we speak of a sense of timing, sensitiveness to the needs and capacities of human beings, political and historical genius, in short the kind of human wisdom, ability to conduct one's life or fit means to ends, with which, as Faust found, mere knowledge of facts – learning, science – was not at all identical. Trial and error occur here, as in the sciences, as in the growth of scholarship. What Karl Popper calls the hypothetico-deductive method plays a central part here, and so do deduction and induction in their orthodox senses. But there is an element of improvisation, of playing by ear, of being able to size up the situation, of knowing when to leap and when to remain still, for which no formulae, no nostrums, no general recipes, no skill in identifying specific situations as instances of general laws can be a substitute.[1]

[1] This kind of knowledge, or practical genius, which statesmen and historians equally need if they are to succeed in understanding the societies of their own or other times, of the past and perhaps of the future, is not the same as that referred to in the celebrated distinction drawn by Gilbert Ryle between knowing that and knowing how. To know how to do something – to possess or acquire a skill or a knack – does not imply an ability to describe why one is acting as one is; a man who knows how to ride a bicycle need not be able to explain what he is doing or why his behaviour leads to the results he desires. But a statesman faced with a critical situation and forced to choose between alternative courses, or a historian who rejects some explanation of past events as fanciful or superficial because events cannot have happened in the manner indicated, or because the explanation does not disclose the relationships of the truly crucial factors, does in some sense judge the situation, assess it so that he can answer objectors, can give reasons for rejecting alternative solutions, and yet cannot demonstrate the truth of what he is saying by reference to theories or systems of knowledge, except to some inconsiderable degree – certainly not in a sense in which scientists or scholars must be ready to do it. And yet in scholarship, for instance, there are strong analogies to the kind of understanding of which I speak. The scholar's process of, say, amending a corrupt text seems to me not altogether unlike the analysis or diagnosis of a social situation. Here, too, no doubt, one cannot do without

The rationalists of the eighteenth century have often been accused, and with reason, of ignoring this truth, and of supposing that the phenomena of social and individual life could be deduced from initial conditions plus scientific laws, like heavenly bodies in the Newtonian system. The truth they ignored was the existence of too great a gap between the generalisation and the concrete situation – the simplicity of the former, the excessive complexity of the latter. But some among their critics are in no better case. No doubt Helvétius and Robespierre and Comte and Lenin erred in supposing that applied science would solve all human ills. But Burke and Maistre and Tolstoy and T. S. Eliot, who perceive the fallacies of this position, tend themselves to suggest that although the key of science is no key, yet a true method of unlocking the mystery exists – in reliance upon tradition, or revelation and faith,

method, scientific system: marks in manuscripts are compared to other marks, structures of sentences to other structures; induction can take the place of memory, hypothetico-deductive tests the place of guesswork. Yet when Porson amended the text of Aristophanes with such spectacular success, his sense of Aristophanes' style – an awareness of what Aristophanes could and what he could not have said – could not have been performed by an 'artificial brain', no matter how many general propositions about ancient Greek comedy had been fed into it, how many manuscripts and papyri and critical editions had been added thereto. Had he not possessed his prodigious learning Porson might not have conceived his solutions; but his capacity for finding them depended on an ability to co-ordinate an untold number of dimly articulated data – and then to take the crucial step, or undergo the crucial experience – to discriminate and articulate to himself a pattern which provided all or many of the desiderata. That is what is meant by calling his guesswork inspired. In principle a great many of the characteristics of Aristophanes' style which entered into his imaginative activity in a semi-conscious fashion could be laid bare, enumerated and labelled, and their connections systematically worked out. In practice this is obviously impossible, because the facts are too minute, there are too many of them, too few persons are adept at such pearl-diving operations, and so forth. Much the same is the case with regard to solutions of problems of history and human action. There is, in one sense, no empirical reason why such processes should not be fully describable and reducible to sciences; why the work of genius, inspiration, imagination – both that of generalisation on the one hand, and that of scrupulous minute fitting of fragments into a pattern on the other – should not be done by machines. But our experience would have to be altogether different – its multi-faceted, 'many-level' structure would have to be radically altered for this to be possible. And when possibilities as radical as this are contemplated – which the imagination can scarcely compass – it is perhaps improper to call them empirical. They belong to the ultimate, most general characteristics of normal human experience, which we cannot assume, on the basis of human experience to date, to be alterable; these characteristics are sometimes known as categories rather than empirical facts.

or an 'organic' view of life, or utter simplicity and simple Christian faith, or divining the hidden stream of Christian civilisation. But if we are right all such solutions are false in principle. There is no substitute for a sense of reality.[1] Many activities may be propaedeutic to it, as archaeology and palaeography are to history. Historians and men of action draw their information whence they can. Scientific, statistical methods and microscopic biographical detail – none of these is irrelevant, all may increase this sense of what belongs where. Indeed, without a minimum of plain information of this type there is nothing but ignorance. Nevertheless, the sense of reality or of history which enables us to detect the relationships of actual things and persons is acquaintance with particulars, while all theory deals with attributes and idealised entities – with the general.

This is perceived by many thinkers, but only Hegel attempted to wed the two by speaking of the universal as 'concrete', by dismissing actual science for dealing with abstractions and propounding the possibility of another altogether superior one which, without ceasing to be general, would enable the scientist (that is, metaphysician) to reason his way by infallible steps to the heart of the concrete particular – the actual situation, which he would understand in all its complexity and fullness and richness, as clearly and exhaustively, and with the same kind of demonstrative certainty, as he grasped rigorously deductive systems. By this monstrous paradox a state of mind was conceived in which contradictory attributes – the formal and the material; theory and practice; deduction and direct acquaintance; that which is here and now, the actual situation, as well as that which is there and then, divided from it by time and space; thought and observation; actual experience and generalisations from it; subject and object; things and words – all were proclaimed to be one and indivisible, the object of a transcendental wisdom, the *Geist* coming to consciousness of itself, which would supersede all the lame and broken efforts to treat the fragments of reality one by one, or, worse still, as if each contained a whole. Nevertheless, in this very effort to cut through the knot by what, at the best, is a sensational conjuring-trick, Hegel did something towards exposing the exaggerated claims of the positivism of his time, which identified all knowledge

---

[1] T. S. Eliot said that men cannot face too much reality; but great historians, novelists and other artists do face it more than others.

with the methods of the natural sciences, culminating in a system of general propositions covering the universe and accounting for all there was.

From this kind of positivism most Utopias of our time have flowed. What is it that we mean when we call a thinker Utopian, or when we accuse a historian of giving an unrealistic, over-doctrinaire account of events? After all, no modern Utopian can be accused of wishing to defy the laws of physics. It is not laws like gravitation or electromagnetism that modern Utopians have ignored. What then have addicts to such systems sinned against? Not certainly the laws of sociology, for very few such have as yet been established, even by the least rigorous, most impressionistic of 'scientific' procedures. Indeed, the excessive belief in their existence is often one of the marks of lack of realism – as is shown on every occasion when men of action successfully defy them and knock over yet another false sociological model. It seems truer to say that to be Utopian is to suggest that courses can be followed which, in fact, cannot, and to argue this from theoretical premises and in the face of the 'concrete' evidence of the 'facts'. That is certainly what Napoleon or Bismarck meant when they railed against speculative theorists.

What are these facts which resist our wishes, which make otherwise desirable schemes seem impracticable to men of sense, which make those who nevertheless urge their realisation liable to be called foolish theorists, blind Utopians? There is no doubt that, in arguing about what can and what cannot be done, we tend to say of this or that plan that 'it will inevitably fail' – that is, that it rests on the assumption that human wills, human organisations, will be strong enough to effect this or that, when in fact they will not, since forces too powerful for them will crush and defeat them. What are these forces? Forces which, say, Bismarck or Lord Salisbury or Abraham Lincoln understood, we believe, but which mere fanatics obsessed by theories do not.

There is at least one answer to this question which is certainly false, and that is that Bismarck perceived laws which the fanatics do not, that his relation to them is that of Newton or Darwin to pre-scientific astrologers or alchemists. This is not so. If we knew laws, the laws which govern social or individual life, we could operate within them by using them as we use others in conquering nature, by inventing methods which take full account of such forces – of their relationships and costly effects. This dependable social technology is precisely what we lack. No one really supposes that Bismarck knew more laws of social dynamics, or knew them better, than, say, Comte. On the contrary, it is because Comte believed in them and William James did not that the former is condemned as Utopian. When we speak of some process as inevitable, when we warn people not to pit their wills against the greater power of the historical situation, which they cannot alter, or cannot alter in the manner they desire, what we mean is not that we know facts and laws which we obey, but that we do not; that we are aware, beyond the facts to which the potential reformers point, of a dark mass of factors whose general drift we perceive but whose precise interrelations we cannot formulate, and that any attempt to behave as if only the clear 'top level' factors were significant or crucial, ignoring the hinterland, will lead to frustration of the intended reforms, perhaps to unexpected disaster. When we think of Utopians as pathetically attempting to overturn institutions or alter the nature of individuals or States, the pathos derives not from the fact that there are known laws which such men are blindly defying, but from the fact that they take their knowledge of a small portion of the scene to cover the entire scene; because instead of realising and admitting how small our knowledge is, how even such knowledge as we could hope to possess of the relations of what is clearly visible and what is not cannot be formulated in the form of laws or generalisations, they pretend that all that need be known is known, that they are working with open eyes in a transparent medium, with facts and laws accurately laid out before them, instead of groping, as in fact they are doing, in a half-light where some may see a little further than others but where none sees beyond a certain point, and, like pilots in a mist, must rely upon a general sense of where they are and how to navigate in such weather and in such waters, with such help as they may derive from maps drawn at other dates by men employing different conventions, and by the aid of such instruments as give nothing but the most general information about their situation.

It is one of the greatest and most fatal fallacies of the great system-builders of the nineteenth century, Hegelians and Comtists and, above all, the many Marxist sects, to suppose that if we call something inevitable we mean to indicate the existence of a law. In the natural sciences the concept of inevitability is seldom used, and to identify there what is inevitable with that which conforms to a law may perhaps be valid, and is certainly harmless; but in the sphere of human relations the precise opposite seems to be the case. When we speak of forces too great to be resisted we do not mean that we have come up against an 'iron law'. We mean that there is too much that we do not know, but dimly surmise, about the situation, and that our wills and the means at our disposal may not be efficacious enough to overcome these unknown factors, menacing often precisely because they are too difficult to analyse. We rightly admire those statesmen who, without pretending to detect laws, are able to do more than others to accomplish their plans, because of a superior sense of the contours of these unknown and half-known factors, and of their effect upon this or that actual situation. They are the persons who estimate what effect this or that deliberate human act is likely to have on the particular texture which the situation presents to them; and they assess the texture, and how much they or others will be able to modify it by acts of will – a texture compounded of human and non-human factors in their interplay – without the benefit of laws or theories; for the factors in question are below the level of clear scientific vision, are precisely those which are too complex, too numerous, too minute to be distilled into an elegant deductive structure of natural laws susceptible to mathematical treatment, and are 'formidable', 'inexorable', 'inevitable' precisely because the texture *is* opaque. We cannot tell exactly how plastic it will prove, because every effort to act upon it is a risk and not precisely calculable – the exact opposite of what it would be if there were social laws and we knew them and what we meant by 'inevitable', or that which accorded with them.

The equation which identifies the difficult medium in which we live with something which obeys objective laws, themselves precise, contradicts our normal usage. For Marxists and, indeed, all those who believe that social or individual life is wholly determined by laws at least in principle discoverable, men are weaker than they supposed in their pre-scientific pride; they are calculable, and in principle capable of omniscience. But as we ordinarily think of ourselves, especially as historians or men of action – that is, when we are dealing with particular individuals and things and facts – we see a very different spectacle: of men governed by few natural laws; falling into error, defeated, victims of one another, through ignorance not of laws, but largely of the results of human acts, those being most successful who possess (apart from luck, which is perhaps indispensable) a combination of will-power and a capacity for non-scientific, non-generalising assessment of specific situations *ad hoc*; which leads to a picture of men as free, sometimes strong, and largely ignorant that is the precise contrary of the scientific view of them as weak, determined and potentially omniscient.

The glaring failure of the latter view to conform with what we see life to be like is what causes such suspicion to fall on scientists when they attempt to generalise about history or politics. Their theories are condemned as foolish and doctrinaire and Utopian. What is meant is that all reforms suggested by such considerations, whether of the Left or the Right, fail to take into account the only method by which anything is ever achieved in practice, whether good or bad, the only method of discovery, the answer to the questions which are proper to historians, namely: What do men do and suffer, and why and how? It is the view that answers to these questions can be provided by formulating general laws, from which the past and future of individuals and societies can be successfully predicted, that has led to misconceptions alike in theory and practice: to fanciful, pseudo-scientific histories and theories of human behaviour, abstract and formal at the expense of the facts, and to revolutions and wars and ideological campaigns conducted on the basis of dogmatic certainty about their out-come – vast misconceptions which have cost the lives, liberty and happiness of a great many innocent human beings.

# POLITICAL JUDGEMENT

WHAT IS it to have good judgement in politics? What is it to be politically wise, or gifted, to be a political genius, or even to be no more than politically competent, to know how to get things done? Perhaps one way of looking for the answer is by considering what we are saying when we denounce statesmen, or pity them, for not possessing these qualities. We sometimes complain that they are blinded by prejudice or passion, but blinded to what? We say that they don't understand the times they live in, or that they are resisting something called 'the logic of the facts', or 'trying to put the clock back', or that 'history is against them', or that they are ignorant or incapable of learning, or else unpractical idealists, visionaries, Utopians, hypnotised by the dream of some fabulous past or some unrealisable future. All such expressions and metaphors seem to presuppose that there is something to know (of which the critic has some notion) which these unfortunate persons have somehow not managed to grasp, whether it is the inexorable movement of some cosmic clock which no man can alter, or some pattern of things in time or space, or in some more mysterious medium – 'the realm of the Spirit' or 'ultimate reality' – which one must first understand if one is to avoid frustration.

But what is this knowledge? Is it knowledge of a science? Are there really laws to be discovered, rules to be learnt? Can statesmen be taught something called political science – the science of the relationships of human beings to each other and to their environment – which consists, like other sciences, of systems of verified hypotheses, organised under laws, that enable one, by the use of further experiment and observation, to discover other facts, and to verify new hypotheses?

Certainly that was the notion, either concealed or open, of both Hobbes and Spinoza, each in his own fashion, and of their followers – a notion that grew more and more powerful in the eighteenth and nineteenth centuries, when the natural sciences acquired enormous prestige, and attempts were made to maintain that anything not capable of being reduced to a natural science could not properly be called knowledge at all. The more ambitious and extreme scientific determinists – Holbach, Helvétius, La Mettrie – used to think that, given enough knowledge of universal human nature and of the laws of social behaviour, and enough knowledge of the state of given human beings at a given time, one could scientifically calculate how these human beings, or at any rate large groups of them – entire societies or classes – would behave under some other given set of circumstances. It was argued, and this seemed reasonable enough at the time, that just as knowledge of mechanics was indispensable to engineers or architects or inventors, so knowledge of social mechanics was necessary for anyone – statesmen, for example – who wished to get large bodies of men to do this or that. For without it what had they to rely on but casual impressions, half-remembered, unverified recollections, guesswork, mere rules of thumb, unscientific hypotheses? One must, no doubt, make do with these if one has no proper scientific method at one's disposal; but one should realise that this is no better than unorganised conjectures about nature made by primitive peoples, or by the inhabitants of Europe during the Dark Ages – grotesquely inadequate tools superseded by the earliest advances of true science. And there are those (in institutions of higher learning) who have thought this, and think this still, in our own times.

Less ambitious thinkers, influenced by the fathers of the life sciences at the turn of the eighteenth century, conceived of the science of society as being rather more like a kind of social anatomy. To be a good doctor it is necessary, but not sufficient, to know anatomical theory. For one must also know how to apply it to specific cases – to particular patients, suffering from particular forms of a particular disease. This cannot be wholly learnt from books or professors, it requires considerable personal experience and natural aptitude. Nevertheless, neither experience nor natural gifts can ever be a complete substitute for knowledge of a developed science – pathology, say, or anatomy. To know only the theory might not be enough to enable one to heal the sick, but to be ignorant of it is fatal. By analogy with medicine, such faults as bad political judgement, lack of realism, Utopianism, attempts to arrest progress, and so on were duly conceived as deriving from ignorance or defiance of the laws of social development – laws of social biology (which conceives of society as an organism rather than a mechanism), or of the corresponding science of politics.

The scientifically inclined philosophers of the eighteenth century believed passionately in just such laws; and tried to account for human behaviour wholly in terms of the identifiable effects of education, of natural environment, and of the calculable results of the play of appetites and passions. However, this approach turned out to explain so small a part of the actual behaviour of human beings at times when it seemed most in need of explanation – during and after the Jacobin Terror – and failed so conspicuously to predict or analyse such major phenomena as the growth and violence of nationalism, the uniqueness of, and the conflicts between, various cultures, and the events leading to wars and revolutions, and displayed so little understanding of what may broadly be called spiritual or emotional life (whether of individuals or of whole peoples), and the unpredictable play of irrational factors, that new hypotheses inevitably entered the field, each claiming to overthrow all the others, and to be the last and definitive word on the subject.

Messianic preachers – prophets – such as Saint-Simon, Fourier, Comte, dogmatic thinkers such as Hegel, Marx, Spengler, histori-cally-minded theological thinkers from Bossuet to Toynbee, the popularisers of Darwin, the adaptors of this or that dominant school of sociology or psychology – all have attempted to step into the breach caused by the failure of the eighteenth-century philoso-phers to construct a proper, successful science of society. Each of these new nineteenth-century apostles laid some claim to exclusive possession of the truth. What they all have in common is the belief that there is one great universal pattern, and one unique method of apprehending it, knowledge of which would have saved statesmen many an error, and humanity many a hideous tragedy.

It was not exactly denied that such statesmen as Colbert, or Richelieu, or Washington, or Pitt, or Bismarck, seem to have done well enough without this knowledge, just as bridges had obviously been built before the principles of mechanics were discovered, and diseases had been cured by men who appeared to know no anatomy. It was admitted that much could be – and had been – achieved by the inspired guesses of individual men of genius, and by their instinctive skills; but, so it was argued, particularly towards the end of the nineteenth century, there was no need to look to so precarious a source of light. The principles upon which these great men acted, even though they may not have known it, so some optimistic sociologists have maintained, can be extracted and reduced to an accurate science, very much as the principles of biology or mechanics must once have been established.

According to this view, political judgement need never again be a matter of instinct and flair and sudden illuminations and strokes of unanalysable genius; rather it should henceforth be built upon the foundations of indubitable knowledge. Opinions might differ about whether this new knowledge was empirical or a priori, whether it derived its authority from the methods of natural science or from metaphysics; but in either form it amounted to what Herbert Spencer called the sciences of social statics and social dynamics. Those who applied it were social engineers; the mysterious art of government was to be mysterious no longer: it could be taught, learnt, applied; it was a matter of professional competence and specialisation.

This thesis would be more plausible if the newly discovered laws did not, as a rule, turn out either to be ancient truisms – such as that most revolutions are followed by reaction (which amounts to not much more than the virtual tautology that most movements come to an end at some time, and are then followed by something else, often in some opposite direction) – or else to be constantly upset, and violently upset, by events, leaving the theoretical systems in ruins. Perhaps nobody did so much to undermine confidence in a dependable science of human relations as the great tyrants of our day – Lenin, Stalin, Hitler. If belief in the laws of history and 'scientific socialism' really did help Lenin or Stalin, it helped them not so much as a form of knowledge, but in the way that a fanatical faith in almost any dogma can be of help to determined men, by justifying ruthless acts and suppressing doubts and scruples.

Between them, Stalin and Hitler left scarcely stone upon stone of the once splendid edifice of the inexorable laws of history. Hitler, after all, almost succeeded in his professed aim of undoing the results of the French Revolution. The Russian Revolution violently twisted the whole of Western society out of what, until that time, seemed to most observers a fairly orderly course – twisted it into an irregular movement, followed by a dramatic collapse, foretold as little by Marxist as by any other 'scientific' prophets. It is easy enough to arrange the past in a symmetrical way – Voltaire's famous cynical epigram to the effect that history is so many tricks played upon the dead is not as superficial as it seems.[1] A true science, though, must be able not merely to rearrange the past but to predict the future. To classify facts, to order them in neat patterns, is not quite yet a science.

We are told that the great earthquake that destroyed Lisbon in the mid-eighteenth century shook Voltaire's faith in inevitable human progress. Similarly the great destructive political upheavals of our own time have instilled terrible doubts about the feasibility of a reliable science of human behaviour for the guidance of men of action – be they industrialists or social-welfare officers or statesmen. The subject evidently had to be re-examined afresh: the assumption that an exact science of social behaviour was merely a matter of time and ingenuity no longer seemed quite so self-evident. What method should this science pursue? Clearly not deductive: there existed no accepted axioms from which the whole of human behaviour could be deduced by means of agreed logical rules. Not even the most dogmatic theologian would claim as much as that. Inductive, then? Laws based on the survey of a large collection of empirical data? Or on hypothetical-deductive methods not very easily applicable to the complexities of human affairs?

In theory, no doubt, such laws should have been discoverable, but in practice this looked less promising. If I am a statesman faced with an agonising choice of possible courses of action in a critical situation, will I really find it useful – even if I can afford to wait that long for the answer – to employ a team of specialists in political science to assemble for me from past history all kinds of cases analogous to my situation, from which I or they must then abstract what these cases have in common, deriving from this exercise relevant laws of human behaviour? The instances for such induction – or for the construction of hypotheses intended to systematise historical knowledge – would, because human experience is so various, not be numerous; and the dismissal even from these instances of all that is unique to each, and the retention only of that which is common, would produce a very thin, generalised residue, and one far too unspecific to be of much help in a practical dilemma.

Obviously what matters is to understand a particular situation in

---

[1] 'Un historien est un babillard qui fait des tracasseries aux morts.' *The Complete Works of Voltaire*, vol. 82 (Geneva and Toronto, 1968), p. 452.

its full uniqueness, the particular men and events and dangers, the particular hopes and fears which are actively at work in a particular place at a particular time: in Paris in 1791, in Petrograd in 1917, in Budapest in 1956, in Prague in 1968 or in Moscow in 1991. We need not attend systematically to whatever it is that these have in common with other events and other situations, which may resemble them in some respects, but may happen to lack exactly that which makes all the difference at a particular moment, in a particular place. If I am driving a car in desperate haste, and come to a rickety-looking bridge, and must make up my mind whether it will bear my weight, some knowledge of the principles of engineering would no doubt be useful. But even so I can scarcely afford to stop to survey and calculate. To be useful to me in a crisis such knowledge must have given rise to a semi-instinctive skill – like the ability to read without simultaneous awareness of the rules of the language.

Still, in engineering some laws can, after all, be formulated, even though I do not need to keep them constantly in mind. In the realm of political action, laws are far and few indeed: skills are everything. What makes statesmen, like drivers of cars, successful is that they do not think in general terms – that is, they do not primarily ask themselves in what respect a given situation is like or unlike other situations in the long course of human history (which is what historical sociologists, or theologians in historical clothing, such as Vico or Toynbee, are fond of doing). Their merit is that they grasp the unique combination of characteristics that constitute this particular situation – this and no other. What they are said to be able to do is to understand the character of a particular movement, of a particular individual, of a unique state of affairs, of a unique atmosphere, of some particular combination of economic, political, personal factors; and we do not readily suppose that this capacity can literally be taught.

We speak of, say, an exceptional sensitiveness to certain kinds of fact, we resort to metaphors. We speak of some people as possessing antennae, as it were, that communicate to them the specific contours and texture of a particular political or social situation. We speak of the possession of a good political eye, or nose, or ear, of a political sense which love or ambition or hate may bring into play, of a sense that crisis and danger sharpen (or alternatively blunt), to which experience is crucial, a particular gift, possibly not altogether unlike that of artists or creative writers. We mean nothing occult or metaphysical; we do not mean a magic eye able to penetrate into something that ordinary minds cannot apprehend; we mean something perfectly ordinary, empirical, and quasi-aesthetic in the way that it works.

The gift we mean entails, above all, a capacity for integrating a vast amalgam of constantly changing, multicoloured, evanescent, perpetually overlapping data, too many, too swift, too inter-mingled to be caught and pinned down and labelled like so many individual butterflies. To integrate in this sense is to see the data (those identified by scientific knowledge as well as by direct perception) as elements in a single pattern, with their implications, to see them as symptoms of past and future possibilities, to see them pragmatically – that is, in terms of what you or others can or will do to them, and what they can or will do to others or to you. To seize a situation in this sense one needs to *see*, to be given a kind of direct, almost sensuous contact with the relevant data, and not merely to recognise their general characteristics, to classify them or reason about them, or analyse them, or reach conclusions and formulate theories about them.

To be able to do this well seems to me to be a gift akin to that of some novelists, that which makes such writers as, for example, Tolstoy or Proust convey a sense of direct acquaintance with the texture of life; not just the sense of a chaotic flow of experience, but a highly developed discrimination of what matters from the rest, whether from the point of view of the writer or that of the characters he describes. Above all this is an acute sense of what fits with what, what springs from what, what leads to what; how things seem to vary to different observers, what the effect of such experience upon them may be; what the result is likely to be in a concrete situation of the interplay of human beings and impersonal forces – geographical or biological or psychological or whatever they may be. It is a sense for what is qualitative rather than quantitative, for what is specific rather than general; it is a species of direct acquaintance, as distinct from a capacity for description or calculation or inference; it is what is variously called natural wisdom, imaginative understanding, insight, perceptiveness, and, more misleadingly, intuition (which dangerously suggests some almost magical faculty), as opposed to the markedly different virtues – very great as these are – of theoretical knowledge or learning, erudition, powers of reasoning and generalisation, intel-lectual genius.

The quality I am attempting to describe is that special understanding of public life (or for that matter private life) which successful statesmen have, whether they are wicked or virtuous – that which Bismarck had (surely a conspicuous example, in the last century, of a politician endowed with considerable political judgement), or Talleyrand or Franklin Roosevelt, or, for that matter, men such as Cavour or Disraeli, Gladstone or Atatürk, in common with the great psychological novelists, something which is conspicuously lacking in men of more purely theoretical genius such as Newton or Einstein or Russell, or even Freud. This is true even of Lenin, despite the huge weight of theory with which he burdened himself.

What are we to call this kind of capacity? Practical wisdom, practical reason, perhaps, a sense of what will 'work', and what will not. It is a capacity, in the first place, for synthesis rather than analysis, for knowledge in the sense in which trainers know their animals, or parents their children, or conductors their orchestras, as opposed to that in which chemists know the contents of their test tubes, or mathematicians know the rules that their symbols obey. Those who lack this, whatever other qualities they may possess, no matter how clever, learned, imaginative, kind, noble, attractive, gifted in other ways they may be, are correctly regarded as politically inept – in the sense in which Joseph II of Austria was inept (and he was certainly a morally better man than, say, his contemporaries Frederick the Great and the Empress Catherine II of Russia, who were far more successful in attaining their ends, and far more benevolently disposed towards mankind) or in which the Puritans, or James II, or Robespierre (or, for that matter, Hitler or even Lenin in the end) proved to be inept at realising at least their positive ends.

What is it that the Emperor Augustus or Bismarck knew and the Emperor Claudius or Joseph II did not? Very probably the Emperor Joseph was intellectually more distinguished and far better read than Bismarck, and Claudius may have known many more facts than Augustus. But Bismarck (or Augustus) had the power of integrating or synthesising the fleeting, broken, infinitely various wisps and fragments that make up life at any level, just as every human being, to some extent, must integrate them (if he is to survive at all), without stopping to analyse how he does what he does, and whether there is a theoretical justification for his activity. Everyone must do it, but Bismarck did it over a much larger field, against a wider horizon of possible courses of action, with far greater power – to a degree, in fact, which is quite correctly described as that of genius. Moreover, the bits and pieces which require to be integrated – that is, seen as fitting with other bits and pieces, and not compatible with yet others, in the way in which, in fact, they do fit and fail to fit in reality – these basic ingredients of life are in a sense too familiar, we are too much with them, they are too close to us, they form the texture of the semi-conscious and unconscious levels of our life, and for that reason they tend to resist tidy classification.

Of course, whatever can be isolated, looked at, inspected, should be. We need not be obscurantist. I do not wish to say or hint, as some romantic thinkers have, that something is lost in the very act of investigating, analysing and bringing to light, that there is some virtue in darkness as such, that the most important things are too deep for words, and should be left untouched, that it is somehow blasphemous to enunciate them.[1] This I believe to be a false and on the whole deleterious doctrine. Whatever can be illuminated, made articulate, incorporated in a proper science, should of course be so. 'We murder to dissect,' wrote Wordsworth[2] – at times we do; at other times dissection reveals truths. There are vast regions of reality which only scientific methods, hypotheses, established truths, can reveal, account for, explain, and indeed control. What science can achieve must be welcomed. In historical studies, in classical scholarship, in archaeology, linguistics, demography, the study of collective behaviour, in many other fields of human life and endeavour, scientific methods can give indispensable information.

I do not hold with those who maintain that natural science, and the technology based upon it, somehow distorts our vision, and prevents us from direct contact with reality – 'being' – which pre-Socratic Greeks or medieval Europeans saw face to face. This seems to me an absurd nostalgic delusion. My argument is only that not everything, in practice, can be – indeed that a great deal cannot be – grasped by the sciences. For, as Tolstoy taught us long ago, the particles are too minute, too heterogeneous, succeed each other too rapidly, occur in combinations of too great a complexity, are too

---

[1] In this spirit Keats wrote: 'Do not all charms fly / At the mere touch of cold philosophy? . . . Philosophy will clip an Angel's wings, / Conquer all mysteries by rule and line . . .'. *Lamia* (1820), part 2, line 229.

[2] In 'The Tables Turned' (1798).

much part and parcel of what we are and do, to be capable of submitting to the required degree of abstraction, that minimum of generalisation and formalisation – idealisation – which any science must exact. After all, Frederick of Prussia and Catherine the Great founded scientific academies (which are still famous and important) with the help of French and Swiss scientists – but did not seek to learn from them how to govern. And although the father of sociology, the eminent Auguste Comte himself, certainly knew a great many more facts and laws than any politician, his theories are today nothing but a sad, huge, oddly-shaped fossil in the stream of knowledge, a kind of curiosity in a museum, whereas Bismarck's political gifts – if I may return to this far from admirable man, because he is perhaps the most effective of all nineteenth-century statesmen – are, alas, only too familiar amongst us still. There is no natural science of politics any more than a natural science of ethics. Natural science cannot answer all questions.

All I am concerned to deny, or at least to doubt, is the truth of Freud's dictum that while science cannot explain everything, nothing else can do so. Bismarck understood something which, let us say, Darwin or James Clerk Maxwell did not need to understand, something about the public medium in which he acted, and he understood it as sculptors understand stone or clay; understood, that is, in this particular case, the potential reactions of relevant bodies of Germans or Frenchmen or Italians or Russians, and understood this without, so far as we know, any conscious inference or careful regard to the laws of history, or laws of any kind, and without recourse to any other specific key or nostrum – not those recommended by Maistre, or Hegel or Nietzsche or Bergson or some of their modern irrationalist successors, any more than those of their enemies, the friends of science. He was successful because he had the particular gift of using his experience and observation to guess successfully how things would turn out.

Scientists, at least *qua* scientists, do not need this talent. Indeed their training often makes them peculiarly unfit in this respect. Those who are scientifically trained often seem to hold Utopian political views precisely because of a belief that methods or models which work well in their particular fields will apply to the entire sphere of human action, or if not this particular method or this particular model, then some other method, some other model of a more or less similar kind. If natural scientists are at times naïve in politics, this may be due to the influence of an insensibly made, but

nevertheless misleading, identification of what works in the formal
and deductive disciplines, or in laboratories, with what works in
the organisation of human life.

I repeat: to deny that laboratories or scientific models offer
something – sometimes a great deal – of value for social organisation or political action is sheer obscurantism; but to maintain that
they have more to teach us than any other form of experience is an
equally blind form of doctrinaire fanaticism which has sometimes
led to the torture of innocent men by pseudo-scientific monoma-
niacs in pursuit of the millennium. When we say of the men of
1789 in France, or of 1917 in Russia, that they were too doctrinaire,
that they relied too much on theories – whether eighteenth-century
theories such as Rousseau's, or nineteenth-century theories such as
Marx's – we do not mean that although these particular theories
were indeed defective, better ones could in principle be discovered,
and that these better theories really would at last do the job of
making men happy and free and wise, so that they would not need,
any longer, to depend so desperately on the improvisations of
gifted leaders, leaders who are so few and far between, and so liable
to megalomania and terrible mistakes.

What we mean is the opposite: that theories, in this sense, are not
appropriate as such in these situations. It is as if we were to look
for a theory of tea-tasting, a science of architecture. The factors to
be evaluated are in these cases too many, and it is on skill in
integrating them, in the sense I have described, that everything
depends, whatever may be our creed or our purpose – whether we
are utilitarians or liberals, communists or mystical theocrats, or
those who have lost their way in some dark Heideggerian forest.
Sciences, theories no doubt do sometimes help, but they cannot be
even a partial substitute for a perceptual gift, for a capacity for
taking in the total pattern of a human situation, of the way in
which things hang together – a talent to which, the finer, the more
uncannily acute it is, the power of abstraction and analysis seems
alien, if not positively hostile.

A scientifically trained observer can of course always analyse a
particular social abuse, or suggest a particular remedy, but he can
do little, as a scientist, to predict what general effects the application of a given remedy or the elimination of a given source of
misery or injustice is going to have on other – especially on
remote – parts of our total social system. We begin by trying to
alter what we can see, but the tremors which our action starts

sometimes run through the entire depth of our society; levels to which we pay no conscious attention are stirred, and all kinds of unintended results ensue. It is semi-instinctive knowledge of these lower depths, knowledge of the intricate connections between the upper surface and other, remoter layers of social or individual life (which Burke was perhaps the first to emphasise, if only to turn his perception to his own traditionalist purposes), that is an indispensable ingredient of good political judgement.

We rightly fear those bold reformers who are too obsessed by their vision to pay attention to the medium in which they work, and who ignore imponderables – John of Leiden, the Puritans, Robespierre, Lenin, Hitler, Stalin. For there is a literal sense in which they know not what they do (and do not care either). And we are rightly apt to put more trust in the equally bold empiricists, Henry IV of France, Peter the Great, Frederick of Prussia, Napoleon, Cavour, Lincoln, Lloyd George, Masaryk, Franklin Roosevelt (if we are on their side at all), because we see that they understand their material. Is this not what is meant by political genius? Or genius in other provinces of human activity? This is not a contrast between conservatism and radicalism, or between caution and audacity, but between types of gift. As there are differences of gifts, so there are different types of folly. Two of these types are in direct contradiction, and in a curious and paradoxical fashion.

The paradox is this: in the realm presided over by the natural sciences, certain laws and principles are recognised as having been established by proper methods – that is, methods recognised as reliable by scientific specialists. Those who deny or defy these laws or methods – people, say, who believe in a flat earth, or do not believe in gravitation – are quite rightly regarded as cranks or lunatics. But in ordinary life, and perhaps in some of the humanities – studies such as history, or philosophy, or law (which differ from the sciences if only because they do not seem to establish – or even want to establish – wider and wider generalisations about the world) – those are Utopian who place excessive faith in laws and methods derived from alien fields, mostly from the natural sciences, and apply them with great confidence and somewhat mechanically. The arts of life – not least of politics – as well as some among the humane studies turn out to possess their own special methods and techniques, their own criteria of success and failure. Utopianism, lack of realism, bad judgement here consist not in failing to apply the methods of natural science, but, on the contrary, in over-applying them. Here failure comes from resisting that which works best in each field, from ignoring or opposing it either in favour of some systematic method or principle claiming universal validity – say the methods of natural science (as Comte did), or of historical theology or social development (as Marx did) – or else from a wish to defy all principles, all methods as such, from simply advocating trust in a lucky star or personal inspiration: that is, mere irrational-ism.

To be rational in any sphere, to display good judgement in it, is to apply those methods which have turned out to work best in it. What is rational in a scientist is therefore often Utopian in a historian or a politician (that is, it systematically fails to obtain the desired result), and vice versa. This pragmatic platitude entails consequences that not everyone is ready to accept. Should states-men be scientific? Should scientists be put in authority, as Plato or Saint-Simon or H. G. Wells wanted? Equally, we might ask, should gardeners be scientific, should cooks? Botany helps garden-ers, laws of dietetics may help cooks, but excessive reliance on these sciences will lead them – and their clients – to their doom. The excellence of cooks and gardeners still depends today most largely upon their artistic endowment and, like that of politicians, on their capacity to improvise. Most of the suspicion of intellec-tuals in politics springs from the belief, not entirely false, that, owing to a strong desire to see life in some simple, symmetrical fashion, they put too much faith in the beneficent results of applying directly to life conclusions obtained by operations in some theoretical sphere. And the corollary of this over-reliance on theory, a corollary alas too often corroborated by experience, is that if the facts – that is, the behaviour of living human beings – are recalcitrant to such experiment, the experimenter becomes annoyed, and tries to alter the facts to fit the theory, which, in practice, means a kind of vivisection of societies until they become what the theory originally declared that the experiment should have caused them to be. The theory is 'saved', indeed, but at too high a cost in useless human suffering; yet since it is applied in the first place, ostensibly at least, to save men from the hardships which, it is alleged, more haphazard methods would bring about, the result is self-defeating. So long as there is no science of politics in sight, attempts to substitute counterfeit science for individual judgement not only lead to failure, and, at times, major disasters, but also discredit the real sciences, and undermine faith in human reason.

The passionate advocacy of unattainable ideals may, even if it is Utopian, break open the barriers of blind tradition and transform the values of human beings, but the advocacy of pseudo-scientific or other kinds of falsely certified means – methods of the sort advertised by metaphysical or other kinds of bogus prospectuses – can only do harm. There is a story – I don't know how true – that when the Prime Minister Lord Salisbury was one day asked on what principle he decided whether to go to war, he replied that, in order to decide whether or not to take an umbrella, he looked at the sky. Perhaps this goes too far. If a reliable science of political weather-forecasting existed, this would, no doubt, be condemned as too subjective a procedure. But, for reasons which I have tried to give, such a science, even if it is not impossible in principle, is still very far to seek. And to act as if it already existed, or was merely round the corner, is an appalling and gratuitous handicap to all political movements, whatever their principles and whatever their purposes – from the most reactionary to the most violently revolutionary – and leads to avoidable suffering.

To demand or preach mechanical precision, even in principle, in a field incapable of it is to be blind and to mislead others. Moreover, there is always the part played by pure luck – which, mysteriously enough, men of good judgement seem to enjoy rather more often than others. This, too, is perhaps worth pondering.

# PHILOSOPHY
# AND GOVERNMENT REPRESSION

APART FROM the question of what rights are in themselves, or how human beings come to have them or to own them or to lose them, it may be asked: Why should philosophers have a special claim to the right to express themselves? Why they rather than artists or historians or scientists or ordinary men? Freedom of speech – or of expression by means other than words – may be an absolute end, needing no justification in terms of any other purpose, and worth fighting for, some would add dying for, for its own sake, independently of its value in making people happy or wise or strong. That is what I should wish to say myself. But this is a point of view which has seldom held the field in human affairs; more frequently there has been a tendency to believe in some single ideal – social or political or religious – to which everything was to be sacrificed, and among the first the freedom for individual self-expression, because it was, quite rightly, seen to constitute a grave danger to the kind of social conformity which uncritical service to a single ideal in the end requires. But be that as it may – whether or not individual freedom is a goal worth defending against the jealous and exclusive claims of even the noblest form of the single final human goal – the question remains: Why should philosophers need special protection from social repression? Is there a special correlation between, say, political liberty and philosophical genius? Would Socrates have risen to even greater heights in a society less terrified of the dangers to the Athenian way of life? Would Aristotle have done better in a republic, or Descartes in conditions of religious freedom, or Spinoza in a society where no one was liable to be excommunicated for his beliefs? After all, some of the boldest, most original and most subversive statements ever made were articulated in Paris in the eighteenth century where both State and Church exercised unlimited censorship. Immanuel Kant introduced the greatest philosophical revolution of our times as a citizen of a State where complete freedom of expression was by no means encouraged, as he himself came to know only too well; and conversely conditions of genuine freedom of expression – as they obtained in many countries of Europe in the nineteenth century – did not, in England or the French Republic or Switzerland or the kingdom of Italy, lead to that magnificent flowering of philosophical talent which those optimistic rationalists who directly connect the growth of freedom with the progress of philosophy must have expected.

I am sure that no genuine correlation can be established except of that elementary kind, for which statistical evidence does not seem indispensable, whereby it is clear that too much repression prevents too many persons from saying what they want, and gradually atrophies their power of comprehension and expression; from which nothing follows save the trivial fact that if you prevent people from thinking, and dull their imagination, they will remain frightened or stupid or infantile and produce little of value in any province. But the converse does not seem to follow: all that we seem able to gather from history is that the arts, the sciences and human thought in general flourish both in periods of freedom and in periods of intermittent or inefficient oppression; and particularly when a despotic regime has lost confidence in itself and is visibly moving towards its fall – in England in the seventeenth century, in France in the eighteenth, in Russia in the nineteenth. But even this is not universally true: it was not so in the declining years of the Roman Empire; nor, so far as I know, in the last years of the empires of China or Turkey, or the last years of the Spanish monarchy. I see no profit in trying to extract historical generalisations from such empirical data, calculated to show that freedom and philosophy are somehow indissolubly connected. The variety of human life and of the types of society is too great – each case must be examined on its merits – and those who seek to establish great sociological uniformities of this type have, thus far, contributed more to the sum of human error than to either truth or entertainment.

And yet there *is* a connection, and a very profound one, between the activity of philosophers and social liberty and State control. It seems to me to follow from what philosophy is, rather than from an artificial schema of what society is and what the pattern of history is and how philosophy does or should fit into them. Consequently I intend to leave for the moment the subject of what freedom is, and whether philosophy needs it and contributes towards it, and whether it is a good thing or dangerous to the stability of society; and say a few words about the nature of philosophy itself, from which I propose later to try to draw some conclusions, which seem to me to be of importance, about the connection between philosophical activity and State control in any form.

Many attempts have been made to define and describe philosophical activity, and perhaps one further attempt will not do great harm or put too great a strain on the patience of my readers. It seems to me that philosophy is peculiar in that it has no fixed technique – no discipline, no set of operational rules in the sense in which the sciences, both empirical and formal, possess them; in the sense in which they can be taught to pupils who can, if they are intelligent and retentive enough, then begin to apply them on their own. And the reason for this is not far to seek: it is that, as soon as a subject does acquire rules of this kind, it is sloughed off by philosophy and falls into one of two receptacles on either side of it, either into the realm of the empirical sciences or into that of the formal a priori ones.

It seems clear that whatever philosophy deals with, it does not concern itself with questions of the kind to which answers can be established by empirical observation; it does not seek to establish matters of fact, once it is clear that an answer to a given question can be found only by some kind of observation – whether of the normal, common-sense, kind, by which I find out whether it is raining or whether I can remember *Lycidas* by heart or have forgotten it; or by slightly more elaborate techniques, by which I find out whether a given country is rich or poor, or whether a given molecule consists of these or those minuter particles, or by which I discover the age of the earth or of the universe, or the relation of one musical style to another, or the causes of a great historical event, or the effect of some unnoticed psychological trait in the mind of a given individual. In all these cases it is quite clear how I must proceed in order to establish the facts – namely by some species of empirical investigation – and once this is so it is clear that the questions are not philosophical questions (whatever philosophical implications they may turn out to have), but questions of fact to be established by the use of appropriate techniques; so that understanding what the question means is itself in part a knowledge of the kind of technique that is relevant to the establishing of an answer.

Equally there is a class of disciplines of a formal type – deductive and not inductive or analogical or feeding upon direct inspection – which again are not part of the subject-matter of philosophy. Wherever the technique of establishing the answer is formal, as in arithmetic, or logic or heraldry, or any other deductive field (say, chess, or any other game obeying rules) – that is, where the answer is to be found by applying specific transformation rules in a field where the axioms and the methods of reasoning are laid down, as it were, beforehand – there too philosophy has no place.

The history of the sciences, both deductive and inductive, has consisted largely, if not entirely, in the way in which groups of related questions to which the answers have previously not been altogether clear are suddenly seen to depend for their answer upon methods which are clearly either empirical or formal; once this is perceived these subjects leave the general field of undifferentiated human enquiry, presided over by philosophy, and set up as independent sciences on their own, with specific techniques, specific rules and teachable methods of procedure. What is left remains the rich but confusing province of philosophy proper, which deals with the whole gamut of questions where the method of solution is not clear, not given as part of the formulation of the question itself.

If I am asked about the physical composition of a planet, or the prospects for life on earth, or whether there are living creatures on Mars, I may not know the answer, but I know – or someone knows – how to discover it, or what specific obstacles there are to the answering of such questions, what data are lacking to such answers, how one would proceed if such data were available; the only difficulty resides in the actual availability of the means to the obtaining of the answer, lack of data or absence of the tools required, not in the obscurity of the question itself, nor in uncertainty as to what method to adopt or where the answer should be looked for. Similarly, if someone asks the solution to some logical or mathematical problem, I know precisely in what region the answer is to be looked for and what the proper techniques to be employed are, and any difficulty there may be will reside in the feebleness of my intellectual resources – I know how such problems are solved and what kind of mental powers are necessary to their solution. But if I am asked whether absolute goodness exists; or whether the material world is real; or what infinity is; or why I cannot go back into the past, or be in two places at once; or whether you can ever know fully what I think or what I feel as I know these things; or whether freedom is better than happiness, or justice, and what justice is – when questions of this type are asked the difficulty is not about the absence of material means for their solution, whether lack of physical capacity (for example, to fly to other planets, to make relevant observations and come back again) or lack of powers of memory, or intellectual analysis, or money (with which to build adequate instruments and the like): the principal difficulty is to know where to look for the answer at all; to know how even to begin to set about looking for a satisfactory solution. It is doubt about what would constitute a satisfactory answer, let alone what the true answer would be. It is when we are in this kind of mental perplexity, when it is clear that the problem is not empirical, at however sophisticated a level, nor one to be solved by mere application of deductive techniques which could in theory be performed by an electronic device – it is then that we are in the presence of a genuine philosophical problem.

It may be that careful thought and elucidation of the problem will succeed in relegating it to one of the two great roads on either side of the central causeway – will show that it is an empirical problem properly to be dealt with by one of the sciences, or by some new science not yet established; or alternatively that it is a logical or mathematical or some other kind of deductive question. This is how philosophy has gradually sloughed off a great many of the questions with which, at various periods, it was beset. Psychology and sociology are the latest of these: and presently logic itself will doubtless become detached and take flight, as mathematics has, as an independent discipline, leaving only the problems of its 'foundations' – themselves not analysable in purely logical ways – to the great source of all problems in general, the philosophically troubled intellect.

In so far as the first mark of a genuinely philosophical question is that it does not, as it were, carry the technical means to its own solution within itself – so that the first difficulty is to establish what it is that we are asking, what it is that is troubling us, what kind of answers we would take as even the appropriate kind of solutions to this problem rather than something totally irrelevant to them (irrespective of whether they were true or false) – the solutions to such questions cannot be provided by creating an army of experts, who, gifted with reasonable intelligence, assiduity, devotion, can set about performing the semi-mechanical work required, as routine scientists or routine historians can perform their work without inspiration or genius or originality of the highest order, and can indeed teach others to perform useful labours without the need of these exceptional attributes.

The major successes of philosophy are constituted not by the discovery of new techniques for the purpose of providing solutions for the questions asked earlier but not sufficiently answered – as Newton provided answers to questions asked before his time, but answered less skilfully, or not answered at all, by his predecessors. The major triumphs of philosophy are achieved by thinkers who do one of two things: either (a) reformulate the questions themselves, by themselves having, and binding upon others, a new vision of the world or some portion of it which itself liberates the intellect from the state of intellectual quasi-cramp which is the original problem, and allows of what is called a new synthesis, a new vision of the relationships of the entities concerned which automatically of itself solves or resolves the original problem; or (b) alternatively do the opposite, namely, finding a situation in which certain dogmatic solutions to questions have been accepted as true, they by some violent shock upset the previously existing 'synthesis' and force upon the attention of other human beings a new and disturbing vision which creates tormenting problems where there was contentment before, and causes people to be troubled and restless where previously they were blind or uninterested.

Both these procedures are totally different from those either of empirical scientists, increasing our knowledge of the external universe, or of the logicians and mathematicians who increase our knowledge or our techniques for the arrangement of what we do know; although, of course, no human activity is wholly distinct from any other, and the kind of synthetic or analytic, combinatory or disruptive genius which philosophers have possessed plays its part in every other province of human thought and, indeed, feeling. Yet there *is* a radical difference between philosophy and other pursuits. I do not mean to imply that in the sciences, or in history, it is enough to proceed by careful observation, patient accumulation of the facts, skilful and ingenious application of techniques which have proved successful in the past, together with such improvements as experience or imagination suggests; in short that skill, devotion, honesty, energy, fixity of purpose are sufficient without inspired conjectures and a sudden insight by genius. But it is, nevertheless, possible in these provinces to advance without inspiration, without the unpredictable leap of imaginative genius. When once a science has been placed on rational and consistent foundations, and a technique of observation, research, hypothesis, experiment successfully elaborated, the great pioneers can teach others less gifted, less enterprising, the proper procedures. A combination of moral and intellectual gifts somewhat below the highest order can often yield useful results and advance knowledge and disseminate light in important ways. An unimaginative historian who composes a painstaking account of, say, the development of an industry in a particular locality, or the development of the art of war in a particular portion of, let us say, the Mediterranean in the later Middle Ages, may not be doing something original or arresting, but he is making a contribution to knowledge, something which others can weave into a more ambitious pattern, for what he is doing is not merely not wasted, but is in its own humble way of positive value. But this is not true in philosophy. In philosophy proper there are no approved techniques, no possibility of uninspired progress, no value in the mechanical or quasi-mechanical application of proven methods to new subject-matter in co-operation with others working as a team (as in some of the natural sciences) or simply for the purpose of providing material for some more powerful or imaginative mind, as on the historical side.

Philosophy is not concerned with the discovering and the ordering of facts, and the inferring of other facts from them, as the sciences are, nor with the weaving of symbolic patterns, as the formal disciplines are. It is concerned with the formulation of problems which are genuine simply because they are felt as such, and the solution of these by *ad hoc* methods dictated by the nature of the problem itself, by the kind of demands which it makes, by the kind of perplexity which it causes; and the greatest of philosophers have done this, whether consciously or not, by altering the point of view from which the problem seemed a problem; by shifting emphasis, by transposing, by shifting the vision of those who are perplexed, in such a way that they perceived distinctions which had hitherto not been visible, or came to see that the distinction upon which they had laid much stress did not in fact exist, or rested upon muddles or lack of insight.

The sense in which, for instance, the greatest revolutionary in modern philosophy – Descartes – altered the history of the subject was not by patient accumulation of facts, or by experiment, or by observation, or by endless trial and error, but by a great act of rebellion. His new method, however he arrived at it, was such that those who accepted it as a source of light found that the vexing problems of scholastic philosophy were not so much solved as rendered irrelevant or meaningless, or shown to be confusions resting upon distinctions which themselves derived from the mechanical use of words or concepts without examining what it was they applied to or in what context they were useful or made sense. Whereas Newton revolutionised modern physics by integrating hitherto disconnected generalisations into a set of a few powerful central formulae, whence so much followed deductively as to render it the most powerful single instrument for the increase of human knowledge in our epoch, Descartes did not integrate, did not simply replace a certain number of isolated truths by a central integrating single theorem or theorems from which the rest deductively followed; he altered the point of view from which philosophical, metaphysical, theological problems had been conceived, and thereby created a host of new problems, some of which in their turn were destined to be superseded and exploded by just such methods as he himself had used.

Philosophical problems arise because concepts and words and thoughts and ways of formulating and arguing about the world and about oneself come into special sorts of collision. This they may do because there was some original contradiction in some early half-conscious formulation or use of such thoughts or such symbols; or because key words have become obsolete – continue to be used when the circumstances with which they were intimately interwoven no longer exist; or because they have become the subject-matter of such occupations as metaphysics or theology, which have tended to develop such concepts or words without paying attention to the situation in which they were born and to which they applied, and in which they played a part, and have therefore tended to create an independent mythology of which such concepts are the inhabitants and which, sooner or later, because they are no longer related to the world in which alone they had real significance, become a source of perplexity – often an unexplained nightmare, something the reason for whose existence no one can any longer remember or account for. This was the condition of scholastic philosophy at many points in the Middle Ages, but particularly towards the end of the sixteenth century, when some of its own practitioners had, in a sense, lost interest in what they were doing, largely because they no longer understood the reasons for the elaborate manipulation of hollow symbols which much of it had by this time become.

To take so vast a step as to liberate oneself from the incubus of an entire system of symbols – and it is scarcely possible to distinguish symbols from thoughts – to shake oneself free of so obsessive a framework, requires genius and intellectual strength and independence of the highest order. The new construction, if it is created by a man of creative as well as destructive talent, has an immense and liberating effect upon his contemporaries, since it removes from them the weight of a no longer intelligible past, and a use of language which cramps the intellect and causes the kind of frustrating perplexity which is very different from those real problems which carry the seeds of their own solution in their own formulation. The new system, born of an act of rebellion, then becomes a kind of new orthodoxy, and disciples spring up on all sides, eager to apply the new technique to provinces to which the original man of genius had perhaps not conceived of applying them. This is sometimes successful, and sometimes leads to a new and equally arid and obfuscating scholasticism. Once the new orthodoxy has won the day, this in its turn, by making concepts rigid, by creating an ossified system of symbols no longer flexible in response to the situations which had originally led to the revolt, creates new frustrations, new insoluble problems, new philosophical perplexities.

The error is perpetually perpetrated whereby philosophy is conceived as a discipline analogous to the most successful pursuits of the day – typically some given science – conceived, say, as being analogous to physics or to biology or to history. The old overthrown philosophy is indeed regarded as a mass of superstition and error; but the new is hopefully accepted as 'scientific' – modelled upon the most successful disciplines of its time – and it is then thought that, just as in the sciences there are techniques communicable to the disciples of the great pathfinders, so in philosophy it is equally possible to train armies of specialists equipped with the latest techniques, using their skills in ways agreed amongst them for the purpose of a collective discovery and dissemination of the final truth.

But this very belief, like the process which embodies it, which has so often led to spectacular success in the sciences, or in history, or in deductive disciplines like mathematics or logic, is, owing to the basic sanity upon which it rests, nothing short of a disaster in philosophy. For the nature of philosophical problems (if I am right) is that they are precisely those problems which are not soluble by the application of ready-made techniques, precisely those questions which puzzle and oppress because they cannot be dealt with by the techniques so successful in the sciences or elsewhere, or by any techniques; and in this way are more akin to the 'problems' of art than to those of science. The supposition that there is a single, final method of dealing with problems which themselves arise from the changing texture of life and of thought and of feeling and of words, of concepts and opinions, of usage and attitude – this supposition is precisely what itself leads to a hardening of the arteries, to excessive dogmatism about the proper use of philosophical terminology, and is itself a cause of that mental agony which philosophical problems at their most acute essentially are. Then there is a new rebellion, the old philosophical luggage is thrown overboard, the victorious and triumphant and liberating methods of an earlier day are quite correctly labelled as dead scholastic logomachy, and men of genius break through the old despotic orthodoxy, set mental bones straight, and create a new language in terms of which the old problems dissolve, and new problems in due course come into being. In the course of this operation some questions are seen to be either empirical or formal, and are, as it were, cast overboard to the right or to the left, and cease thereupon to be part of the subject-matter of philosophy. But despite this systematic parricide much remains, although it is reformulated and reappears in a new guise, in which it can be thought about in terms more adapted to the contemporary experience of the thinkers who grapple with it.

But the pattern of the history of philosophy remains much the same. In a situation where too many problems have become traditional, insoluble, in which nothing but trivial and minor labours are indulged in, and there is a feeling of asphyxiation due to the fact that the major problems seem hopelessly insoluble, and lead to intellectual gloom rather than the stimulation of intellectual power, some great revolutionary arises and breaks through the existing forms. Leibniz was, for instance, such a one, and nothing is more common than the next stage of this particular process, when his devoted disciple, Christian Wolff, proceeded to promise a new rationalist millennium by applying the principles of Leibniz as far and as wide as he could. He drew up programmes for rational theology and rational aesthetics, rational ethics, rational history, rational physics and so forth. Any upheaval in old subjects causes some intellectual ferment, some light, some freedom; and no doubt the beginning of the eighteenth century on the continent of Europe did see a great upsurge of intellectual vitality as thinker after thinker responded to the promise of a new harmonious synthesis. Presently the Wolffian movement developed into an arid orthodoxy as dry, as mechanical, as scholastic and incapable of yielding truth or intellectual excitement as the scholasticism which it had itself so contemptuously and so justifiably destroyed. Then Kant performed upon it the same bold and violent operation as Leibniz and the rationalists of the seventeenth century had performed in their own day.

These liberating operations are the great moments of advance in the subject; but there is here no cumulative technique, no progress, no advance towards some single rational goal, as had been fondly hoped in the seventeenth and eighteenth centuries. Because Descartes or Spinoza or Leibniz showed their genius in destroying the work of their predecessors it does not follow that for their own day and time St Thomas or Albertus Magnus or Duns Scotus or William of Occam had not performed similar liberating tasks. Locke and Berkeley had certainly inflicted defeats upon the orthodox rationalism of the seventeenth century; but then Kant, and perhaps even some among the German romantic philosophers, blew up a large portion of the construction of the English empiricists. In his turn Russell destroyed the greater part of the impressive-looking edifice of traditional metaphysics, and modern linguistic analysts have done much to destroy the foundations – at least the philosophical foundations – upon which Russell had so confidently built.[1]

This is the kind of thing which tends to get philosophy into disrepute. It is felt that the great philosophers are men of considerable intellectual genius, and yet it is noticed that there is no single line of progress, that philosophical disagreements are as sharp and

[1] I am told that Heidegger undermined traditional epistemology in this fashion: but since I do not understand his language or views, I am in no position to comment on this.

as profound as they have ever been; that there is no agreed corpus of growing knowledge, as in the sciences; that the discussion often seems merely verbal; and that there are perpetual 'throwbacks' in philosophy whereby philosophers in the twentieth century go back to those in the eighteenth to draw weapons against those of the nineteenth, whereby the resurrection occurs of thinkers of the past with whom alliances are made across the centuries against new and old heresies of other times and other places. From this it is concluded that there is here some aberration of the human spirit, that nothing solid is being built, and that all that occurs is empty verbal discussion, mere talk, without a rigorous technique to ensure that the results arrived at are guaranteed, solidly embedded in the great edifice of human knowledge. From this in turn one of two conclusions is drawn. One is that philosophy is amusing, sometimes inspired talk which has no 'scientific' value, a species of personal confession, a kind of individual poetry on the part of persons (for example, nineteenth-century romantic writers) who prefer to express themselves in metaphysical prose rather than in verse. On the other side there are those who do demand some rigour and discipline and solid achievement, and therefore seek at last to put philosophy on the sound foundation of the sciences and make it something, if not quite as respectable, at any rate tending towards the solidity and the trustworthiness of, say, chemistry, or at least biology.

Both these attitudes rest upon a misunderstanding of what philosophy is and what it can do. Philosophy is an attempt, and has always been an attempt, to find ways of thinking and talking which, by revealing similarities hitherto unnoticed, and differences hitherto unremarked (sometimes by drawing new analogies with hitherto unthought-of models, or pointing with new emphasis at ignored or underestimated differences between the models hitherto followed and the objects alleged to be like them), cause a transformation of outlook sufficient to alter radically attitudes and ways of thought and speech, and in this way solve or dissolve problems, redistribute subjects, reformulate and reclassify relationships between objects, and transform our vision of the world. This, as in the analogous case of the arts, is something which can be performed only within and for each generation separately, for the vision of one generation must always, if formulated in words, frozen into techniques, established as an orthodoxy, become a prison-house for the next or next but one; and therefore no 'progress' in the precise sense can be expected; each generation requires its own osteopathic operation, its own new insights, its own self-liberation, its own powerful men of genius to transfigure its vision, establish new relationships and new differences. That is why third-rate historians, fourth-rate chemists, even fifth-rate artists, painters, composers, architects, may be of some value; for all these subjects have their own techniques and operate at their own proper level, which may be low, but remains a level. But there is no such thing as third-rate or fourth-rate rebellion, there is no such thing as a trivial effort to cause a major upheaval. That is why the third- and fourth-rate philosophers, who are really engaged in applying the techniques of their predecessors who are dead and gone, as if they were practising a science, as if they were being chemists or engineers, are not so much unsuccessful or unimportant, or unnecessary or superfluous, as positively obstructive, the very persons whose activity often breeds those perplexities and darknesses and problems, those superstitious and dogmatic and often specious and mechanical answers to them, whose sole value is that they act as a spur and a stimulus to the new rebellion, to the men of genius who break through the asphyxia of dogmatism in a subject whose very essence it is to be a liberator and not a constrictor.

This has its own implications, of a perhaps unnoticed kind, with regard to State control. The business of control is to preserve the status quo – to guarantee some established situation, to protect what is regarded as the best, most harmonious correlation of interests, combination of factors, that can in the circumstances be achieved. The purpose of it is stability, peace, contentment. The principal function of philosophy at its best is to break through, liberate, upset. And the mere fact that the method with which it does its upsetting seems abstract and intellectual and often unrelated to the burning practical problems of the day is not a sufficient guarantee against its ultimate influence. For it is difficult to promise that those who are revolutionary and irreverent in one sphere will remain docile and conformist in others. Kant did his best to say nothing too startling in the realm of politics. But his uncompromising ethical conclusions, and to some degree his metaphysical position as well, led to the most upsetting and revolutionary consequences shortly after his own death. Hegel certainly tried, as someone once said,[1] to trim his sails, to steer his course unobtrusively in the peaceful inland lake of aesthetics and metaphysics, and to attract as little notice as possible with his revolutionary doctrines in the realm of politics. But the Marxist and Fascist consequences of applying certain principles of Hegel (however distorted) are not in doubt. In this sense philosophers are necessarily subversive. Others may remain conformist and do work of great value. Certainly painters and architects, even physicists and geographers, chemists and astronomers, biographers and composers, may remain peacefully within the set bounds of some accepted tradition, and within its rigorous framework create immortal masterpieces; or, if not masterpieces, pleasing works, of at any rate temporary value, of a third- or fourth-rate order, works that nevertheless have their place in the universe, which cannot live on major works of genius alone.

This peaceful conformity with his environment, this gentle function within an accepted traditional framework, is not, alas, open to the philosopher. If that is the kind of activity in which he wishes to indulge – and it can be worthy enough and inspired enough – he must cease from philosophy and apply himself to some other work. For as a philosopher he is bound to subvert, break through, destroy, liberate, let in air from outside. And even though in his lifetime he may appear mild, academic and unconcerned with the affairs of the world, his effect upon it is likely to be more destructive, more revolutionary, more far-reaching than that of a great many people who appear to make far more noise. This is not simply an instance of the general influence of ideas as such. Of course ideas are powerful, in particular when they embody – are part and parcel of – strong trends, whether material or spiritual, which are transforming societies and individuals, and work with them and as part of them and not against them or outside them. What I wish to emphasise is the peculiar disruptive power of philosophical ideas.

Perhaps the most dramatic expression was given to this by Heinrich Heine, when in his account of the philosophical schools of Germany he paints an apocalyptic vision of the vast destruction to come, when the great god Thor lifts his hammer to smash Western civilisation, and the armed followers of Fichte, Schelling

[1] Alexander Herzen, Sobranie sochinenii v tridsati tomakh, vol. 9 (Moscow, 1956), p. 21.

and Hegel burst out against the civilised Latin West and lay waste
its ancient culture. He compares Kant to Robespierre and warns
the French not to despise the humble philosopher in his study,
who in peace and silence meditates in terms of apparently harmless
abstractions, but then, like Rousseau and Kant, lights the fuse
which leads to the beheading of a king and world-wide explosions.
Tolstoy once coarsely remarked that to the cobbler nothing is like
leather, and university professors tend to magnify the influence of
ideas upon history simply because these are the wares in which
they professionally deal. Although this was no doubt a just protest
against the placing of exaggerated value upon theories and doctrines, and the neglect of other factors – social, spiritual, economic,
psychological – and networks of factors too minute and numerous
and unanalysable to have had names and classifications applied to
them at all, it does ignore the function and effects of philosophical
activity. For, let me repeat, the problems which philosophers deal
with are not technological in character: that is to say they are not of
such a kind as can plainly be solved by the proper application to
them of methods of discovery which can, as it were, be patented
and taught and gradually improved with time, as the methods of
the sciences or of mathematics or even of history or philology have
been improved and perfected. For all such questions are either
empirical – questions of what happens and how and when and
under what circumstances and in company with what – or formal,
that is, questions of consistency, validity, demonstrability, the most
convenient method of expression, and so forth. But philosophical
questions do not arise in this way at all. They arise because some
kind of crossing of intellectual lines has occurred – some kind of
collision, at times on a grand, paralysing scale, of the traffic of
ideas. Philosophical questions have a certain desperateness about
them, are accompanied by a degree of emotional pressure, a craving
for an answer whose very nature is not clear, a sense at once of
urgency and insolubility which indicates not a quest for facts, for
information about the world or about oneself, nor for the comple-
tion of some formal pattern, the ordering of symbols, the bringing
of them into the required relations with each other, but rather that
there is a conflict – some inner conflict of ideas, of concepts or
ways of thought – either, within a discipline, minor collisions
between subsidiary concepts, the current local symbolism; or, in
the case of major crises, a head-on crash, a confusion and
interreaction of entire conceptual systems, of whole methods of

looking at the world and of describing it, which leads to the so-called 'perennial' problems such as free will versus determinism, theism and atheism, materialism and immaterialism, liberty and order, authority and equality, happiness and justice, self-sacrifice and the pursuit of happiness.

The problems depend to a much greater extent than scientific or mathematical ones upon the particular ways of thinking, on the particular sets of concepts and categories, prevailing in a given culture or language in a given country at a particular time. All problems depend to some degree upon the ways in which people think and act; but the external universe and men's relations to it, although they have no doubt changed throughout historic time, have altered less than ways of thought and of language, whose inner history is in part the history of those problems which are properly called philosophical. And because the problems are not requests for information or greater technical proficiency, deductive or inductive, the 'solutions' sometimes take the form of artistic or religious or metaphysical experience, which liberates those who are oppressed from the particular mental stress which a philosophical problem necessarily, to some degree, always is. For there are many ways of ridding oneself of obsessive anxieties of this kind, and one of them is not by finding a solution but by some method of obliterating the problem itself – the method so frequently used by governments of an authoritarian kind, naturally nervous of ferment and discontent among their subjects, who instead of allowing unpredictable solutions to be propounded, seek to protect the security and stability of their regimes by educating their populations into ignoring or forgetting their troublesome problems, by ironing them out instead of solving them. This, no doubt, is one way in which the State can render men incurious, conformist, obedient, harmonious, but also deprive them of the powers of choice, of creation, of the pursuit of individual ends, of all that we call personal freedom – in favour of all that which, since the Renaissance, liberals in every land have rightly regarded as dark and oppressive, whether they found it in the European Middle Ages, in Asiatic tyrannies, in Fascist and Communist regimes of our own day, or in petty tyrannies and persecutions of originality and the serious quest for the truth, which are so great a menace, even in the democracies, particularly in the greatest among them, of today.

The other path is that which has been taken by the great thinkers of mankind. It is that of breaking through the obstacles to thought and clearing the confusions and refitting the stage by some revolutionary transformation of thought, engendered by those with minds sufficiently imaginative and fresh to be able to rethink their position, to look at the situation in some radically new fashion, from some radically new angle from which everything is seen in what is called 'a different light', so that what seemed insoluble problems are seen to be merely dark shadows apparently cast by no longer real entities which, from the new vantage point, are no longer visible at all.

Because philosophy at its most effective consists in radical transpositions of this type – and the more fundamental, that is to say the less liable to normal self-examination, the categories or concepts transposed in this way are, the profounder we think a philosophy to be – its effect is necessarily in the direction of wider freedom, of upsetting of existing values and habits, of destroying boundaries, transforming familiar contours, which is at once exhilarating and disturbing. No doubt this occurs also outside the realms of philosophy proper, in the arts, the sciences and other provinces of human activity. What I should like to maintain is that, although it may happen there, it need not happen necessarily; an art can be strong and creative and give birth to men of great genius without needing to be revolutionary. Beethoven was no doubt a highly revolutionary and upsetting composer who transformed the nature not merely of symphonic music but of the thought – aesthetic, moral and political – of his time, by creating new ideals and leading the way to new attitudes, a new romanticism, new forms of hero-worship, new notions of what constitutes artistic and personal freedom, integrity, the self-immolation of the artist. But such phenomena are not essential to music. Bach, it might be said, was a composer of magnificent genius, but in a sense a consolidator – a conservative, a creator of order, a source of strength to the tradition, not of revolutionary upheaval. And Ranke, that Bach among historians, similarly preserved more than he destroyed. Men of genius may be creative or destructive, may be liberating or enslaving, or both in one; it is only among philosophers that men of authentic genius are necessarily to a large degree destructive of past tradition. Great philosophers always transform, upset and destroy. It is only the small philosophers who defend vested interests, apply rules, squeeze into procrustean beds, try desperately to fit a great many incompatible, conflicting, contradictory notions into some formal and schematic orthodoxy which is a misapplication of some original revolutionary vision. And when I say misapplication I mean that all attempts to construct orthodoxies out of such visions are necessarily *ipso facto* misapplications.

That is the most important point, it seems to me, about all philosophical activity – that there can in it be no orthodoxy, that there can be no methods capable of indefinite improvement, so that we can say that each generation begins peacefully where the previous generations have left the great work unfinished, so that it can be said that there is continuous progress, and the philosophers of the seventeenth century have improved upon the work of those of the sixteenth, and those of the twentieth have brought to fruition the tasks left unfinished in the nineteenth. This cannot, if I am right, in principle be true. It makes no more sense than saying that Tennyson continued – and improved – the poetry of Aeschylus or Virgil, or that impressionist and post-impressionist painters are an 'advance on' or a 'retrogression from' the painters of the Renaissance, or the sculptors of the Middle Ages, or Benin.

This is what constitutes the uniqueness of philosophy: that its whole work is, and has always been, addressed to each generation with its peculiar problems, created by the particular intellectual or political or social or psychological circumstances of its own time; that originality in philosophy always consisted in the liberation of those beset by problems from some cramping orthodoxy – itself the ossified relic of some previous period – which failed to answer or tended to distort questions which have arisen since, perhaps themselves stimulated by the insufficiency of the prevailing philosophy, by its dogmatism or its obscurity, or its incapacity to respond to some of the problems of its own time. That is why many virtues are of little use in philosophy: patience, industry, capacity for taking pains, a retentive memory, skill in ordering material; all these excellent qualities which are needed by historians, logicians, natural scientists sometimes tend to become enemies of the truth in philosophy. For in that subject there is no 'research', properly speaking. This applies only to the history of ideas and of their origins and propagation, not to original philosophical thought. That is why in philosophy only the first-rate are of use, only the bold, uncommon intellects which possess what Russell once called the capacity for the dissociation of ideas – for the dissolution of concepts which have traditionally travelled tied in bundles – for the questioning of truths so familiar, so thoroughly taken for granted, that the mere suggestion that they could be questioned, that they could be analysed, that their ingredients could be taken apart, sends electric shocks through the frame of ordinary common sense or traditional philosophical thought.

In philosophy alone the plodding, competent, solid workers who cling to accepted methods, and half-consciously seek to preserve familiar landmarks, and work within a system of inherited concepts and categories, are a positive obstruction and a menace – the most formidable of all obstacles to progress. The world, one likes to think, has been created for some given purpose and everything in it plays some necessary part. If you ask what necessary part the second- and third- and fourth-rate philosophers, and those, even, below that line, can have been created to play, perhaps the answer is that, if they did not exist, the possibility of those great creative rebellions which mark the stages of human thought would never have occurred. For the task of the great philosophers who break through the orthodoxy is to sweep away the painstaking edifices of their honourable but limited predecessors, who, whether consciously or unconsciously, tend to imprison thought within their own tidy but fatally misconceived constructions.

If this is so, if it is only in philosophy that true creativeness is always identical with an act of rebellion, a transformation and transposition which in relation to tradition is always subversive – if this is so, then indeed there is a peculiar connection between philosophy and liberty, philosophy and non-conformity, philosophy and the need for freedom from repression, whether by the State or any other suppressing agency, which is relatively absent from other disciplines and is indeed unique. For it seems clear that great creative art can not merely flourish under tyranny but adapt itself to it, that even so sensitive a subject as history, needing correlation of truths unpalatable to a given regime, can nevertheless, if not flourish, at any rate continue and generate useful if not arresting works under a despotism. Certainly the natural sciences can be pursued under tyrannies – it is only the most extreme forms of suppression of thought, those despotisms which make all original activity, all forms of self-expression, dangerous or impossible, that succeed in destroying these human activities as well.

Therefore to denounce slavery because it is fatal to the arts or the sciences seems to me a kind of hypocrisy. I do not think that a sufficiently strict correlation can be established historically to prove slavery is fatal to these activities. If we denounce slavery we do so because it is slavery, because we believe in the value of giving human beings the right to choose what they think and how they live within certain limits as a sacred end in itself, and for no utilitarian reason at all. Slavery, cruelty, oppression; the humiliation and degradation of human beings and the vivisection of them by the State, by the 'engineers of human souls' (as Stalin once so expressively called them), in order that there might be no disharmonies and collisions, and variety be replaced by uniformity, and individual differences by a single world-embracing discipline – these are detestable because they are what they are, because we believe in the opposite, because they offend against our scale of values, against those ends for the sake of which we live and some of us are prepared to die, those ends the suppression of which would make our life literally not worth living; for this reason, and not because it is discouraging to the arts or hampering to the sciences – these seem to me feeble and artificial arguments inherited from those far-off eighteenth-century days when it was thought that all virtues were not merely compatible with each other but entailed each other, and that freedom was desirable because without it one could not have justice or virtue or happiness or knowledge; that knowledge was desirable because without it these other virtues could not be. Since then we have learnt that not all good things are compatible with one another; and that if we seek them we seek them for their own sakes and not because they form a part of some imaginary harmony which a baseless optimist idealism has led us to expect and the attempts to introduce which into the world have already cost it so much needless suffering and frustration.

With philosophy the case is different. There absence of freedom is literally fatal. Human beings are liable to ask themselves questions – about how the world is made and about how they should lead their lives, about what constitutes truth and how their thoughts relate to the real world, about the foundations of the arts and the sciences, about the concepts and categories in terms of which they think and speak. So long as they ask these questions they will claim a natural right to get them answered. This natural right, like all natural rights, flows from the fact that this is how human beings are mentally constituted and that the satisfaction of this kind of curiosity – the pursuit of this province of the truth – is one of the ends which they pursue for their own sake and which make their lives worth living. Any attempt to prevent that activity – to prevent the upsetting of accepted values, the freest possible discussion of ultimate issues, by whatever methods and in whatever terms seem most promising, most illuminating, seem to afford paths out of the impasses which are philosophical problems, to lead forth out of the dead ends which so many genuine philosophical perplexities turn out to be – any attempt to do that, whether in the name of the security and happiness of the community, or of the sacredness of established traditions, or of one of those great and hollow abstractions to which human lives have been sacrificed so often – the claims of nation or race, or manifest destiny, or history or progress, or the Church or the proletariat, or law and order, or any of the other catchwords the exposure and destruction of which has been one of the great glories of critical philosophy – that is a genuine suppression of a basic interest and need and craving of human beings.

That is why periods of conformity, of the application and re-application of methods and categories no longer suitable to their subject-matter – a process that necessarily becomes mechanical, and in the end meaningless, through mere repetition, however scrupulous and sincere – are the blankest patches in the history of human thought. The Middle Ages in Europe, where the censorship was the most severe and conformity most effectively promoted and observed, is a period of this type. Much in it survives and is justly admired to this day. Its art, its statues and its architecture, its social institutions, its poetry, and to some degree its prose, even its music, have a certain eternal value. But its thought is a great and arid waste compared to that of the periods which precede and follow it. To that degree the liberal interpretation of history, the notion of these ages as dark and of the Renaissance as a gradual lifting of the night, is not a falsification. May Erigena, Aquinas, Duns Scotus, Anselm forgive me – but which of these is of real interest except to specialists? Perhaps William of Occam, but that is because he rebelled. Many though the glories of the Middle Ages may be, and superior though they may be in many respects to the disordered world of the present, in the province of thought its record is not equal to those of its predecessors or successors. For all philosophy, because of its function as a liberator of human beings from the inevitable perplexities caused by the intellectual predicaments they get into (because of the continuous development of ideas, and of the meanings of the words that express them), is necessarily a breaking of bonds. Those who believe that final truths may be reached, that there is some ideal order of life on earth which may be attained, that all that is necessary is to establish it, by whatever means, whether peaceful or violent – all those who believe that such finality, whether of life or of thought and feeling, is in principle attainable will, however benevolent their desires, however pure their hearts, however noble and disinterested their ideals, always end by repressing and destroying human beings in their march towards the Promised Land.

Against fanatics of this order – the most dangerous to human freedom, whether they be secular Utopians or theocratic bigots – philosophy is the surest weapon and prophylactic. For its whole history is a warning against the assumption that there are permanent questions and final solutions. In each generation it performs its indispensable task of destroying the integuments of orthodoxies which are the congealed answers to dead or obsolescent questions; and to each generation it provides its own new revolutionary solutions, welcomed, and justly, as revelations of genius in their own day; but probably destined, like the others, to become instruments of tyranny after their day is past and requiring to be overthrown in their turn. There is something arrogant and something unrealistic in demanding solutions which shall be sufficient not merely for one day and time and place but for ever. That is why any attempt to repress philosophers – to replace their tentative answers with final solutions, to silence them or canalise their thought along prearranged channels in the name of some perennial value or fixed scheme of things – is a sure sign that humanity is about to be slaughtered on the altar of some dogma, some false belief in an ultimate salvation. That is why philosophical activity, a perpetual search for new answers in new situations, the recognition that such human situations are perpetually altering, that the present must not be sacrificed either to the past or to the future, is so closely bound up with the existence of a minimum area of civil liberty within which an individual may think and do what he pleases because he pleases it.

If there were a final solution, a final pattern in which society could be arranged, to rebel against which would be sinful, for it was ultimate salvation, liberty would become a sin. By refuting this sinister view, by furnishing perpetual examples of its falsity, philosophy serves the cause of liberty, at least in the work of its best representatives, more faithfully, because this is part of its very essence and not simply a by-product; it is a necessary condition of its activity, by contrast with other provinces of human thought. It needs no justification, it is indispensable to human beings and an end in itself. And the very notion of justification, of the need for evidence and proof of the value of this or that activity, is its own creation. But for those to whom no activity can be self-justified, who seek some social value in everything which is done before they let it pass the barrier of their moral judgement, the unique nexus between philosophical activity and the minimum degree of liberty which a society needs to be called free at all will perhaps serve as an answer. Certainly no society will be wholly secure, wholly safe on rocklike foundations, while philosophers are allowed to roam at large. But their suppression will kill liberty too. That is why all the enemies of freedom automatically round upon intellectuals, like the Communists and Fascists, and make them their first victims; rightly, for they are the great disseminators of those critical ideas which as a rule the great philosophers are the first to formulate. All others may be brought into conformity with the new despotism; only they, whether they want to or not, are in principle incapable of being assimilated into it. This is glory enough for any human activity.

# SOCIALISM AND SOCIALIST THEORIES

SOCIALISM IS a body of Western teaching and practice resting upon the belief that most social evils are due to unequal, or excessively unequal, distribution of material resources; and that these evils can be cured only by the transference, gradual or immediate, total or partial, of the ownership of property and of the means of production, exchange and distribution from private to public control.

I

Socialist or communist ideas and movements (the terms were largely interchangeable until the twentieth century) were fed from many streams: thus the notion that the concentration of power or wealth in the hands of a minority in a community leads to the exploitation of, and injustice to, the majority, is almost as ancient as social thought itself. The Old Testament and the sacred and secular writings of other ancient faiths and cultures contain denunciations of the wickedness and rapacity of the powerful rich as well as practical provisions against the growth of excessive inequalities of wealth. The theme constantly recurs that the pursuit of riches defeats the proper ends of man and perverts his vision of his true condition and purpose: hence the total or partial condemnation of the ownership of worldly goods in the theory and practice of the Essene sects among the Jews of the Roman period, in certain passages of the New Testament, by some early Christian teachers, and by the founders of monastic orders dedicated to poverty and the community of goods as a prerequisite of holy living. Similarly Plato advocates the abolition of private property among the guardians of his ideal State because the possession of, or desire for, private property tends to corrupt the individual, obscure his moral and intellectual vision and make him incapable of pursuing truth and the rational organisation of society. Platonist, Cynic, Stoic and Christian writers are at one in maintaining that private property must be controlled or abolished, not because its possession is of supreme importance but, on the contrary, because it is unimportant in comparison with the social or spiritual values which its existence or accumulation tends to obstruct. Thus Zeno, the founder of Stoicism, advocated anarchism because political authority and the right to property were contrary to the life of reason. The opposite – the cardinal importance of property – animates those who assail uncontrolled acquisition of property because of the poverty, oppression and misery which it brings on the labouring sections of the community. Such explosions as slave revolts in the ancient world (and social ideas at times connected with them) and peasant risings during the Middle Ages served to force upon the attention of the rest of European society the conditions of injustice and degradation in which the vast majority of its members were compelled to live.

As feudalism gave way to private initiative and the institutions of modern capitalism, social thinkers began to condemn the evils of unbridled competition, less because of its incompatibility with the spiritual life than because they concluded that property relations determined other social, political and economic factors in society, and consequently that any radical reform designed to bring social justice and happiness, and to remove irrational divisions between human beings, would have to begin by altering the conditions of the use and exchange of property in the State. Hence in More's *Utopia*, in Campanella's *City of the Sun* and Harrington's *Oceana*, the creation of communal ownership is an indispensable measure, since the property relations of existing societies are regarded as being mainly responsible for the injustices prevalent in them, and the material conditions of human happiness, so far from being considered to be negligible as compared to spiritual factors, begin to be regarded as decisive. This tendency grows more marked with the rise of philosophical and social doctrines which seek to explain the laws of nature and the behaviour of man by the operation of material and tangible rather than palpable occult or spiritual causes.

In the ferment of the religious, social and political conflicts of the seventeenth century and the rationalist or empiricist criticism of all established institutions in the eighteenth century, the basis of the right to property was bound to be questioned. Was the right to property an inalienable 'natural right' of the individual? Or might the State dispose of it as it wished? Was it conferred by the authority of the scriptures, or of natural law, or of a royal sovereign or of some other human or superhuman institution, and how did this square with the Christian doctrine that God had given the earth to all men and not only to some? Was it the result of free agreement between individuals or simply a matter of brute force? Locke had advanced the theory that men had a right to property with which they had 'mixed their labour' and that the value of commodities was created by the labour expended upon making them; the consequences he drew favoured the owners of property. But before him the Diggers led by Winstanley had, during the Commonwealth, demanded the right of communal exploitation of State properties on the ground that the entire community and not specific individuals were entitled to the possession of 'the earth and all the fruits thereof'; similar views had been uttered by leaders of Protestant religious sects in Germany and elsewhere. In part this was still the social protest against the iniquities of the rich and powerful heard in every generation, but it also derived from a doctrine gradually growing articulate, that the right to private property was neither God-given nor inherent nor 'natural', but a human artifice, and the further view that the only path to happiness and justice lay through the abolition of private property, and communal ownership and control.

II

In the eighteenth century these doctrines found explicit formulation: in the works of the abbé Mably private property is denounced as the chief source of the evil that men do to their fellows and, with many an example drawn from the semi-communist constitution of ancient Sparta and from the writings of Plato and his followers, the thesis is developed that only through communal ownership of the means of material production can justice be ensured and the minority of the strong prevented from oppressing and thwarting the full development and liberty of the weaker majority. In a similar strain Morelly in his *Le Code de la nature* develops the doctrine that the sole source of injustice and misery is the unequal distribution of property, with the corollary, soon to be drawn by others, that the political liberty and removal of political and social privilege for which the great eighteenth-century radicals – Voltaire, Diderot, Helvétius and the *encyclopédistes* in general – fought with passion and eloquence would avail nothing unless accompanied by guarantees against the unequal accumulation of property in private hands. Morelly declared that this could be secured only by the establishment of common ownership. Like Mably, he does not confine himself to general principles. Like all inventors of Utopias he goes into the minute details of the ideal State, prescribes specific functions to various classes of its citizens, elaborates a severe penal code and recommends various transitional measures whereby the desired transformation of existing society into a rigidly regimented ideal community may most easily and painlessly be brought about.

Such aspirations were decisively influenced by the deeply stirring and, despite their confusions, illuminating tracts of Rousseau, who did not advance a coherent, unified social and economic doctrine but preached on the text that the greatest criminal was he who first drew a boundary round a field and called it his own. Rousseau did not advocate the abolition of private property; but he denounced competition, blatant inequality, the unbridled accumulation of property and power, and the acquisitive instinct which caused it, as central sources of political and moral evil; from this to the thesis that property should be held in common was but a short step.

The French Revolution did not encourage communism: among the sacred rights of every man and citizen was that of property; and although Robespierre passed a law which seemed to impose State control upon the acquisition and enjoyment of resources by the individual, communism was opposed by nearly all the principal revolutionary sects. There was, however, at least one small group of revolutionaries, deeply influenced by Morelly and Rousseau, who, under the leadership of 'Gracchus' Babeuf, believed that the Revolution, which had intended to liberate the individual and introduce equality between all sections of society, had plainly failed in its purpose, as the most casual glance at the corruption and despotism prevalent in France during the *Directoire* would show. To them it seemed that the Revolution had clearly been betrayed, and betrayed by those who had put their own wealth and power before the interest of the people. The vast transfers of the property which had belonged to the proscribed classes, the aristocracy, the Church and the enemies of the Revolution, had evidently gone to fill the pockets of the new rich; there was neither liberty nor equality; for the former could not exist without the latter. Robespierre's task must be carried through to the end, and the only way of guaranteeing political liberty was by securing economic equality. From this Babeuf and his pure-hearted and fanatical friends deduced their immediate duty – to abolish private property and transfer all the resources of France (ultimately no doubt of mankind) to the community as a whole, to be disposed of by its democratically appointed representatives in accordance with the laws of equity and justice. In 1796 they entered into a conspiracy to overthrow the *Directoire* and declare a communist republic. They were betrayed by one of their number and duly arrested; the ringleaders were executed. Nevertheless the 'conspiracy of the equals' was an event of cardinal importance. It was the first attempt to translate communist doctrine, which had previously played its part merely as an element in the general radical literature of the time, into actual practice. The shock to public opinion was considerable, and from that moment communist doctrine began to be taken seriously as something more than unworldly idealism or a merely theoretical threat to the existing order. Not all of Babeuf's followers were executed, and one of them, Buonarroti, survived the Restoration and impregnated a good many of the revolutionaries and reformers of the nineteenth century with the simple and violent ideas of his master.

Socialism, from a doctrine which, whatever view might be taken of its merits, had earlier almost universally been recognised as too impracticable to be more than a Utopian dream, began a new career in the nineteenth century as a revolutionary and, in the view both of its champions and of its opponents, as a by no means unattainable goal. A great fillip to socialist doctrines was given by the general loosening of the social and economic structure of Europe brought about by the Revolution and by the Napoleonic conquests and reforms. The Bourbon Restoration frustrated so great a majority of the newly emancipated French middle class that it caused a violent intellectual ferment among Frenchmen not normally of a revolutionary temper. One of the most imaginative and radical expositions of the new ideas about society which the Revolution had generated, and the Restoration tried to resist, exists in the works of the Comte Henri de Saint-Simon.

Saint-Simon is not an enemy to private accumulation, and so not strictly a socialist, but he originated a great many doctrines which later socialism took over, and as a pioneer of the new European (and American) outlook he had an influence second to that of no other thinker of his time. He was a man of chaotic life and scarcely less chaotic and undisciplined thought, interspersed with insights of genius. He was neither a democrat nor a liberal. Unlike the rationalists of the eighteenth century, he did not believe in the steady progress of human enlightenment, culminating in the ideals of the *Encyclopédie*. One of the first thinkers with an acute sense of historical evolution, he believed in an alternation of periods of progress and disintegration; by progress he meant the development of institutions which fitted and stimulated the growth of tendencies brought about by technological inventions and discoveries. He was sufficiently a child of the eighteenth century to believe in the omnipotence of reason; but by reason he meant the rational organisation of society, and by rational organisation the planning of a social order by those whose technical knowledge best equipped them to understand the material and spiritual needs and possibilities of their own times. The fundamental factors of history, according to him, consist in the interplay of economic forces: more precisely in the interplay and conflict of social classes, each of which represents a distinct economic, social and spiritual demand in the society of its time. If in the Middle Ages kings, soldiers, priests and lawyers represented classes expressive of the dominant economic forces of their time, and armed with the most advanced technical resources then available, modern industrial and scientific development had rendered these classes obsolete. The natural leaders of contemporary society, representing the new and decisive social forces which the industrial revolution had released, were industrialists, bankers, scientists, technicians, artists, international traders; they and they alone understood and, indeed, incarnated the new forces at play, they and they alone should be entrusted with the conscious organisation of the new society. Misery and injustice sprang from idleness and ignorance and their by-product, inefficiency. The survivals of a crumbling feudalism could not adequately serve a society which had, as a result of an unparalleled advance in scientific techniques, become capable of producing infinitely greater wealth, together with resources for its exploitation, than any dreamt of in any previous society. Political forms were but the outer shape of the real connections, social and economic, between human beings, and it required men of organising genius to transform these political forms to fit the new social and economic realities. Unless there was organisation and rational planning, there would be waste, conflict and misery. The warfare between economic classes which had shaped previous history was not inevitable. Under a rational plan of production and distribution of material goods, of education, of scientific research, the interests of all individuals would become reconciled. Idleness is the deadliest of all sins. The only citizens who truly matter are the producers, whether manual or intellectual: the rest are drones and parasites, obsolete survivals from the past, or else the fools and knaves and misfits who cannot adapt themselves to the new world created by new forces of production.

Hence Saint-Simon advocated at various stages of his life various forms of a totally planned society, directed by captains of industry or finance and scientific experts, and aided by the imaginative power of artists – the only true benefactors of mankind – who by acting together would create a world in which the faculties of man, hitherto frustrated by crippling environments, could at last find a rich and complete fulfilment. This 'technocracy' would be founded, not on the unhistorical and therefore often inapplicable principles of a Benthamite utilitarianism, but on a profound understanding of the factors, chiefly technological, which determine social change, and transform the needs and character of men, and consequently of the particular historical stage which mankind had reached. It would plan the future of mankind in accordance with the vast new possibilities of material development which alone could produce the infinite plenty from which all could draw inexhaustibly. The abolition of scarcity would lead to a state of complete economic contentment, without which political liberty and political equality are hollow slogans.

Saint-Simon, unlike Babeuf, did not advocate the abolition or even curtailment of private property, nor yet the equality of mankind. On the contrary, he believed in the virtue of the infinite expansion of individual enterprise, and the immense superiority of scientists, bankers, industrialists and artists of genius to the mass of mankind. But he advocated a completely planned production and distribution of economic resources. He asserted that individuals, left to themselves, tend to get in each other's way and diminish productivity, and denied that they possessed natural rights against a central planning body. He regarded the moral, religious, artistic and intellectual development of humanity as directly dependent upon the progress of the new industrial system, freed from wasteful class conflict; and he placed all his hopes upon the rational control of it by men of genius.

These theses, despite the obscure and fanciful imagery in which they are often expressed – or perhaps because of it – profoundly influenced all subsequent collectivist thought. His followers Enfantin and Bazard repeated their master's denunciation of equality and unchanging, universal human 'rights', advocated the rewarding of individuals according to their industry and ability, demanded association and hierarchical organisation of society – in fact, a kind of State capitalism, rigidly controlled by scientifically trained experts – and above all urged abolition of inheritance, whereby in due course the existing irrational organisation of private property would come to an end. Saint-Simon's vision is a half mystical, half scientific Utopia, in which reason is victorious over superstition and prejudice, and material resources are developed to their fullest extent under the direction of a kind of world trust or cartel, regulated by an omniscient, wise, benevolent central planning board in control of all aspects of social and economic life. At once scientific and authoritarian, this body will change humanity, will cause mankind freely to fulfil and realise its whole nature, sensuous, emotional and intellectual, and so end all self-destructive asceticism, false spirituality and other worldliness, by restoring to the body its pre-Christian rights – by the 'rehabilitation of the flesh'. It was a dream destined to have a profound influence upon the socialist and communist experiments of the twentieth century, but running sharply counter to the liberal, individualist and democratic thought of the later nineteenth century, which tended to look upon it as a despotism too inhuman to be realisable, as J. S. Mill looked on its later development by Saint-Simon's disciple Auguste Comte. It was not for nothing that Engels called Saint-Simon's doctrine 'an administration of things', not of men.

III

Scarcely less important was the influence of an even stranger and less realistic system builder than Saint-Simon, Charles Fourier. While Saint-Simon was a nobleman and a man of broad and sweeping vision, who conceived society in terms of a new, scientific industrial feudalism with bankers and scientists in the place of soldiers and priests, Fourier was of lower-middle-class origin, lived in perpetual financial difficulties and had a far more intimate acquaintance with the miseries and iniquities of the social system of his time.

The main problem which troubled Fourier, like other early

nineteenth-century thinkers, was the failure of the French Revolution to confer the benefits which it had promised so lavishly. But whereas Saint-Simon was opposed to popular government, which seemed to him no better than irrational mob rule, Fourier was more democratically inclined. His criticisms and his Utopian vision spring mainly from the sense of outrage to his desire for justice and his natural benevolence caused by the spectacle of human exploitation and brutality, of the stupid waste of effort and resources, of extremes of frustration and helpless poverty side by side with ill-gotten wealth, a scene which Stendhal and Balzac painted at a later stage of its development.

Fourier possessed a violent, unbridled and eccentric imagination; his cosmological, psychological, botanical and zoological speculations are fantastic to the point of lunacy. In the course of a penetrating and realistic sociological exposition he discusses the influence of the putrescence of the moon upon human diet, invents cycles of twenty thousand ascending or descending orders of cosmic progress or reaction, foreshadows the appearance of new races of beasts useful to man, amiable 'anti-lions', busily performing menial tasks for their masters, 'anti-whales' engaged in towing ships across the Atlantic in a day (the sea water having been meanwhile magically transformed into an ocean of lemonade). Nevertheless Fourier's basic criticisms of industrial society are full of unforgettably bright flashes of insight, and their influence has proved remarkably powerful.

Fourier's main thesis is that the root evil in society is competition: at the very moment in which mankind is producing unparalleled quantities of material goods, misery and poverty are increasing by leaps and bounds; the more productive the inventions of scientists and technicians, the greater the exploitation of the weak by the strong, of the many by the few; the more primitive and resourceless a society, the more kindly and patriarchal are relations between individuals and classes; the more mankind knows and produces, the more cruelty, suffering and immorality it brings into the world. There is only one explanation for this. Because men compete and fight each other instead of working in association, they have created a system by which success for one man is possible only through the failure of another. One man's meat can satisfy him only by being another man's poison. How does the manufacturer become rich? By selling as much as he can as dearly as he can. The greater the scarcity in the market, the higher the price he can exact. Hence he will build up monopolies and will even destroy some of his commodities to raise the price of the rest. Moreover he will be encouraged to adulterate his goods so that they may be used up as rapidly as possible and thereby stimulate the demand for more. The shoemaker will see to it that the shoes he sells fall to pieces as quickly as possible; the builder, that his building collapses reasonably early. The doctor will hope for the widest possible spread of disease; he will avoid anything which cures the patient too quickly or completely; the lawyer and the judge will hope for the maximum quantity of discord, crime, litigation. The method of competition is the cutting of throats. So long as the purpose of society is not welfare but acquisition, the attempt by each individual to enrich himself must lead to the maximum of chaos and therefore to waste, conflict and misery. The middlemen, the bureaucrats, the officials, the soldiers, the journalists produce nothing useful. They can exist only as parasites, by battening on the destructive instincts, the vices and the follies of mankind; they have a vested interest in useless ferment and disorder.

This can be remedied only by inducing men to form themselves into mutually beneficial associations where the advantage of each contributes to the happiness of the social whole. Men become rapacious and hostile to one another, greedy, unscrupulous, ruthless, sycophantic and dishonest only because bad education and bad institutions blind them to the natural harmony of their interests. Man is by nature good, that is, all his instincts, appetites, feelings, tendencies can be fulfilled harmoniously provided they are given the environment and purpose for which they crave. The purpose of education is to fulfil natural human needs, not to cripple them by forcing them in unnatural directions. We disapprove of theft, but theft is due only to scarcity. Where there is plenty, the gifts of ingenuity and imagination which at present go into stealing can be diverted into constructive channels which will delight their owner instead of, as now, riddling him with fears. We rack our brains to find ways of getting workers in a factory to perform so many hours of grinding monotonous labour; fatigue kills the creative impulse, monotony is the death of the imagination and productive instinct. Men would achieve far more if their work were made more varied, if each man were carefully chosen to do that to which his natural talents incline him. The despotism of the capitalist, and the sullen hatred and liability to crime of his brutalised workmen, are due only to maldistribution of talents, the bad organisation of the productive faculties of man. There is no character which cannot be successfully canalised into activities useful to society by a sufficiently careful educationally formative system.

To put an end to the horrors of industrial standardisation Fourier advocates that men live in associations of about eight hundred families – such a co-operative group being called the 'phalanx' – in attractive buildings called 'phalansteries' surrounded by gardens, fields and groves, in which much of the heavy work is done by machinery, the lighter tasks by members specially trained, never working for more than a few hours a day, and provided with all the necessities and luxuries which a normal well-developed human being would require to satisfy his material, moral, spiritual and intellectual needs. The phalansteries, by using methods of co-operation, will introduce scientific rationalisation; infinitely richer results will be achieved by centralised, but not over-centralised, production by means of machinery than by individual handicrafts and the chaotic scattering of unbalanced resources. Everything becomes rationalised. The principle of competition is gone, and happy, free, voluntary association has taken its place. The phalansteries are organised into wider and wider wholes, national frontiers are transcended and mankind becomes a free federation of free associations of self-subsistent co-operative producers and distributors, living under healthy conditions and the enlightened guidance of benevolent educators who have grasped the principle that, to be efficient, men must enjoy their work, and that there are few tasks that need doing that someone or other cannot be found or trained to enjoy.[1]

Fourier's actual Utopia is in many details fantastic; but the basic theses (which owe much to Rousseau) – that the industrial revolution produced a society which spent much of its energy in defeating its own ends; that unbridled competition is not the most efficient means of producing either prosperity or happiness; that most men are the victims of man-made institutions whose purposes they do not understand or have forgotten; that men work best and are most human when they do that which they enjoy most; that

[1] For instance, he says, those who love gossip could be made telegraph operators, children who love to play in mud could be made happy scavengers – and so on.

men are happiest when they are most creative, and that association conduces to this in many instances more effectively than the ferocious competition of a *laissez-faire* society – all these have had an immeasurable influence upon both socialist and liberal thought and practice. Fourier's doctrines, which led to the establishment of idealistically conceived but short-lived colonies in the United States, profoundly affected radical thought in America; the New Deal inaugurated by Roosevelt in 1932 was full of Saint-Simonian and Fourierist notions. Fourier exercised influence in Russia, where the ideal of an harmonious and egalitarian association of producers, that is, workers and planners, in a society free from the despotism both of the bureaucracy and the police and of that exercised by a competitive capitalism, struck deep root in the 1840s and fed both the romantic 'populist' and the 'scientific' socialist oppositions to the government (indeed Dostoevsky was all but condemned to death for belonging to an association for the spreading of Fourierist doctrines). In France he helped to shape the ideas of Proudhon, and through his works shaped the outlook of the founders of the anti-political syndicalist and co-operative movements, whose influence was scarcely smaller than that of political socialism itself. The emphasis on the virtues of association, of vocational training and distribution, of industrial psychology, of the centralisation and rationalisation of economic life in self-subsistent, small, semi-rural co-operatives, rather than the vast, urban centralised industrial units of Saint-Simon; the ending of purely private enterprise and moral regeneration through the liberation of the creative, human faculties of the flesh as well as of the spirit – all these ideas are seeds of socialism. But Fourier detested communism and revolutionary methods; he believed in moral conversion and social peace between opposed classes on the basis of common ideals; he defended private property and wished to create it in abundance rather than abolish it. His follower Considérant stressed the element of class struggle; the development of capitalism threw more and more propertyless proletarians into the vast reservoir of pauperised workers with no rights and no hopes: there were 'two nations' struggling in every community and their interests sharply conflicted at every point; but this war could be concluded peacefully, if need be by State intervention, by the expedient of guaranteeing a minimum subsistence to labour and the freedom of religion and association, thought and speech to all citizens; by regrouping society into communities of co-operative producers, eternal peace and plenty could be ensured.

A somewhat similar doctrine but with a greater stress on collectivism is to be found in the writings of Pierre Leroux. He believed with a mystical fervour in State control and socially committed art. The State must regulate economic life and take from everyone according to his capacity and give to everyone according to his need. It is contrary to divine law that thirty-four million Frenchmen should be exploited by some hundred thousand of their fellows and that the inequalities of income should grow greater with every year. Leroux's views had a decisive influence on the social novels of George Sand.

Views similar to those of Fourier (but without the absurdities) were held by the Welsh manufacturer Robert Owen, who, unlike Fourier, triumphantly demonstrated their validity in practice. By improving the conditions of his cotton-spinners in New Lanark, by establishing minimum wages, creating a unique and boldly original system of social services at the grimmest period of the Industrial Revolution, by creating conditions of health, honesty and confidence by the most generous and efficient exercise of paternalistic control, Owen created a model industrial community. Its standard of living was higher than any then prevalent either in England or in Europe and, in view of the very tangible profits which it made for its owners, it attracted world-wide attention. Not content with this practical demonstration of the principles of rational and humanitarian planning, Owen sought to universalise his experience and gradually came to the conclusion that unless private property was abolished altogether – and with it such irrational and anti-social institutions as marriage and organised religion – mankind was doomed to the misery spread by ignorance and competition. He believed, like the rationalists of the previous century, that all that a man was he owed to his environment, and especially to education or lack of it, and that the dissemination of the truth would of itself virtually avail to cure all evils. Like Saint-Simon, Owen ruined himself financially towards the end of his long and devotedly altruistic life, spent in preaching atheism, collectivism by free association and love freed from the marriage bond, as the principles upon which a new model world must be founded. His 'parallelograms', so called because of the shape of the buildings he advocated, were the British equivalent of Fourier's phalansteries. As in the case of Fourier, the fantastic elements in Owen's doctrines were in

time forgotten. The fruitful elements – the blessings of co-operation, the increased productivity and efficiency due to the raising of
material, moral and intellectual standards in the form of health,
educational and other social services, social insurance and so
forth – were the foundation of workers' co-operative movements
in many countries, and of more humane and more scientific
principles and methods of industrial legislation and management;
indeed the term 'socialism' itself occurs for the first time in an
Owenite journal as a vague name for communal solidarity as
against private gain.

The intellectual centre of Europe in the nineteenth century was
Paris, where the next step in the development of socialist ideas was
made by Louis Blanc. His principal innovation consisted in the
thesis that all forms of reform or revolution which sought to
substitute industrial or other forms of co-operation for the action
of the State were necessarily impracticable, as the State had in the
course of time accumulated such powers of control and coercion –
the army, police, financial machinery – that all efforts to overthrow
it by either persuasion or violence in favour of some other
institution must necessarily be vain. Nevertheless Blanc, although
he was opposed to revolution, recognised the necessity of the
radical transformation of society from its condition of chaos and
injustice. He paints a picture, scarcely less horrifying than Fourier's
most lurid descriptions, of unbridled competition in which battles
are fought not merely between employers and employed, but
between the town worker subsisting on the edge of employment
and the poor peasant who leaves the village to compete with him
for the few available jobs, between groups of workers themselves,
between individuals within as well as outside every trade and
profession. The present order of society is that of the jungle: eat or
be eaten, beat or be beaten, every man's hand against his neigh-
bour.

There is only one cure for this. Since the State is too powerful to
be overthrown, it must be turned into an instrument of liberation
and progress. The State itself must take over trades and industries;
by creating model factories, model banks, model enterprises of
every kind, it will, by displaying the qualities of honesty, efficiency
and scientific management of which Owen had shown the utility,
enter into competition with private enterprise, and by its superior
efficiency and resources drive it out of the field. There is no need
for general nationalisation, which can be done only at the cost of

violence and bloodshed. State capitalism on a limited scale –
although Blanc would have rejected such words – would have the
automatic effect of gradually eliminating and taking over the
necessarily less efficient private firms, and so a painless transition
to State capitalism would inevitably occur. Capitalists would
peacefully capitulate and a rational system would succeed the
present chaos. Agriculture should probably be organised along
Fourierist lines of federated co-operatives.

Still more ambitious is the thought of Constantin Pécqueur. Like
Blanc, he thought the State should take over social and industrial
organisation. Like Fourier, he believed that each man should be
fitted for those tasks to which he was most naturally congenial. In
his scheme the State regulates the relations of producers and
consumers, *laissez-faire* being condemned as being a mere right to
rob and to destroy. The complete vision of later socialism is
beginning to emerge. The frontiers of a nation are, according to
Pécqueur, an artificial curb to the full free association of all
mankind. When all men are engaged in the tasks to which they are
most suited, the economic causes of war, due to the blind greed of
competition, become eliminated. Heredity, privilege, religious and
social prejudice die in a society organised on rational principles.
Class war is overcome by economic association regulated by the
State. Patriotism is replaced by world loyalty. The division of
labour and production occurs on a world scale. Humanity lives in
one socialised world.

The communism of Étienne Cabet is a variation upon this
theme, but far more rigid and totalitarian. The State owns all the
main sources of wealth and the means of production and assigns
tasks to individual citizens. There is equal pay for all, and a heavy
taxation of the rich. Violence is condemned but complete State
control enjoined in Cabet's ideal State, called Icaria. There is rigid
control of publication and a severe State censorship. All citizens are
equal and their property may not be violently expropriated. The
transition to the perfect State should occur by increased taxation
and abolition of military budgets. Cabet's attempts to establish a
colony of this kind in Texas failed, but the idea of a rigidly
organised communist State probably had its due influence on
Marx.

While Blanc, Leroux, Cabet and their followers confined themselves to theorising and social experiment and denounced violence,
Auguste Blanqui organised armed risings. He saw injustice,

oppression and exploitation round him, distrusted palliatives and the powers of persuasion and believed in the violent overthrow of the wicked order by organised revolution. In order to do this he spent his entire life in perfecting himself as a professional revolutionary, in studying the technique of revolution and in gathering followers whom, during the intervals between his lengthy terms in prison, he trained in the art of insurrection. He was a disciple of the followers of Babeuf, a militant atheist and an advocate of professionally trained revolutionary élites. He believed in the abolition of private property, but still more in the abolition of the capitalist State in which everything, consciously or unconsciously, was weighted in favour of the possessing classes. His main objective was to smash the existing order and all its institutions. The bourgeoisie would not yield without a fight: consequently it must be attacked by force; this was a democratic procedure, since the oppressed, in whose name the liberators were acting, vastly outnumbered the ruling class.

How, after the success of the revolution, society would be organised, he did not seem clearly to conceive; he vaguely believed in the direct application of democratic methods on the part of the liberated agricultural and industrial slaves. While he did not contribute anything of significance to socialist doctrine, his criticism of ineffectual reformism and his work as an agitator and political incendiary left a profound mark upon every branch of militant socialism. The Paris rising in 1839, the revolution in June 1848, and still more the Paris Commune of 1871 all bear the imprint of his technique as organiser and militant activist, above all in turning scattered discontent into concerted revolutionary violence.

IV

Parallel to the development of French communist ideas and apart from the internationally celebrated Owen, there exists a native British socialist tradition. Among the most prominent names is that of Thomas Spence, who preached against the evils of excessive encroachment by landlords over the properties of the vanishing yeomanry, and offered as a remedy the restoration of the alleged ancient rights of parishes to communal ownership of the land. His vision of the government was as a kind of federation of parish councils with consequent elimination of centralised control and of all forms of State bureaucracy. William Ogilvie was a mild reformer, who denounced the tendency whereby more and more land was accumulated in fewer and fewer hands, principally in the hands of the idle rich, whom he calls 'freebooters' and condemns in scathing language. His remedy is scarcely socialist, since the society he contemplates is a modified feudalism in which everyone is to own about 40 acres of land, to which a rent and prescriptive duties to the overlord are attached. Nevertheless this type of condemnation of ill-gotten landed wealth fed the stream of socialist sentiment.

More searching and formidable were five British writers, sometimes classed together as forerunners of Marxism. Charles Hall pointed out that the fruits of productive labour were distributed to capitalists and workers in the proportion of eight to one. The fact that seven-eighths of what was produced should go to the master, who does not appear to deserve it, is due to the control of the State by the wealthy, wealth being the power of forcing others to part with what rightly belongs to them. The exercise of this power must tend to make the rich richer and the poor poorer, increasing their degradation. Education, being in the hands of the owners, tends to perpetuate inequality. Wars spring from acquisitive motives and widen still further the existing gulf of inequality. Hall's remedy, like that of Ogilvie, is the establishment of small peasant proprietors on the land and the reform of a system whereby trade largely consists in exporting the necessities of the poor in order to import the luxuries of the rich.

William Thompson put into bold relief the conflict between the 'natural right' of the worker to the 'total product of his labour' and the claims of economic freedom, whereby anything could be legally bartered by anyone anywhere at any time for anything else, which justified capitalism. He represents the capitalist as forcing the workers to live on as little as possible, while he consumes the residue himself. Thompson offers no clear remedy for this, and is the first to employ the term, later to be made notorious by Marxists, of 'surplus value', although here it means the increase in productivity created by machinery, all of which goes to the employer and is used by him in conspiracy with other employers, both in his own country and internationally, to force the living standard of labour lower still.

This theme is emphasised even more strongly by Thomas Hodgskin, a former naval officer whose views are a mixture of abhorrence of all State control and interference as such and the desire to see the control, not the abolition, of private property, by the elimination of the wholly unproductive owner or middleman who squeezes unearned income out of the producer; he must be replaced by the 'master', that is, the manager of an enterprise, and by the genuine trader, both the last classes being entitled to remuneration, but one far smaller than that granted them in the existing order.

In his pamphlet *Labour's Wrongs and Labour's Remedy*, published in 1839, J. F. Bray, after singing a hymn to labour as the natural function of everything that lives – animals, plants – points out that the class of owners avoids this duty at the expense of the rest of society. The capitalist gets something for nothing: he does not even expend capital, since his wealth is always growing. The result is plainly no better than legalised robbery. This is to be remedied by altering the laws of inheritance and by a curious sort of communism, whereby everyone enters into a vast, universal profit-sharing organisation, a kind of joint-stock company of the universe. It is a hazy combination of Owenite doctrines with elements of what was later Fabian doctrine.

John Gray formulated a kind of 'iron law' of remuneration, whereby everyone ends by losing, because everything is done in competition and all production is for profit rather than for social use: labour is paid the lowest possible wage; capitalists make the smallest profit allowed by the violent competition of other capitalists; human labour becomes a commodity bought at one price and sold at another; and all leads to the iniquitous absorption of a portion of the fruit of society's labours by unproductive idlers who should be put to socially useful work. Such ideas as the exploitation of man by man, surplus value, the thesis that the distribution of political power and the educational and ethical ideas in a society depend upon its economic structure and not vice versa, that social misery is due to unbridled *laissez-faire*, emerge clearly and sometimes dramatically in the writings of this group of thinkers. To them must be added the name of William Godwin, the father of anarchism, who taught that the rule of reason entitles everyone to take his just due, according to his rightful needs, independently of who might happen to possess it under the unjust and irrational dispensation of the actual social order. His notion of the distribution of resources according to a rationalist ethic goes back to

Mably and Plato and forms a strong link in the tradition of philosophical anarchism.

The ideas of these social rebels fell on fruitful soil. The combination of economic and political instability in Europe after the Napoleonic Wars increased discontent with existing regimes, and this, in almost direct proportion to the degree of political suppression prevalent in a given State, stimulated the creation of conspiracies. They began, as a rule, with moderate liberal and democratic aims but gradually, with the increase of repression on one side, and economic, social and political bitterness and despair on the other, began to take more and more uncompromising forms. In France political censorship under the July monarchy was relatively mild, so that socialist theses were openly preached by radical writers and journalists, and even by priests such as Lamennais, the greatest figure in Christian socialism, and the abbé Constant; revolutionary plots were correspondingly few and unimportant. Presently these ideas crossed into the German-speaking States where, owing to the severe counter-measures of Metternich and the Prussian government, they were driven underground.

A secret society with purely communist aims was established by German émigrés in Paris as early as 1836. Radical intellectuals, such as Hess and Grün, spread communist ideas in German middle-class, especially academic, circles. To some degree these views infected even the Polish nationalists then struggling against Russian oppression; in Russia herself, semi-feudal as she was, vague socialist notions began to grow articulate in the 1830s among the radical intelligentsia of Moscow and St Petersburg. In Italy and Spain the fight against authoritarian governments still took predominantly nationalist and liberal forms; in England the Chartist movement represented a clear-cut programme embraced eagerly by the victims of the Industrial Revolution in their hatred of the utter degradation and misery which the sudden and sensationally rapid development of industry had brought on growing sections of politically helpless factory workers and industrial labourers. From a mere abstract doctrine advanced by isolated thinkers, socialism began to be identified with the actual demands of the increasingly menacing multitude of discontented workers, and socialists began to look on themselves as the natural political leaders of the coming final, revolutionary transformation of society. Communist or socialist ideas – the terms, as mentioned above, were not at that time clearly distinguished – infected equally university intellectuals (particularly in Germany) and groups of disaffected workers and artisans. Small semi-legal or illegal circles were established, and pamphlets and clandestine propaganda circulated: the radical journalist Heinzen and the apocalyptic itinerant tailor Weitling were typical representatives of these social groups. But by far the most eloquent and influential spokesmen of this attitude were Proudhon in France and, among the Germans, Karl Marx and Ferdinand Lassalle.

Proudhon emphasised the inevitability of antagonism between the classes – on the one side the possessors, who controlled the machinery of public life, political, economic, social, religious and intellectual, on the other the vast majority whom they mercilessly and stupidly exploited. He looked upon all States as such as being pure instruments of oppression and advocated the view that true liberty, impossible without true economic equality, was unattainable until the State was abolished and the productive elements in society were transformed into free associations pledged to mutual aid. In language full of paradoxes, derived from a superficial acquaintance with Hegel, Proudhon maintained that history, like all other processes of nature, moved not as a smooth progression but in a path determined by, indeed consisting of, the conflict of contradictory forces; this continuous strife every now and then mounts to revolutionary leaps – crises whose resolution by an upward shift of level constitutes progress.

As a characteristic inner contradiction of society, Proudhon, in the book which opens with his famous paradox, 'Property is theft', exposes the self-frustrating nature of capitalism – in their desperation to increase their wealth the unscrupulous few have effected the suppression of the creative instincts of the many, and ultimately destroy themselves too. To try to remedy this by substituting a no less authoritarian collectivist communist system whereby the State still rigidly controls its citizens, albeit in the interests of the proletarians, as advocated for example by Louis Blanc, is to spread the disease, since State communism destroys the individual no less surely than did unbridled capitalism. The State is wholly evil, being wholly coercive, and is therefore useless even as a weapon against itself. Proudhon's point of view is diametrically opposed to that adopted by Blanc and later by the Russian revolutionary exile Peter Tkachev, who maintained against advocates of voluntary co-operation that the State was too powerful to be either ignored or resisted, and must be turned to its own use by the revolution if the latter is to be successful.

Proudhon insists on the right to a limited quantity of private property and on the preservation of the inviolable rights of the family, of which he takes a patriarchal view, not unlike Rousseau, with the same insistence on the subordinate status of women: these are institutions designed to guarantee the individual against the brutal and excessive encroachment of both the State and rapacious capitalism. To restore individual and class self-respect and give full scope to the creative energies of mankind, all central coercive authority must be destroyed and replaced by a condition of peaceful economic co-operation. To Proudhon such encroachment or exploitation means anything which confers undue power upon the exploiter, whether it be rent, interest or any other form of extortion, whereby the weaker party, that is, the proletarians or the poor, are made to give up something for nothing in order to avoid starvation or the loss of personal freedom. This evil is not curable by compulsory association in the sense preached by Saint-Simonians or communists, since that would vest too much power in the hands of the organisers, and so dehumanise – destroy the bodies and souls of – the workers. This goes with Proudhon's theory of value, whereby objects should exchange in direct proportion to the hours of labour spent on their production, and credit should be widely extended at the lowest possible rate of interest, if possible none at all, by the freely collaborating combinations of the producers themselves.

Anything, even war, is good which intensifies a man's individual qualities, develops his free, creative personality; industrial exploitation, which demeans individuals and crushes their resistance, is the ultimate evil. This violent individualist self-assertiveness links Proudhon, in an unforeseen manner, with Nietzsche, Fascist irrationalism and nostalgic medievalism, through which in Roman Catholic countries he has had a recognisable influence no smaller than that of Bakunin. Proudhon's teachings do not form a coherent doctrine, but the denunciation of unlimited property rights, which echoes Rousseau and Fourier, and of political centralisation, and his eloquent pleas for a decentralised economic system founded on workers' co-operation, have had a profound effect on social thought and action, particularly in Latin countries, and formed the basis of the anarchist and syndicalist movements, which became the traditional opponents of centralised political socialism and communism.

V

Undoubtedly the most celebrated and influential of all modern socialist thinkers is Karl Marx. He created the most lasting body of coherent socialist doctrine, and based an international organisation with revolutionary aims upon it. The most arresting exposition of his views is in the *Communist Manifesto*, which, with Friedrich Engels, he composed towards the end of 1847 at the request of one of the small communist groups of exiled German workers then to be found in Western Europe. As a bold new synthesis of ideas, which had previously circulated in a loose uncoordinated form – for example, those of Rousseau, Saint-Simon, Fourier, Hodgskin – it is a unique polemical masterpiece. Its main theses are these. The history of human society is a history of the struggle between economically determined classes – this much was discovered by bourgeois historians, but they have failed to point out that in our day it is a struggle between the bourgeoisie and the proletariat, which the latter is bound to win. This war takes a political form, since political power is that whereby one class seeks to defeat the other, and the modern State is simply the instrument to execute the will of the dominant class. The vast modern development of industrial resources has destroyed the traditional feudal and domestic character of economic life and has created a world market to feed which immense monopolistic industrial structures have been built; and these in their turn have, without meaning to do so, inevitably organised the workers of various countries, races and ways of life into one huge army of propertyless labour.

What determines the lives of individuals and societies is the relation in which they stand towards one another in the productive process. Hence the only true scientific analysis of contemporary society is an analysis of the historical relationship to one another of the various participants – producers, consumers, workers, employers, middlemen – entering into the productive process. As Lenin was later to say, the basic question for Marx is who exploits whom; all else is a by-product of this. The intellectual, moral, religious, artistic activity of an individual or a society is the 'superstructure', that is, not the cause but the effect of the material factors of production, dependent upon them, and liable to blind men to their true position in the world, namely, to the material causes which ultimately, though not always obviously, determine the course of their lives and their characters. The permanent conflict of which Hegel had spoken is in truth a conflict between material, economic and social interests; when these struggles reach one of their periodic crises there is a revolutionary explosion which means that the outer relations which form the social, industrial, political, intellectual, above all economic structure of a society are no longer adequate for the productive forces working within. A revolution occurs and new forms, better fitted to aid the development of these forces, come into being.

The capitalist system is a transient phenomenon riddled with inner conflict: individual capitalists can develop only by defeating one another in ever more deadly competition which involves governments and continents in internecine struggles. In pursuit of its own industrial purposes it has trained a vast army of workers whose very organisation makes them at once more and more alienated from the actual goals and values of the society of which they are ostensibly members, and, at the same time, progressively better organised and consequently a more powerful menace to their masters.

The accumulation of capital rests on the systematic robbery and dehumanisation of the workers. The value of a material commodity exchanged in the world's markets is constituted by the socially required labour expended upon its production. The labourer himself has become such a commodity, that is, his value is estimated in terms of the labour required to keep him alive and adequately efficient; but he produces more than the cost of his upkeep. The surplus of the value which he creates over the value of what he consumes is the 'surplus value' which the capitalist takes away from him. Unlike the workers of the classical or medieval economies, he is cut off from his tools, from the products of his own labour, in the end from his own powers of production, all of which are owned and exchanged by others, whose purposes ignore or brutally frustrate his own minimal needs as a human being. Human beings are treated as useful commodities, their gifts are bought and sold for cash. This is justified by a pseudo-science, called by the bourgeois 'economics', which treats historically changing relations between men as timeless, unchangeable laws that govern quantities or processes called goods, commodities, money, supply, demand and so forth.

As competition grows more and more cut-throat, greater and greater concentration of capitalist enterprise into monopolies and cartels is bound to occur in order to lower costs. Capitalists must progressively grow at once less numerous and more powerful, workers more numerous, more impoverished, more concentrated, better organised by the industrial system itself; by a grim Hegelian paradox capitalism is compassing its own doom, creating its own gravediggers. The proletariat is bound in the course of time to acquire such power, centralisation, organisation, international solidarity and effective revolutionary indignation that it will find it inevitable and relatively easy to take over the whole economic system by removing the dwindling number of capitalists from their centralised position of control, thus at last obtaining the full fruit of its labour for its own use. In this way, as Marx put it in *Capital*, 'The expropriators are expropriated.'

Since the proletarians are the lowest class in the economic scale, with their final victory the class struggle will come to an end, for with the liquidation of the bourgeoisie there will be no other class for them to oppose. When this occurs, the State, which is the instrument whereby one class oppresses another, will become otiose; human energies will be liberated from the struggle between the classes (the motor of all previous historical change), identical according to Marxist doctrine with the struggle for economic power and even existence. With no one to exploit, and the fruits of agriculture, trade and industry, of the arts and sciences of mankind, growing ever more plentiful, man will at last enjoy full liberty, within which he will be able to develop his faculties (no longer distorted by being turned against one another in the unnatural wars of men against men which alienate them from their common human purpose) to their fullest and richest extent: prehistory will end, human history will begin.

Marx developed these ideas in a series of works beginning with attacks on the French and German Utopian socialists, on the Hegelian leftists, on Hess, on Proudhon and on various semi-liberal sympathisers. Their main errors seemed to him to consist in misunderstanding the nature of the world in which they lived and therefore the causes of historical change, which made some of them suppose that the existing State could be turned to use by the revolution; or alternatively that reconciliation between the classes was feasible. This Marx proclaims to be a blunder which inevitably leads to the frustration of those who hold it, and to the spreading of error which must confuse the issue and betray the working class. The modern State is necessarily a bourgeois instrument and cannot be employed by workers without perverting their purpose in the process. As for attempts at reform, these, whether moderate or extreme, are, according to Marx, equally futile, since they presuppose the possibility of values common to the opposed classes, some sort of common good for which co-operation can be organised: but this is a fatal illusion with which the masters have bemused the slaves. The reformers assume by a similar fallacy that the existing system can be altered without being destroyed, but every existing institution bears the seeds of its destruction within itself, as Hegel had taught; until the final dissolution of the class war by the victory of the proletariat, no institution has more than transient historical value. Hence to attempt to improve by reforms, like all efforts at changing men's habits by peaceful persuasion or education, is to build upon a volcano; history will sweep away these blind attempts to construct edifices out of crumbling materials.

Marx, quite consistently, is opposed to all appeals to moral sentiment or, except for tactical reasons, to temporary common interest between the classes. Morality like everything else is determined by the condition of the productive system. The only rational appeal is to that future form of human life endowed with its own proper moral system, which history – the next step, that is, in the development of the forces of human production and consequently of the human relations determined by them – will inexorably bring. By bending all available effort to the enlightenment of the workers about these truths (notably by making them adequately conscious of the class struggle and of their own position in it), and by organising them into a militant revolutionary army, this inevitable process may be accelerated and the birth pangs of the new society made less painful. These views, originally stated in treatises composed before 1848, some of which were published posthumously (for example, *On The Jewish Question*, the *Economic and Philosophical Manuscripts*, *The German Ideology*, *The Holy Family*) found their fullest expression in Marx's later works, notably *A Contribution to the Critique of Political Economy*, *Capital*, the *Critique of the Gotha Programme*, as well as in the more popularly written expositions by Friedrich Engels.

VI

The revolutions of 1848 which spread like wildfire over Italy and
France and the German-speaking States soon offered a test of
Marx's analysis. They often began with an alliance of liberal and
radical nationalist democrats with socialists of various hues. Both
in France and in Germany a split between the socialists and the
bourgeois democrats and liberals developed, and the revolutions
ended with the forcible suppression of the socialists, often by an
alliance of liberals and moderate radicals with more reactionary
forces. In the period of profound disillusionment which followed
the failure of the revolutions of 1848–9, socialism appeared to
vanish from the scene and was by many given up for dead.

It was during this period that Ferdinand Lassalle founded his
German Workers' Union. His views were similar to those of Marx.
His most memorable thesis was that 'the iron law of wages', which
he had derived from liberal economists, must always force capitalists, under conditions of ruthless competition, to lower the cost of
production so far as economically possible, and with it the
workers' wages. This meant that all appeals to their humanity or
their self-interest were bound to fail, and the workers had only
themselves to lean upon. He accepted Louis Blanc's view that only
political methods can be effective and that the proper aim of a
workers' party therefore must be to recapture the machinery of the
State. Lassalle was also much influenced by the version of the 'iron
law' given by Rodbertus, a Pomeranian landowner, who taught
that untrammelled *laissez-faire* leads inevitably to the acquisition
of an ever-increasing proportion of social product – goods and
services – by the owners, owing to the operation of a system
whereby the workers are allowed only a bare subsistence wage
while the value of what they produce is continually increasing. It
leads also to indirect taxation, which falls more heavily on workers
than on owners and therefore causes underconsumption and
periodic economic world crises. This can be remedied only by
rational planning of economic life, which only the State can do
effectively. The workers must not demand 'the full fruit of their
labour', because the social process of production, into which
elements other than labour enter, cannot be split up into ingredients; so that unless the social process as a whole is rationally
organised, labour cannot alone expect to get its proper reward. But
this can be realised only by peaceful methods which it may take

centuries to evolve. To cover the interval Rodbertus suggested various palliatives which became the commonplaces of all non-socialist left-wing parties in Europe.

Marx maintained that the modern State was an instrument of capitalist oppression and could not, even if captured, be used by the victorious workers, but must be transformed into the 'dictatorship of the proletariat' – a transitional stage wherein the political party representing the workers' interests would defend the victorious revolution against the revenge of its defeated enemy until the enemy was rendered powerless and the need for such a dictatorship disappeared. Lassalle, following Rodbertus, sought direct State intervention in resisting *laissez-faire* capitalism and organising the collective welfare of the workers along socialist lines, and stands at the opposite pole of thought to that of Proudhon and his followers, who, like Bakunin and the anarchists, looked on the State as the embodiment and source of all evil, and advocated solely non-political economic organisation and pressure upon the government. Lassalle was a fiery orator and an immensely capable organiser. His German Workers' Union became the first formidable political party, seeking parliamentary representation by the votes of the citizens, founded on explicit socialist teaching. It continued to grow in strength after his death in a duel in 1864.

VII

Apart from this, the decade after 1848 represents a dead period in the history of socialism. The unorganised French socialists, defeated after their abortive rising in June 1848, were persecuted, exiled or silent. This applied beyond France to all save Lassalle's followers in the later 1850s. In the 1860s the men of 1848 began to show signs of life again, and in 1864 in London Marx helped to found the International Working Men's Association with which the history of modern socialism begins. This was composed of delegates of trade-union and other workers' organisations from various European countries, pledged not only to the improvement of working-class conditions but to the transformation of political conditions. It was dominated by Marx, who found his most formidable opponent in the Russian anarchist Mikhail Bakunin.

Bakunin went further than Proudhon in opposition to all forms of State control or indeed any coercion at all. He believed that since the use of organised force was the principal obstacle to justice and freedom, anything at all likely to lead men to revolt against their masters (including man's natural love of destruction, or the activities of bandits and desperadoes, who are natural enemies of the imposed political order) should be encouraged, until in one final revolutionary act all authority was destroyed – after which man's natural reason, goodness and love of liberty would assert themselves and people would live for ever in free and happy federative, co-operative, non-political associations. These views played a considerable part in creating anarchist and syndicalist parties.

As a result of the growing conflict between Marx and Bakunin the First International finally succumbed in 1876, after some ten years' active existence, in the course of which it had achieved a certain degree of international labour solidarity but little else. Meanwhile a German socialist party, in opposition to the *étatiste* workers led by Lassalle, was created by Marx's followers in Germany. Eventually a fusion between Lassalle's followers and those of Marx was arranged (at the Gotha congress of 1875 and the Erfurt congress of 1891) and a united Social Democratic Party emerged in Germany, so formidable that in 1878 Bismarck took fright and enacted anti-socialist legislation against it.

In France, the growth of socialism as a revolutionary party of the workers was given a new direction by the Paris Commune of 1871. This arose after the defeat of France by Germany in 1870 and was a rebellion by radical parties in Paris against the liberal government of Thiers. Members of Marx's international organisation took relatively little part in the revolt. It was mainly organised by left-wing neo-Jacobin radicals, Proudhonists, the followers of Blanqui, who believed in terrorism and revolution wherever and whenever possible, together with less identifiable revolutionary elements. The Commune was crushed after a brief and furious resistance and its followers were executed and exiled in large numbers. Although Marx disapproved of the tactics and theoretical errors of the Communards, he recognised it as the first revolutionary government established to promote socialist principles and establish the dictatorship of the proletariat, and celebrated its martyrs in two eloquent pamphlets.

The violence of the Commune so shocked conservative, liberal and even socialist European opinion that the avowed adhesion to it of the Marxists, and the less obvious sympathies of socialists vaguely identified with Marxism, tended to compromise socialism in progressive circles for some years. When the Socialist (Second) International was re-established in 1889, a very different mood prevailed. Economic conditions had improved for the majority of workers in most European countries. Marx and the militants were for the most part dead or forgotten. The main purpose of the workers of European countries, few of which were governed with a degree of despotism which had been common earlier in the century and still existed in Russia or Spain, lay in the general improvement of their economic status, education, social services and so forth. Independently of each other, but springing from the same general conditions, there were born a number of national 'reformist' socialist movements.

In England, where there had never been a properly constituted socialist party, the Social Democratic Federation, which had been founded by such followers of Marx as H. M. Hyndman and such quasi-Marxist sympathisers as William Morris and Belfort Bax, and later the Socialist League, soon yielded in influence to the Fabian Society, founded by Sidney and Beatrice Webb, Sydney Olivier, Bernard Shaw and other radical intellectuals, and attached more firmly to Ricardo's doctrine of rent than to the Marxist theory of surplus value. The Fabians believed, not in revolution, which under British conditions seemed impracticable, but in the gradual increase of State and municipal control over individual enterprise and in the adaptation of already existing forms of social control, for example, in the civil service, local government and other public organisations, leading, it was hoped, to a growing process of collective control by rational experts over the entire social and economic life of the nation. The Fabians sometimes spoke as if all State control as such led to socialism; they approved of joint-stock companies, because these already represented a form of collective organisation all the easier to nationalise, and they echoed the views of Louis Blanc in supposing that private enterprise would find itself eliminated, not by specific socialist legislation or expropriation, but simply by the more efficient working of public corporations, municipalities and county councils, which would defeat the old-fashioned capitalist by beating him at his own game with his own weapons. This doctrine of socialism by gradual permeation of government departments and local and municipal institutions denied the very basis of Marx's socialism, with its stress on the inevitability of class war and revolution, and asserted against it the possibility of piecemeal socialisation and nationalisation.

Although the Independent Labour Party, founded in 1893, was more sympathetic to militant Marxism than to the Fabian belief in the 'inevitability of gradualness', it did not in practice engage in revolutionary activity. The English trade unions, mainly concerned with the improvement of their members' standards of living, could be won, it was thought, only by a party which did not jeopardise this aim by open conspiracy against the State, and the alliance between trade unionism and socialism in England was effected by an organisational and ideological compromise which has lasted to this day, duly condemned by faithful Marxists as a betrayal of socialism. Although some Marxists occasionally conceded that the revolution when it came might not necessarily be violent – a point which Marx himself had made in connection with highly industrialised countries such as England or Holland – yet it was a far cry from this to faith in the slow process of conversion and enlightenment, held by Fabians and trade unionists, who between them were most instrumental in founding, in 1900, the Labour Representative Committee from which the British Labour Party developed.

An interesting but short-lived movement in England was that of guild socialism, which sought to combine Marxist belief in class warfare, and the necessity for socialisation of all means of production and distribution, with an attempt to return to a somewhat earlier tradition with its roots in medieval economic organisation, and which has persisted in syndicalism and the co-operative movement; namely, the attempt to place control of economic life, not in the hands of the elected representatives of all the citizens as such, but in the hands of producers (and, to some degree, consumers) organised in accordance with their occupation or craft. Under this doctrine, a man would be represented by elected deputies in all the aspects of his various activities: inasmuch as he belonged to more than one association as producer, consumer or disinterested specialist or amateur, he would be able to vote for persons who would represent all these various functions of his life. In order to prevent the danger of a monotonous and uniform bureaucratic centralisation and the destruction of individual values by a collectivist State, wider scope and means of self-realisation would be given to human needs and interests in all their rich diversity by a reasonable degree of local and functional self-government, maximum practical de-centralisation, and the encouragement of the fullest and most imaginative forms of personal self-expression and the liberty of individuals and associations. The guild socialists accepted the Labour Party's programme of achieving public control of the means of production, distribution and exchange in Britain by peaceful parliamentary methods.

In France a more revolutionary tradition persisted: after the débâcle of 1871 the orthodox Marxists were reorganised by Jules Guesde and Marx's son-in-law, Paul Lafargue, and carried on political warfare against the ideologically more flexible groups led by Paul Brousse, who inclined towards a more Proudhonist and apolitical interpretation of the role of the working class. In 1890 there existed as many as six factions of the socialist party in France, divided between Marxists, Blanquists, Allemanists, Broussists (sometimes called 'Possibilists' because of their alleged tendency to opportunist alliances with non-socialist radicals), and dissident factions of these. They were as one in being atheist, republican, internationalist, and in varying degrees stood for communist or collectivist principles. Only the Marxists, however, were strictly revolutionary, although this was also claimed by the various syndicalist bodies which continued the anti-political tradition of Proudhon and Bakunin; they drew inspiration from the violently anti-parliamentarian doctrines of Georges Sorel, who warned the workers against the contaminating influence of liberal democracy and urged them to confine themselves to implacable economic warfare by union actions – strikes and other forms of resistance – within their factories and workshops, which would preserve their moral purity and heroism, and render them saviours of a corrupt and decadent society. Like the syndicalist Lagardelle, Sorel set before them the goal of the 'general strike'; this, like the 'second coming' to early Christians, was to function as a myth, a flag, belief in which could inspire all feeling and activity even if it never actually materialised; Sorel accepted Marx's apocalyptic vision and his militancy and rejected his rationalism.

The French socialists had begun to elect deputies to the chamber some years before their British brothers had succeeded in electing a socialist to parliament; the most violent controversy in their ranks occurred in 1899 when Millerand, a prominent evolutionary socialist, had agreed without the authorisation of his party to serve in a radical ministry. This split French socialism into the intransigent Marxist Parti Socialiste de France, led by Guesde, and the Parti Socialiste Français, led by Jean Jaurès, which recognised the possibility of temporary alliances with non-socialist progressive parties. When however, the conference of the Socialist International in 1904 condemned all compromises of this type, Jaurès accepted his defeat and helped to reunite the party into a single organisation. Since then, the socialist party of France has continued with various fortunes as a legal political party. After the end of the First World War a great many socialists entered the Communist Party. The conservative elements of French socialism gradually left its ranks, and disappeared for the most part into the wholly non-Marxist party of Radical Socialists.

VIII

In Germany Marxist principles were represented by such men as August Bebel and Karl Kautsky, who formally subscribed to the principles of class war and pledged themselves to the revolution. The gradualist heresy in Germany was enunciated most fully by the 'revisionist' Eduard Bernstein, who in the 1890s pointed out more clearly than anyone before him the apparent non-fulfilment of various Marxist prophecies. Facts were facts, he insisted, and while Marx had offered a correct analysis of historical change, and had predicted the universal rise of big business, he and Engels had misunderstood much else. Thus while control of finance and industry was indeed being increasingly concentrated in fewer and fewer hands, the number of small shareholders in joint-stock companies and other enterprises appeared to be increasing just as fast; the standard of living of the workers, instead of declining under the pressure of the 'iron law of wages', was steadily rising; in agriculture middle-sized individual holdings, so far from being absorbed in vast centralised estates, were actually increasing in number, at any rate in Western Europe; the middle class, so far from being squeezed out by the pincer-movement of labour and big business, as Marx predicted, was on the contrary absorbing into itself the workers who, as they grew more prosperous, tended to become shareholders in these same capitalist enterprises. The gulf between the classes, so far from widening, was becoming cluttered up with islands and bridges of various types which transformed its original nature unrecognisably.

Bernstein saw no reason for believing that the historical process was as inevitable as the rigid Marxists asserted, nor did he see in the liberal State the instrument used by one class to suppress another; on the contrary he viewed even trade unions with suspicion, as liable to become no less selfish and antagonistic to the interests of society as a whole than individual capitalists, and preached the virtues of universal suffrage and the growth of true social democracy, which would enable the workers to satisfy their needs by the simple expedient of majorities obtainable in parliamentary elections. On these grounds Bernstein attacked the guild socialists for suggesting, for example, that factory managers should be elected by the factory, because this put too much arbitrary control in the hands of one section of society, the producers against the consumers, and led to inefficiency as well; nor did he subscribe to the Marxist slogan that the proletarian has no country. He pointed out that the international solidarity of the working class was not a very powerful bond when it came to international action, that an increase of democracy within a country softened its class conflicts and created an internal solidarity between the citizens, bound to make the worker in the long run as free and active and influential a member of his community as anyone else.

This process might take time but it could be shortened only by the spread of democracy and not by the narrow tactics of bitter class warfare. The political pressure which the socialist party in the Reichstag was able to exercise appeared to be reasonably effective in satisfying individual working-class claims. So far from a wider chasm opening between capital and labour, capitalism itself appeared to be in the mood of concession, and if the workers' movement persisted along the path of gradual political and economic development, it had a better opportunity of transforming society according to its ideals than by fomenting a revolutionary situation. Bernstein's formula 'the end is nothing, the movement everything' represented this belief, according to which the mere growth of socialist public enterprises in a capitalist world, with corresponding increase of their political and economic power, would obviate the need for violent expropriation. Nor were some of the ideals of the average socialist – liberty, political and juridicial equality, economic security and equality of opportunity, internationalism, anti-imperialism and peace – so very different from those of the average left-wing liberal. Hence the desirability of collaboration with other political parties sympathetic to the workers' outlook, as did in fact occur in Britain, France and the Scandinavian countries. Naturally this view earned Bernstein the implacable hostility of Marxists and revolutionary syndicalists, but it had a decisive effect upon the German social democratic movement and was a cause and symptom both of its strength and of its weakness.

Even in Russia, the political and social condition of which was in some respects medieval, this gradualist socialism made some headway. The first properly socialist party in Russia, which had inherited the tradition of unorganised liberalism, populism and the revolutionary – to some degree, agrarian – terrorism of earlier decades, was the Russian Social Democratic Party founded by Georgy Plekhanov, Leo Deutsch and Vera Zasulich in 1898. This was originally a Marxist party which maintained that Russia was to be saved from autocracy and exploitation only by the organised proletariat of the growing Russian industries, and not by the development of the emancipated peasant communes into modern forms of communal agrarian ownership, as urged by earlier radicals and revolutionaries, from such gradualists as Herzen and Lavrov to such 'activists' as Chernyshevsky and the assassins of the emperor Alexander II. In Russia, too, socialist gradualism had its proponents in such intellectuals as Struve, Prokopovich and Kuskova, who defended 'economic' and legal trade-union action against the bitter attacks of such orthodox Marxists as Plekhanov and Lenin. The earlier tradition of appeal to moral feeling, and the belief that it was possible to avoid the horrors of industrialism by a direct transition from the peasant communes to organised agrarian socialism, was carried on by the Social Revolutionary Party which did not accept the Marxist doctrine of the inevitability of the class war, and believed in the possibility of transforming Russia by democratic, that is, parliamentary, means into a joint industrial and agrarian democracy, the creation of which individual terrorism against the unyielding oppression of the tsarist autocracy would materially assist. Oddly enough anarchism, despite the part played by Bakunin and Kropotkin, never obtained a real foothold in the Russian Empire.

In Latin countries the influence of Bakunin and Proudhon was more powerful than that of Marx: although Italy and Spain had social democratic parties, the main body of revolutionary socialists belonged to various syndicalist and anarchist groups, inspired by faith in economic warfare against the bourgeoisie and in proletarian self-help, occasionally taking the forms of sabotage and strikes, as being more effective forms of social pressure than open political struggle. In the United States the Industrial Workers of the World, whose followers occasionally perpetrated terrorist acts, also represented a form of syndicalist activity.

Certain new tendencies had in the meanwhile made themselves felt. Social and economic theorists such as J. A. Hobson, V. I. Lenin, Rudolf Hilferding and Rosa Luxemburg had added to Marx's theory a doctrine about the uneven development of imperialism and its effects on class war. Since imperialism in their view was caused by the pursuit of fields for investment by financial and industrial capital, and since in this race some countries had captured territory, native labour and natural wealth before others, the possibility of conflict between the capitalist classes of various countries – the new 'hungry' powers against the old 'sated' ones – had drawn appreciably nearer. Moreover, within the ranks of the Russian Social Democratic Party a crucial split had occurred. Lenin, who led the left wing, demanded a greater degree of authoritarian centralisation on the part of the executive of the Party, as well as the elimination from its control of all but professional whole-time revolutionaries who were to lay down the policy to be followed by the legal and overt trade-union and political Marxists in Russia itself. Plekhanov, the leading theorist of the Party, and Martov, one of its best pamphleteers and organisers, believed in a less hierarchical, more democratic organisation. The Party split into Bolsheviks led by Lenin and Mensheviks led by Martov and later also by Plekhanov. On ultimate ends – a revolution to be followed by a bourgeois republic, with Marxists remorselessly driving for total socialisation – both sections appeared to be agreed.

The First World War created a crisis in the ranks of European socialists: not many days before the outbreak of hostilities, French and German socialists had pledged each other to avert war by displaying their solidarity against their respective governments. This pledge had proved vain, and all but a few socialist deputies of Germany as of France voted for war credits in 1914, although the former showed some signs of restiveness as the war wore on. Dissident socialist organisations which had condemned the war as an imperialist conflict, alien and antagonistic to the interests of the workers, met in two conferences in the Swiss cities of Zimmerwald (in 1915) and Kienthal (in 1916). These were attended by Lenin and his Bolshevik followers and the 'left Mensheviks' (Martovites), while Plekhanov and the orthodox Russian social democrats supported the French comrades led by Guesde, and pledged their support to the Entente inasmuch as it was fighting on the side of liberty and international ideals against Prussian militarism, autocracy and the suppression of struggling nationalities by Austria-Hungary.

When the Russian democratic revolution overthrew the tsar in 1917, the Mensheviks maintained that Russia must, in accordance with the Marxist analysis of history, first go through the phase of bourgeois democracy under which alone its industrial and agricultural organisation could develop along Western European lines, thereby strengthening and educating the proletariat until the hour when it became a majority and technological progress had rendered it ready to take over full control. They maintained that socialism presupposed far greater industrial development than Russia had reached; that Marx had warned against coups in conditions of scarcity as likely to lead merely to the replacement of capitalists by the State as exploiter of labour; that the proletariat was as yet too ill-organised, uneducated and weak to be able to govern democratically. This patently held still more of the peasants, who were scarcely capable of playing their Marxist part even within the bourgeois democratic republic. To seize power without adequate mass support was, according to the Mensheviks, mere Blanquist or Bonapartist opportunism, and contradicted the democratic basis of socialism.

Against this Lenin and Trotsky, by now his closest collaborator, maintained that, unless the socialist party seized power in what was to them plainly a revolutionary situation and established a dictatorship in the name of the proletariat, it would be discredited and demoralised. The inevitable capitalist phase must indeed occur; but it must proceed, not under a liberal bourgeoisie harried by the workers' organisation, but under direct proletarian control; unless the soviets seized power immediately, as the Commune had done in 1871, the revolution would, as in 1905, collapse.

The all-Russian soviet of workers, peasants and soldiers, which, as in the revolution of 1905, had been elected with indefinite functions, now acted as a kind of alternative source of authority by the side of the provisional liberal government; the Bolsheviks, with support from the left wing of the Social Revolutionaries, urged that it alone truly represented the proletariat and the masses, and was therefore the only truly democratic body to be found in the general chaos. Moreover, had not Marx himself agreed that if a Russian revolution set off a world conflagration, it might survive without the necessity of an interim bourgeois democratic phase? Lenin in 1917–18 confidently believed so: the warning voices of the orthodox socialist parties of Western Europe were not to be listened to; for they, and the orthodox Russian social democrats with them, had, in Lenin's eyes, betrayed the cause in 1914.

Lenin's successful seizure of power in October 1917 split the world socialist movement into two sharply antagonistic factions. Since the leaders of the Second International had not resisted and, in some cases, had supported the war, since its principal theorist, the leader of the orthodox German Marxists, Karl Kautsky, had attacked the Bolshevik revolution as a betrayal by an extremist minority of social democracy, and for this was denounced by Lenin as a renegade, the Russian Bolsheviks, who had now taken the name of Communists, decided to break with the Second International and the International Federation of Trade Unions which was connected with it, and created their own rival Communist (Third) International and their own world trade-union organisation, the 'Profintern'.

Communist revolutions broke out in Bavaria and Hungary. Abortive attempts in the same direction occurred in Prussia. In 1919 the left-wing German socialists Karl Liebknecht and Rosa Luxemburg were assassinated in Berlin, and their comrades Kurt Eisner and Eugen Leviné in Bavaria, where the Communist republic was suppressed. In Hungary, the Red terror was succeeded by an even more ruthless and brutal White terror; in Russia, a systematic extermination of the opposition to the Communist regime presently took the form of mass executions and imprisonments. In every country labour movements were split into those who declared their solidarity with Lenin's authoritarian dictatorship of the Communist Party and disregard of Western democratic procedures in favour of force and Saint-Simonist direction from the top; those who resisted it as despotic; and those who in varying degrees inclined to one or other of these extremes.

After some years of indecision, in the course of which yet another International sprang up – the so-called '2½ International', with a centre in Vienna – a crystallisation finally occurred into, on the one hand, social democratic parties and their associated trade unions, which continued to believe in democratic, non-violent political and economic action and peaceful agitation, and, on the other, communist parties dedicated to the overthrow of existing non-communist regimes – if need be by violence – and bitterly hostile to all other socialist parties as compromisers and traitors. Trotsky's expulsion from Russia in 1928 led to the emergence of yet another organisation, the Fourth International, which claimed to be the true descendant of both Marx and Lenin, opposed to what it described as the bureaucratic corruption, opportunist deviations and nationalism of the Russian Communist Party headed by Stalin.

Beside small independent groups – of which there have at various times been several in Great Britain, the United States and the Latin countries – there remained outside the socialist movement, but in some ideological sympathy with it, the syndicalist and anarchist parties which continued either a Proudhonist, non-revolutionary, peaceful, mutual-aid tradition, or a Bakuninist tradition of conspiracy, terrorism and opposition to all authority. To meet some specific crisis, temporary alliances between various types of socialism have tended to occur. In 1935–8 the popular front movement in Western Europe sought to unite all anti-Fascist forces, in particular social democrats and communists, into a political alliance against the Fascist States and those forces in democratic countries which might seek to compromise with them. Similarly during the Spanish revolution and civil war in 1935–9 intermittent alliances were struck up between left-wing parties in Spain, ending in the virtual extermination of their rivals by Stalinist Communists, and the victory of the Fascists, led by General Franco.

After the Second World War most socialist and labour parties contained wings or at any rate elements sympathetic to co-operation on a less or more limited basis with communist parties. These tendencies were naturally stronger in Eastern Europe, where Soviet influence was dominant, than in the West, where it was feared. Nevertheless it remained true that the chasm which divided Communists, including the independent national Communist regime of Yugoslavia, from other socialist parties was wider than ever. Orthodox socialism with its democratic organisation, its toleration of differences of view within a common framework, its belief in the acquisition of power by legal and parliamentary means, and in gradual socialisation, above all its steadfast regard for the civil liberties of the individual, pursued a path far distant from

Communism with its rigid hierarchical centralisation, its abhorrence of any degree of political compromise with non-Communists, its rigorous discipline, its machinery for the physical repression of all differences of view or policy among its adherents, above all its faith that the supreme end – the overthrow of all the forms of capitalism – justifies any and every means towards it. As for the foundations of doctrine, no important alteration has occurred in any of the forms of social democratic (non-Communist) belief since 1919, the last occasion on which it was compelled to formulate its position in the face of the charges made against it by the leaders of the Communist International.[1]

---

[1] This essay was first published in 1950, and reissued with revisions in 1966. Some further changes have been made, but it has not been revised again in substance to take account of more recent events, especially the collapse of Communism in Eastern Europe and the former Soviet Union.

# MARXISM AND THE INTERNATIONAL IN THE NINETEENTH CENTURY

THE FIRST International Working Men's Association was created in St Martin's Hall in London on 28 September 1864. Its rules were adopted in the last week in October of the same year by a score of individuals, exceedingly obscure at that date, the majority of whom are, if anything, even less familiar one hundred years after the event.[1] How many, even among well-informed students of nineteenth-century social history, could call to memory the lives, even the names, of Limousin, Dupleix, Lessner and Hermann Jung, Schapper and Bobczynski, or even Levy of Geneva or Major Luigi Wolff? Who remembers the names of the rest of the Communist League? The careers of Tolain, Fribourg, Varlin, De Paepe, Eccarius,[2] Howell, Odger, Cremer may be somewhat better known. Still, it seems unlikely that even the part played by these founding fathers would linger in the memory if it were not for the central figure behind this organisation. It was he who made of this scattered collection of individuals, not over-rich in ideas, or even in organisational ability, an instrument which, if it did not itself alter history, laid the foundations of a movement which did exactly this.

Karl Marx lived in London. He stood head and shoulders above such minor German exiles of communist views as the artisans Eccarius, Lessner, Schapper, who naturally looked up to him as their intellectual leader. The British working-class leaders, such as they were at this time, did not know him well, but some of the more enterprising among them looked on him as a learned revolutionary theorist good at providing and formulating ideas for an international workers' association: consequently he (with his friend Engels) was brought into the movement, played a leading

---

[1] This was written in 1964.

[2] It is worth noting that Eccarius, whom Marx tended to trust as a true revolutionary socialist, seems to have turned out to be a paid agent of the Prussian government.

part in its British section, and so, after fifteen years of obscurity, finally entered as a dominating figure on the public stage of European and world history.

It is ironical to reflect that these crucial moments in the history of international socialism, 1864 and 1903 – when, in this same city, Lenin created the Bolshevik Party – should have occurred in a country whose inhabitants remained, then and later, totally unaware of the historic events that were occurring in their midst, in particular of the fact that decisions were being reached on the basis of doctrines largely founded upon their own social and economic history – decisions in which, in defiance of the part cast for them by Marx and Marxism, they did not, and still do not, play any truly significant role.

Let me recall the circumstances of the time. The period of social reaction which followed the débâcle of 1848 was, on the continent of Europe, by no means spent. In 1864 workers' movements were very weak. Lassalle's striking successes in Germany showed what could be done by genius and energy in the face of legal and social obstruction, but his example was unique. Neither the Frenchmen nor the Englishmen, nor the Belgians nor the Swiss who gathered in St Martin's Hall, had anything like the influence of even secondary leaders of the political parties of their time. Proudhon was in impotent exile in Brussels, Bakunin was engaged in imaginary conspiracies in London or Switzerland. Marx was a poverty-stricken chief of a non-existent sect, burrowing away in the British Museum, author of works none too familiar to professional socialists, let alone to the educated public.

What then was it, it may be asked, that made the First International, and the Marxist doctrines so strongly represented in its preamble, statutes and rules, impress themselves upon men's imaginations; and, more than this, achieve a concrete influence greater than all the other organised social movements of the time – Comtean Positivism, for example, or Utilitarianism or the Saint-Simonian movement, or Christian Socialism, or Liberal Reformism, or the League of Peace and Freedom – some of which were based on clearly argued, clearly stated, all-embracing, reasonable and persuasive doctrines, offering a solution to the perplexed and the oppressed, no less comprehensive, or at times magnificently apocalyptic, than Marxism itself? What, in short, made for the impetus, the success, the overwhelming impact of the Marxist movement? Was it its doctrine or its organisation, or a combination of the two? I shall not attempt an answer, even in brief, to this question, which seems more vital to the survival and prospects of all mankind today than a century ago. Despite the fact that the International was far from being a Marxist organisation in its views – throughout its brief existence it remained a very uneasy alliance of highly disparate ideas, Proudhonist, Jacobin, Bakuninist, populist and, in the case of the trade unions, sometimes too vague to be classified – yet its historical importance derives from its association with Marx's name and doctrine. It was this that created the image and the myth: which historically are at least as potent as the bare truths round which they grow. The phenomenon has a triple aspect: the organisation itself; Marx's doctrines, for which it acted as a platform, and with which it later came to be, a little mythically, identified; and its notoriety and prestige, which Communism as such derived from the deeds and sufferings, and above all the name, of the Paris Commune. Let me begin with the ideas to which the organisation gave so great an impetus.

I propose to discuss these under five heads:

(i) The claim of Marxism to account for human history, and in particular conflict, oppression and misery, in terms that claim to be at once scientific and historical and to lead to foreknowledge of a bright future – the reign of liberty, equality and prosperity in the entire world – in other words a synthesis of scientific method, historical realism and a guarantee of ultimate rewards as real and as certain as any offered by religion or philosophy in the past.

(ii) The provision of concrete ends, in both the short and the long run, which it is natural for men to pursue; in particular the identification of a specific enemy, triumph over whom alone can inaugurate the liberation of mankind.

(iii) The clear division of men into the children of light and the children of darkness; with the corollary that the nature of objective facts, and not free, revocable human decisions on the part of men, are responsible for the fate of the children of darkness, a multitude condemned by history itself to perish; from which it follows that humane efforts to save it are of necessity known to be futile, and therefore irrational.

(iv) The expression in the general values of any society of the interests of a particular class in power; and, in consequence, the inevitable transformation of human morality into a new code, corresponding to the rise of a new class engaged in the final struggle against the forces of social inequality and exploitation, a class whose requirements, since they are identical with those of men as such, overrule all other ethical considerations.

(v) The identification of the interests of a specific human group or class, the workers, the exploited proletariat, perhaps even more simply the poor, with the interests of all mankind as such.

What in fact was created by Marx was a new ecumenical organisation, a kind of anti-Church, with a full apparatus of concepts and categories, capable, at least in theory, of yielding clear and final answers to all possible questions, private and public, scientific and historical, moral and aesthetic, individual and institutional. The gospel of this new establishment, of what Saint-Simon and Comte had dreamt, but which Marx and Engels created, was addressed to the reason and the passions of real persons to whom the expanding industrialism of Europe had already given self-consciousness as a body united by common sufferings and common interests. These were workers in factories and shops, and on the land – those, in short, who did not own their own instruments of production, men whose condition formed the heart of what, in the nineteenth century, came to be called the social question.

While I do not propose to expound the familiar principles of Marxism, I think it as well to remark that they rest upon a metaphysical foundation which is by no means self-evident, a vast assumption which Marx took over from Hegel and classical philosophy, and which he did not himself trouble to argue. This assumption, important not only intrinsically, but on account of the vast influence it has had, is the monistic conception of history.

The Russian Marxist Plekhanov was perfectly right in so describing Marxism, for which, as for the classical thinkers, reality is a single rational system. Not only do those who think in this fashion see history and nature – the two great dimensions of human experience – as explicable in terms of a single, all-embracing system of discoverable laws which govern men and inanimate nature alike, although each branch of the school formulated its own laws, which it claimed to be the first to discover, but Marxism in addition claims (in this respect like Comtean Positivism) that these laws alone could account for the errors in thought and failures and sufferings in practice that have attended the history of mankind thus far;[1] and furthermore can alone distinguish what is progressive from what is reactionary, that is, what is conducive to realising the proper, rationally demonstrable, goals of men from that which obstructs or ignores them. Marxism is based on the assumption that all human problems are capable of solution; that men are permanently so constituted (this is offered as an axiom, both psychological and sociological) as to seek after peace, not war, harmony, not discord, unity, not multiplicity. Strife, conflict, competition between human beings are essentially pathological processes: men may be so built that these tendencies are, at a certain stage of their development, inevitable; what makes them abnormal is that they do not fulfil those ends that men as men cannot avoid having in common – the common and permanent purposes that make men human.

It is this assumption that all human beings have a common nature, change as it may, definable in terms of certain very general, specifically human goals – a doctrine at the root of Aristotle and the Bible no less than Aquinas, Descartes, Luther and the atheists of eighteenth-century Paris – that makes possible talk of frustration, degradation, distortion of human beings. Men have permanent spiritual and material potentialities which they can realise only in one final set of conditions: when they cease from mutual destruction, when they turn their energies from fighting one another and unite them to subdue their environment according to reason; reason being understood as that which understands and seeks the satisfaction of needs that men cannot help possessing, needs misconceived for historically explicable reasons in the past, and misused to justify aggression and oppression. The central – and uncriticised – assumption is that all human ends are, in principle, harmonisable and capable of satisfaction; that men are, or can be and will be, such that the satisfaction of one man's 'natural' ends will one day not frustrate the quest for similar satisfaction by his brothers.

This entails the falsity of all theories that accept the inevitability of conflict, or even, as in the case of Kant, maintain that without strife there is no progress, that it is the struggle for the light which

---

[1] Past errors and suffering are seen as an inevitable prelude, as so many signs and evidences of future felicity: a necessary episode in the great drama of human history, not accidents, not meaningless disasters.

each seeks to shut out from the other that makes trees grow taller. It is directly opposed to every form of 'Social Darwinism'; it denies the hypothesis that it is original sin or inherent evil, or natural aggressiveness, or even the sheer variety and incompatibility of human wants and ideals, that destroys the very possibility of a seamless harmony, a complete unity of wholly rational beings leading lives of frictionless co-operation towards universally accepted and harmonious ends. Hence it is radically opposed to the corollaries of earlier ideas, for example, that the end of political action is not some static perfection, but the adjustment of interests and activities as they arise, when they arise; since, according to such ideas, it is natural to men to pursue different and, at times, incompatible ends; nor is this an evil, for diversity is the price – and perhaps the essence – of free activity. Hence all that political action can achieve is the creation of machinery for the prevention of too much friction, the suffering caused by too many conflicts and collisions, without attempting to suppress them wholly; for to do this, at whatever cost, is to crush men into a bed of Procrustes, to press them into an artificial uniformity that leads to an impoverishment, and occasionally the destruction, of the human spirit. Marxism is opposed to this.

The history of political thought has, to a large degree, consisted in a duel between these two great rival conceptions of society. On one side stand the advocates of pluralism and variety and an open market for ideas, an order of things that involves clashes and the constant need for conciliation, adjustment, balance, an order that is always in a condition of imperfect equilibrium, which is required to be maintained by conscious effort. On the other side are to be found those who believe that this precarious condition is a form of chronic social and personal disease, since health consists in unity, peace, the elimination of the very possibility of disagreement, the recognition of only one end or set of non-conflicting ends as being alone rational, with the corollary that rational disagreement can affect only means – the upholders of the tradition of Plato and the Stoics, the *philosophia perennis* of the Middle Ages, Spinoza and Helvétius, Rousseau and Fichte, and classical political theory. Marx was a faithful son of this tradition from the beginning to the end of his life: his emphasis on the contradictions and conflicts inherent in social development are mere variations on the theme of the uninterrupted progress of humans conceived as a system of beings engaged in understanding and controlling their environment and themselves.

From these classic premisses he drew the most original of all his conclusions, and the most influential – the celebrated doctrine of the unity of theory and practice. What you do is not merely the best evidence of what you think – a better criterion for discovering what you truly believe than anything that you yourself say or think about your own convictions or principles. Marxism has at times been reduced to truisms of this kind, but to do so is to perpetrate a caricature. The Marxist doctrine is that what you do *is* what you believe; practice is not evidence for, it is identical with, belief. To understand something *is* to live, that is, act, in a certain fashion; and vice versa. If such understanding and knowledge belongs to the realm of theory, then it is the activity of thinking along certain lines; if it occurs in the world of action, then it consists of readiness to act in a certain way, the initiation of a certain type of behaviour. Belief, thought, emotion, volition, decision, action are not distinguishable from one another as so many activities or states or processes: they are aspects of the same *praxis* – action upon, or reaction to, the world.

This entails a view of values, and of moral, political and aesthetic goals, that has not always been understood by the simpler-minded of Marx's disciples, and has indeed at times been reduced to vulgar truisms. To be rational, for Marx, is to understand myself, the situation I live in, above all its class structure, and my relation to it. This pattern develops historically into the society of which I am a member; it is as it is in virtue of the relations of its members to one another, relations that are themselves determined by their connection with the productive process. To understand anything is to understand what part it plays in this process, a process that has as its ultimate, objective, unalterable purpose (for Marxism is nothing if it is not teleological) the satisfaction of the true and discoverable interests of men. Moreover to understand is to see the world in the light of it: to live in a certain fashion. There can be only one true answer to any given problem, whether theoretical or practical, one path that is not self-destructive, one social policy or way of life that is rational in any given situation; whatever it may be it must always be directed towards the elimination of strife, to the organisation of human energies, as Saint-Simon had taught, for the attainment of power over nature, not over men, for this fails to fulfil the ends of men, which consist in a harmonious society in which all the ends of all its members are fully realised. This solution alone is rational. All other forms of behaviour are not rational, that is, they lead to various kinds and degrees of self-distortion and frustration. To know what I must do I must know what and where I am in the pattern of the processes of production which determine the shape of every society and of the lives of its members. Values are falsely divorced from facts by the philosophers: for to value is to act. A rational valuation is the correct assessment of ends, means, situations, agents involved in them. To discover these truths is to apply them. It is not, on this view, possible to analyse a situation correctly and fail to behave accordingly, or vice versa, though the process need not always be a self-conscious one. If I cannot know what my true goal is and how to obtain it, I cannot be rational and I cannot determine myself to act in the light of such knowledge.

This is not the crude utilitarianism (sometimes mistakenly attributed to Marx) according to which I say to myself: 'Certain objective laws govern the world and history; I had better find out what these are and adjust myself to them, otherwise I shall be crushed by the Juggernaut of History; and no rational being can want that.' Against this kind of appeal to inevitable forces men's moral consciousness has revolted in every age; for moments occur when men know that it is morally (or even politically) better to defend their absolute principles against any odds, rather than give in and follow prudential rules, and this knowledge remains unshaken when its precepts are called quixotic or Utopian or inexpedient. The Marxist position is a more sophisticated one. Like Hegel, Marx looks upon the division between facts and values as a shallow fallacy: every thought embodies a valuation, no less than every act and every feeling; values are already incarnate in my general attitude to the world, in the total outlook that shapes or is perceptible in all that I think, see, believe, understand, discover, know, say. The notion of value, indeed of the possibility of a value-free activity – detached contemplation, passionless description of what there is, without any attribution of value – is, according to this view, an absurdity. I see what I see with eyes that belong uniquely to my age and its ideals, my culture and its values, my temperament and its drives, and above all, of course, my class and its interests. A realism which rests on the assumption that the facts are objective entities, out there – in neutral space, as it were – and can be viewed as they truly are without any assessment or

interpretation of them – that is, without evaluation – is tantamount
to denying that men are end-pursuing, purposive, intention-form-
ing creatures. The notion of the dispassionate observer, free from
the historical stream that determines him to seek this and avoid
that, causes him to belong to a particular group involved in its
traditions and outlook, or else in revolt against them; the notion, in
short, of the self as a static entity and not as a perpetual activity,
that is, as a perpetual effort to do or be thus and thus – to behave in
this or that fashion vis-à-vis things, one's own characteristics,
above all other persons – is profoundly fallacious. Worse: it is a
disguise for retreat – escape from reality posing as dispassionate
detachment – what Sartre called bad faith. Consequently, only that
valuation, and the activity that expresses it, will be rational which
springs from a correct grasp of my historical position, that is, of
my position in the process determined by whatever is the dominant factor in it – God or the laws of nature, or State, or Church,
or class – and consists in the choice of only those means which,
given this process, can alone effectively promote those ends which
as a rational being I cannot help seeking; cannot help, not in some
mechanical sense in which, say, I cannot help digesting, but in the
sense in which I cannot help reaching logically correct conclusions
if I employ logical methods of reasoning, in which I cannot help
trying to protect myself against dangers if I truly believe that they
threaten me and my purposes.

George Lichtheim is thus perfectly correct in asserting that Marx
did not believe it to be rational to work for the revolution, simply
because it was inevitable; but that he believed it to be inevitable
because the tension between the new state of the forces of
production and old legal or political or economic forces grows
literally unacceptable to those who have grasped what a rationally
organised society must and will be.[1] Thus the conflict between the
increasing socialisation of the means of production on the one
hand (an example of conscious, rational, free human activity
embodying a realistic grasp of how to realise ends that I cannot
help pursuing), and, on the other, the non-socialised means of
distribution, surviving from an earlier economic phase, must issue
in an explosion and a rational solution. This is the deeper, cosmic
sense in which *la raison a toujours raison* (Plekhanov's favourite

[1] George Lichtheim, *Marxism: An Historical and Critical Study* (London and
New York, 1961; 2nd ed. 1964), p. 55.

quotation). This tension, for Marx, makes certain an ultimate revolt by a given society against frustrations which spring from its own unavoidable ignorance or stupidity, and take the form of maintaining institutions originally created by itself in response to real needs, but now no longer capable of fulfilling them, and so transformed into mere impediments to human progress, to the satisfaction of basic human needs in the form which the social process has given them. No doubt this pattern of partial fulfilment breeding its own tensions, and diseases generating their own remedies, is itself inescapable: but it is explicable in terms of men's own nature – the miseries and splendour of men's reason and invention – and not of some external non-human power which shapes men as it does, whether they like it or not. The play is predetermined, but the actors are not marionettes controlled by strings pulled by some outside agency: they determine themselves. Their lines are set them by their predicament, but they understand and mean them, for the ends are their own.

This position, which, on the face of it, is clear, coherent and rounded, conceals an explosive force, a dialectical twist not often explicitly admitted by Marxist thinkers. Facts and values are fused together; men are made what they are by the interplay of historical, social and material-natural factors, and their values are determined by the tasks that history sets any rational creature that possesses, in common with other rational creatures, certain common social ends which it is of the essence of its rationality to have, to understand, to strive for. So far, so good. But if history is a process of perpetual change; if men by pursuing their historical goals alter not merely their environment but themselves also in the course of it, as Marx – following Hegel – argued with brilliance and depth; and if the central motor impulse of human development is class conflict; then social ends, that is, rules, principles, values, during the historical process that leads to the Revolution, must perpetually be altered by the changing relations of classes to each other and of individuals within those classes (for in the end classes are but collections of individuals, and their structure is a function of these individuals' interaction); then there cannot, while the class struggle goes on, exist universal, common human goals. No end or principle can be so immutable and sacred that in a specific situation the demands of the next step in the ascent of self-transforming humanity – a step that, precisely because men are changed by their own efforts, they cannot ever foresee, cannot fully know until they have reached it –

may not justifiably overrule it. This is so until the final rational order of society is reached, and what Marx called 'prehistory' achieves its ultimate goal.

According to this conception the ultimate human end is the freedom of men self-determined by their own unfettered reason, so that progress is to be identified with the triumph of a given section of mankind – say the proletariat – as sole carriers of this rational development; and so it will follow that its interests, because they are identified with the interests of all mankind, are paramount. But – and this is a very crucial 'but' – since these interests, and concrete demands, alter from moment to moment in the vicissitudes of the struggle, if only because they are interests of men who themselves, with their ideals, outlooks, scales of value, are in a state of constant flux, what they dictate cannot be predicted; may differ from everything held sacred today. It is, in the end, this that outraged those who found particular Marxist positions immoral or despotic. No matter how genuinely Herzen and Bakunin, Kropotkin and Lavrov, Jaurès and Martov, Rosa Luxemburg and Karl Liebknecht may have recognised the validity of the class analysis of history, it is evident that they in fact did not believe that values were nothing but functions of changing concrete situations, and directly deducible from them;[1] could not bring themselves to swallow the axiom that the interests of the proletariat as interpreted by competent Marxist analysts acted as a compass pointing inexorably to the morally as well as practically correct policy (for the two must necessarily coincide), in the literal way that truth has often been identified with the varying pronouncements of a privileged priesthood by those religions which believe their Church to be the ultimate and infallible depository of all truth and validity.

Some among these thinkers may at times have believed something resembling this in their studies or on a public platform: but when it followed that, in a particular country and situation, the claims of the peasants were to be ignored because the theory pronounced them – not implausibly – to be a reactionary class; or when the theory – in the name of the historical dialectic – ordered the suppression of the democratic rights of members of working-class parties in favour of the pronouncements of a chosen élite of leaders; or commanded you to sabotage a war fought against men and institutions whom you knew to be enemies of a civilisation

[1] Karl Liebknecht was an avowed neo-Kantian.

which enshrined human values, or without which life seemed to you scarcely worth defending (in 1914 and in 1939), or to suppress elementary human rights if this was required by the Revolution (as sanctioned by Plekhanov in 1903), or to obey a dictatorship of self-appointed Party leaders (as condemned by Rosa Luxemburg in 1918); or required perjury, falsification, alliance with Hitler, murders and massacres of the innocent – all the familiar enormities which provoked the moral crises and bankruptcies and secessions within the Communist Parties – the root of the sense of outrage is always, it seems to me, some lingering belief in the existence of human values more permanent (whether or not absolute) than a constantly altering superstructure determined by a constantly altering economic base. It is this that the earliest heretics, Hess and Grün, Proudhon and the anarchists, could not give up: it was for this that they were anathematised and excommunicated. It was the return to this, relatively non-evolutionary, notion of moral principles that made Bernstein's revisionism appear so serious a danger to orthodox Marxists: his adherence to universal ideals far more than the budget of theoretical errors, false prophecies, tactical and strategic fallacies with which he charged the uncritical disciples of the master. What divided him from the orthodox was his unbreakable conviction that men remote in time and circumstances nevertheless understand each other in terms of a nucleus (or overlapping nuclei) of common human values, that it is possible to understand Hebrew prophets or Greek philosophers or medieval churchmen, or Indian, Chinese, Japanese institutions, despite the vast differences in productive systems that divide these societies from our own. Indeed, Marx too may in his actual life and writings have demonstrated his own acceptance of this undoubted fact, on which all human communication rests: but his doctrine entails the opposite, or at least seemed to do so to some of his most fanatical disciples. When Jules Guesde refused to support the defenders of Dreyfus on the ground that this was an internal quarrel of the bourgeoisie of no possible concern to the proletariat, his behaviour was that of a faithful Marxist doctrinaire. A doctrinaire is a man who is liable to suppress what he may, if he comes across it, suspect to be true; indeed his everyday conduct is based on what his doctrine directs him to think and feel and do. Consequently when Lenin was accused of 'boundless cynicism' by Martov or others of his associates, this was not perhaps entirely just. No one denies that the whole purpose of Lenin's working life was the triumph of the

proletarian revolution as he conceived it. He could and did justify
every one of the acts considered as cynical – from devious political
tactics at the meetings of the Russian Social Democratic Party to
the defence of armed robbery or blackmail by Party members – on
the grounds, considered by him sole and sufficient, of the requirements of the revolutionary movement. If this is condemned as
cynicism, it is so as an offence against a scale of values not
identified with the immediate needs of the militant section of a
class struggling for victory; otherwise it is not cynical, but the code
of a consistent revolutionary Marxist. Lenin may have made
mistakes about tactics; he may, as his opponents said and still say,
have mistaken the true interests of the class he served, or the proper
role of the leaders of this class: but what truly appalled his critics,
including those on the extreme left wing of socialism – Rosa
Luxemburg or Martov – were not intellectual or tactical errors, but
enormities – unforgivable sins against both socialism and morality.

What morality? What had Marx ever said – or Engels, for that
matter – that Lenin specifically denied either in theory or in
practice? At most it could be said that by establishing his rule when
he did, he deviated sharply from doctrine contained in the classical
Social-Democratic schema of the form of the proletarian revolution
in a society in which industrial conditions had not ripened
sufficiently to generate a proletarian majority technically equipped
to take over. But this at worst was a theoretical deviation, a
misreading of history. But cynicism? Or brutality? Those who
used these terms evidently still carried within them traces of an
older moral outlook not compatible with that strictly revolutionary Marxist morality which latter-day champions of Marxist
humanism, based on the early writings of the master, do not stress.

Evolutionary relativism is an intrinsic element of Marx's
thought, early and late. One of the main sources of strength, at
least politically, in Marxism is that despite anything said by Engels,
or Kautsky, or Plekhanov, or the textbooks of Marxism derived
from their writings, there is in Marx's teaching a bold and startling
combination of absolute authority and evolutionary morality: men
in their struggle to subjugate nature change it and themselves and
their values; but what is declared and commanded by those who
direct the struggle and grasp the new values (namely the Communist Party, or those who are held to be its leaders, the élite who
alone fully understand the direction of history) – that is absolute
for their own time. This relativity, whereby each stage of the

process that culminates in the triumph of the proletariat has its historical values, not assimilable to those of another stage, is central: what Marx condemned in bourgeois values was not that they are objectively false, as, let us say, phlogiston theory is false, in the sense of being refutable by timeless criteria, but that they are bourgeois; and therefore false in the sense of expressing or leading to a view of life and a form of action that conflicts with the pattern of human progress, and therefore cannot but distort the facts. Truth, in this sense, resides in the vision of the most progressive men of the age: these are, *ipso facto*, those who identify their interests with those of the most progressive class of their time. The proof of the fact that they see the facts correctly lies in action; the correctness of their interpretation of history and its demands is success in practice, success in advancing humanity towards true, that is, the only truly attainable, human goals. The rules which the crew of the ship obey will change, but the word of the captain and officers, who alone know their destination, is final and irrevocable, and defines what is true and right. This identification of truth and authority with the activity, theoretical or practical, of an identifiable group of human beings had never hitherto been maintained by secular thinkers. Churches have claimed this, indeed, but only by appeal to supernatural sanctions. Marx's epoch-making move was to substitute for the God of the Churches (at once one and absolute, but revealing different aspects of his essence at different moments) the movement of history: to stake everything on this, to identify its authorised interpreters, and to make absolute demands in its and their name. It is this notion of truth as the authority of the group over the individual, or, for practical purposes, of the leaders of the group over the group, that is now[1] prevalent wherever Marxism is dominant, where it has replaced the older notion of an objective truth, for all men to seek and find, testable by public criteria open to all. This is what Marxism has in common with some of the great dogmatic Churches of the world: something that not even Comtism or Saint-Simonianism, not to speak of liberalism or utilitarianism or democratic socialism, or all the other secular – anti-clerical – systems competing with Marxism for the capture of the liberal, progressive and revolutionary section of European opinion (especially those who believe Marxism to be based on the laws of natural science), could successfully compete

[1] 1964.

with. Marxism liberated its adherents from the old, permanent 'bourgeois' morality as effectively as Nietzsche or Nechaev could have demanded. It does not follow that in practice some Social Democrats and Marxists, at least before our own time, could not be good and decent men. This was taken for granted – too much so for some.

## II

To live is to act. To act is to pursue goals, to choose, accept, reject, pursue, resist, escape, be for or against an entire form of life or some ingredients of it. The self-conscious know this, the unself-conscious merely do it; values are therefore part of the very texture of living that includes thinking, feeling, willing; we do not begin by placing ourselves on some Archimedean point outside the world, whence we choose this or that ideal at will, like goods in a shop; we are, as Aristotle had maintained, born into a world and a society; we find ourselves committed to them by the way in which we normally act, by the fact of being where and when and as and what we (and our societies) are; in becoming aware of this we perceive contradictions between facts and our notions or fancies, or between our ideals, or between ends and the means adopted to serve them; and can – that is what being rational consists in – seek to remove these by a fuller understanding of the facts. If we are Hegelian idealists the 'facts' are constituents of a spiritual-cultural process of activity; if we are materialists, they consist of material objects and the laws they obey and efforts by concrete human beings in time and space – themselves natural entities also – to dominate these external objects, including their own bodies and each other. These efforts are designed to achieve the agent's freedom from uncontrolled factors, to enable him to direct himself by 'harnessing' whatever his life depends on, in the first place food, shelter, security, but ultimately whatever else he can control within the physical and psychological boundaries imposed by nature. Hence to divide facts from values as Hume and others have done – the description of what is from what should be – is impossible. Any description of what is, embodies an attitude, that is, a view of it in terms of what should be: we are not contemplating a static garden; we are involved in a movement with a perceptible direction; it can be correctly or incorrectly described; but any description must embody a valuation, that is, a reference to the goals towards which the movement proceeds, and in terms of which alone it can be 'understood', goals that we have not chosen, but which are part of our essence and determine what we ourselves choose or reject.

That is the metaphysical basis equally of the Aristotelian, Hegelian and Marxist systems, nor would the Young Hegelians of the 1830s and early 1840s have dissented from any of it. Nor is the conception of history as based on social classes novel. As Marx himself conceded, this had been a powerful instrument in the hands of the French liberal historians during the Restoration, who had explained social development in terms of the conflicts of classes conceived in more or less economic terms. What was original in Marx's analysis was the notion of bourgeoisie and proletariat as historical categories, due to arise and to vanish at specific historical stages. Proletarians are a class of persons – workers – who are separated from their tools – their means of production – as well as from their raw materials and their product, all of which were owned or taken away from them, by the master; a master who in effect owned his workers, inasmuch as the worker had become, without the institution of legal slavery, a creature whose labour power was itself bought and sold on the market like any other commodity. This class – the proletariat – had lost its moral or social function in society; it was no longer conceived as an element in a social whole with its own unique contribution to the common purpose of this whole to which all the members of a society consciously contributed. According to Marx, labour, or the capacity for it, had become mere material to be 'exploited' – an object, not a subject, a commodity, treated (whatever men might say or think) as if it were a thing, a non-human entity, like wool or leather or a piece of machinery, as something usable, not as a user, as 'human material',[1] not as persons for whose sake everything that is done is, or at least should be, done. This thesis, whether or not it was valid, had important political and moral corollaries.

To begin with, it served to identify the enemy. The motor power of history was held to be the class struggle, a pathological condition for which no one in particular was 'responsible', and one due, according to Marx (and others before him – James Ferguson

---

[1] A phrase that later Marxists were quite naturally to use in a non-pejorative, descriptive sense – this marks the distance of Bukharin, for example, from Marx himself.

for one), to the division of labour which the struggle to control
nature created, a struggle that itself sprang from the *de facto*
physical and mental constitution of men, and more broadly the
facts studied by physics and biology. If class war, then, was the
motor force of human history, it followed that one of the two
struggling classes (why only two? – but that is what Marx taught,
unlike Hegel, who, contrary to popular misconception, allowed a
many-sided conflict) embodied progress, that is, the stage of
human development that came closest – to date – to control over
nature and the self; while its antagonist represented an earlier stage,
further from the goal, and therefore had to be defeated as a class
before the possibility could arise of any further advance towards
the goal – whose absolute validity for its own stage of evolution
could not be questioned. The outlook, beliefs, ideals, institutions,
cultures, religions of men are part and parcel of the historical
situation, that is, conditioned by the development of productive
forces, and are at once active elements in, and the clearest
symptoms of, the particular stage which the class struggle has
reached. Ideals, codes of behaviour, are weapons in the struggle,
conscious or unconscious; that is to say, interests, though often
disguised in the form of lofty abstractions; interests of a particular
class, though often posing as universal human goals; functions of a
particular time and situation, though often 'masquerading' as
unalterable, eternal, universal, natural laws exempt from change.
To show them in their true guise is to 'demystify' them, to unmask,
'demythologise'. But Marx's boldest, and politically most decisive,
stroke was the identification of one particular class with mankind
as such. All previous classes pursued sectional interests: despotic
oriental bureaucracies, Roman patricians and knights, feudal lords,
capitalist accumulators. But the exploited, degraded, dehumanised
proletariat of modern times – the lowest class of all – having no
class below it, represents *man as such*; its class interests, being the
minimum needs of men as such, are the interests of all men, for it
has no interests that conflict with those of any other human group;
deprived to the highest degree compatible with the preservation of
life and animal activity of all sources of human satisfaction, what it
needs and claims is what men as such must have if they are to lead
lives capable of being described as human.

   This leads to a conclusion and a prophecy of radical importance.
All other classes are historical formations destined to pass away,
together with the particular interests of their time and situation, no

matter how much they may look timeless and unalterable. They will perish and with them will vanish the institutions that came into being to serve their particular needs, although they pretended to be embodiments of eternal justice (the legal system) or the eternal laws of supply and demand (the economic system) or eternal truths about man, his purpose and his destiny (priesthoods and Churches). The temporary and class-conditioned character of all these institutions and creeds can be unmasked – history is full of broken relics of such pretensions. But there exists one class – the proletariat – whose interests, since it has no characteristics which are not shared by all other men as such, are the interests of all mankind; its ideals are not a masquerade for something else – concealed sectional interests. It was a brilliant and telling stroke to identify the interests of one particular class with the interests of all men; so that while all previous beliefs and institutions which belonged to this or that social order could be represented as so many conscious or unconscious falsifications of reality – various kinds and degrees of illusion, self-deception or deliberate trickery, designed to prop up the domination of a particular class – one set of beliefs, one form of social structure was exempt from this inexorable decree: those of the working classes, at least those which embodied the acts and opinions of the men who understood the true position and prospects of the proletariat, whether they themselves belonged to it or not. In their case what would necessarily have been the fantasies of any other class turned out to be truths, a correct view of reality and a correct guide to action. An interest is to be classed as mere interest only when it conflicts with other interests; where it is truly universal, it ceases to be a 'mere' interest, and becomes the proper, universally valid, end of man. The liberating knowledge of the truth which earlier doctrines had discovered in the soul of the true believer, or in sacred books, or the pronouncements of the Church, or metaphysical insight, or scientific enlightenment, or the general will of an uncorrupted society, Marx had lodged within something much more concrete – the minds and activities of working men who (with his help) have arrived at an understanding of the world in which they live, its machinery and the unalterable direction of its growth.

One cannot exaggerate the political results of this move: Marx provided the angry, the miserable, the poor, the discontented with a specific enemy – the capitalist exploiter, the bourgeoisie. He proclaimed a holy war which gave the poor and the exploited not only hope, but something specific to do, not simply the task of self-education in the positive sciences (as recommended by, say, Comte) or political pressure through legitimate channels as permitted by constitutionally established authority (as advocated by Mill and the liberals), still less contempt for the values of this world and the attainment of serenity and happiness by unworldly spiritual resignation (as recommended by some at any rate among the Christian teachers), but organisation for ruthless war: with the prospect of blood, sweat and tears, of battles, death and perhaps temporary defeats; but, above all, the guarantee of a happy ending to the story. For the stars in their courses are fighting for this consummation. This none of the rival prophets promised or demanded: Proudhon came nearest to it, but his deep hatred of centralisation led him to prohibit mass organisation and political action. It was as plain to Marx as to Bismarck that the only way to fight power is by power: and power in the modern world requires the organisation of as many human beings as is practicable, and the employment by them or on their behalf of the only instruments capable of crushing resistance – political and military measures. If the institutions and the force of the enemy were to be overcome, it could be done only by the conquest of political power; the enemy could be finally crushed only by an act of coercion, by revolution. The ends of the victors might not themselves be political at all; the State for Marx (as for Bakunin) was always only the jackboot, an instrument of oppression to be done away with as soon as feasible; but the means remained necessarily political, for these were the only effective weapons of the contemporary world, made so by the particular phase of the productive forces and relationships that determined the shape of, at any rate, European society – the particular modern form imposed upon the class war by the intelligible pattern of history herself. This doctrine gave the workers a concrete programme, and more than this, a total *Weltanschauung*, a morality, a metaphysics, a social doctrine, a way of testing and measuring everything that they were offered by teachers and clergymen and politicians and books and all the other forces that form opinion, the total system by which we live, a total substitute for the rival schemas – those offered by the Christian Churches or by liberal atheism, or by nationalism, or by the many confused and uneasy mixtures of all these.

Let me make this point even more sharply. Marx's unique achievement was to split mankind into two worlds, more deeply perhaps than had occurred since the rise of Christianity against paganism. Before Marx it is, I think, true to say that there had existed since, let us say, the Greek Stoics a general assumption in the Western world of the existence of certain common values, values common to all mankind. The assumption of Christian attempts to convert pagans or of Protestant arguments against Catholics, or even between enemies in wars or revolutions, was this: that any man could, in principle, unless he was mentally deficient, understand any other man; that if men were in error, they could be converted by argument; that though a man might be deep in heresy and illusion, something could always be done, or at least attempted, to bring him back to sanity; in extreme cases coercion, torture, might be needed to destroy the obstacles to the perception of the truth – or even death, which would at any rate liberate the heretic's soul and allow it, in the world to come, to see that light which shines equally for all men. In wars and revolutions the appeal might sink to the level of sheer expediency, but still it was assumed that the conquered would surrender by an act of rational choice – because they were endowed with the capacity, present in all men, to understand their own good – to see that in this case they would lose more by resistance than by acknowledging defeat. Whether the argument rested on universal principles, scientific truths founded on observation and reasoning, or sheer superior power, the assumption remained that communication could always be established – the purpose of terror or violence was, at least in theory, conversion to, genuine acceptance of, the point of view of those who used these weapons. The number of those who must be destroyed because they would not be saved must be few: the incurably fanatical, the abnormal, the mad.

But if the class-conflict theory of history was correct, this basic assumption was not true. If I think as I think and act as I do it is because what makes me what I am, whether I know it or not, is my membership of a particular class that is engaged in a struggle for victory or a hopeless attempt at survival in a particular phase of human development; I can scarcely be expected, then, to see the world through the spectacles of another class, the elimination (or at least neutralisation) of which is the whole *raison d'être* of my own class. I am what I am because I am involved in the objective situation of my class on the historical ladder; I cannot be expected to understand even the language used by a spokesman of a class differently conditioned; for try as I might to listen, I am bound to translate it into my own conceptual schema and behave accordingly; so that there will be no true communication. But if this is so, then it is no use trying to explain to the others the errors of their ways, no use arguing, no use hoping that if one can only convince the other side of the hopelessness of their position, of the fact that they are historically doomed, they will abandon the struggle and succumb and be saved. It is still more absurd to bring home to them their wickedness – for this presupposes a minimum universal standard of morality or moral understanding which *ex hypothesi* does not exist, if each class is held to have its own morality.

This, if it is valid, is a radical discovery: for it undermines the basic assumptions of rational dispute, of the possibility of uncoerced consensus which alone justifies democratic government. In a class-divided society, there is in principle no possibility of a rational compromise between groups incapable of understanding, indeed of not seeking to destroy, each other. Hatred, historically inevitable hatred, blows up the entire basis of a unitary State, of society, government, justice, morality, politics, as hitherto conceived. Those whom history has doomed, it has deprived of understanding. They are like the pagans whom Israelites were to eradicate in their entirety, condemned by God utterly. Others had spoken in terms of class conflict – Saint-Simon, Fourier, Owen, Weitling, the 'True Socialists', Hess, Rodbertus, Proudhon, Bakunin had done so. But they allowed the notion to slip in that a pacific solution was, at least in principle, thinkable – that enough argument, enough rationality on everyone's part (however difficult to achieve in practice), and perhaps the other side would understand and abdicate. So Saint-Simon had thought the Jacobin Terror in the great French Revolution could have been avoided if the Jacobins – and 'the rabble' – had not been so uneducated, so stupid as to ignore how much they could have achieved if they had not cut off Lavoisier's head or caused Condorcet's suicide, but on the contrary placed themselves under their guidance. This for Marx was precisely the unhistorical attitude that reduced these thinkers' doctrines to absurdity: for it militated against the deepest of all his beliefs, that history was the history of class struggles. This for him meant that men were formed by their objective situation in history, and could not possibly see what their situation made them unable to see: the Jacobins, however confusedly, represent interests not reconcilable with those of the class to which Lavoisier and

Condorcet belonged, in terms of whose interests, however involuntarily, they thought and acted. Class consciousness was all.

Let me illustrate this by three images. If I am on a mounting escalator, as it were, I can afford to look at the facts without terror, for whatever happens will be evidence, true evidence, of the ultimate victory of my class, if I made my prognosis correctly, as Marx and Engels thought they had done, for my awareness of ascending is not illusory. But if I am on the descending stair I cannot be expected to see the facts in a true light: for they are too frightening. Men, as has so often been remarked (especially by Christian thinkers), cannot face too much reality. Marx thought this true only of those whose defeat was imminent, the downward-tending groups. They try to rationalise their position by every possible means: defend their 'mere' (that is, class-bounded) interests as universal ideals, see their class-created and class-preserving institutions as just or rational, and, indeed, as eternal and unalterable, regard these ephemeral works of men, structures in which men have embodied their temporary vision, religions and Churches, laws and systems of justice, arts and philosophies and social and economic structures, as possessing the stability and inevitability of natural forces, and so treat them as embodying absolute standards of value and truth. This fallacy he called reification, and those who worship such man-made institutions as supernatural, or natural and therefore unalterable, forces he described as being 'alienated', divorced from their own creations, from a society which is their own or their ancestors' handiwork transformed into an external entity, a transcendent authority, an idol to be worshipped.

My second image is that of a man who is drowning: that is surely not the moment to ask him about the temperature of the water, or indeed his views about anything else; he will do anything to save himself, even if it is wholly futile. This, for Marx, is the contemporary position of the bourgeoisie. Debarred as it is by its historical position from seeing reality correctly, it cannot be argued with, cannot be convinced. It can only be despatched to its doom as effectively and swiftly as is feasible, if the next stage, the emancipation of all mankind, is to be achieved as painlessly and rapidly as possible.

Perhaps my third image – from therapeutic medicine – will convey this notion best: a man who understands reality, the nature and incidence of the class conflict that determines the thought and action of entire classes, is like a psychiatrist who understands both himself and the patient; the patient understands neither himself nor the psychiatrist. The psychiatrist has nothing to lose by looking at reality – for only knowledge makes it possible to choose rationally between alternatives. In this case he is the self-conscious proletarian (still more his leaders) who sees that his interests are those of all mankind, that by pressing for them he is pushing open the door to general liberation, that given the inevitable pattern of history he need not shrink from looking: for everything that happens is grist to his mill. The patient, the poor deranged patient, is the doomed capitalist regime which cannot view the facts correctly, for its vision has been impaired by its historical role: it harbours delusions to which it clings pathetically, since they alone enable it to live and think and act at all; if it could see things as they truly are, it would see that it was doomed. Hence it is idle to ask it what it thinks about itself or anything else; the only value of the patient's own observations and ideas is as so many symptoms of its psychical condition which are of help to the physician; as descriptions of reality they are wholly valueless. Yet the madman may, of course, have enough sheer strength left to hurt or destroy the psychiatrist if he does not take care; the psychiatrist must overpower the lunatic; he must provide him with a strait-jacket or kill him, if he is to make the world safe for sane men. Above all, it is no use preaching to the bourgeoisie: it cannot hear, it cannot understand, history has rendered it deaf to reason and blind to reality. That is how classes fall before their successors.

This conception, at one blow, undermines the entire notion of the unity of mankind, the possibility of rational (or any other kind of) argument among men of different outlooks and persuasions: the notion of man which is the heart of all previous views of life; the central pillar on which the entire Western tradition, religious and secular, moral and scientific, had hitherto rested. The Marxist doctrine is a terrible new weapon, for its truth entails that there are entire sections of mankind which are literally expendable. It can only be false humanitarianism to try to rescue classes irrevocably condemned by history. Individuals, of course, can avoid this destruction, and may even be helped to escape – Marx and Engels themselves did, after all, abandon the sinking ship on which they were born for the seaworthy vessel of the proletariat; they crossed over to the party of humanity; so did others. But the class as such is doomed and cannot be rescued. There cannot be mass conversions, for the fate of human groups depends not on free actions – the movements of the spirit – in the heads of men, but on objective social conditions, which guarantee the salvation of one class and the destruction of its rival.

This neo-Calvinist division of mankind into those who can (and will for the most part) be saved and those who cannot, and will (for the most part) perish, is novel and somewhat frightening. When this separation into the elect and the evil who cannot help themselves was translated into racial terms, it led, in our century, to an enormous massacre – a moral and spiritual catastrophe unparalleled in human history. The fact that the rationalist Marx would, of course, have fought this irrationalist wave with all his might as a monstrous nightmare is beside the point at issue. The division of mankind into good sheep and evil and dangerous goats, incapable of turning into sheep, with no hope of salvation, enemies of mankind – and the claim that this sentence of death is based on a scientific examination of the facts – is a turning-point in human history. A doctrine which identifies the enemy and justifies a holy war against men whose 'liquidation' is a service to mankind releases the forces of aggression and destruction on a scale hitherto attained only by fanatical religious movements. But these, at least in theory, preached human solidarity: if the infidel accepted the true faith he was to be welcomed as a brother. But Marxism, since it spoke of objective conditions and not subjective convictions, could not allow this. Neither Marx nor Engels ever spelled out this doctrine: but their followers understood and believed it in the most effective fashion possible – by realising it in practice. The fact that these implications may well have been remote from the minds of the group of men gathered in St Martin's Hall under the eye of Professor Beesly, a left-wing Comtian, who presided over it with great benevolence, does not diminish their validity and historical importance: Lenin, who acted on these assumptions with his customary single-minded consistency, did not in any particular betray the principles of his master. Those who recoiled from such practices recoiled, whether they knew it or not, not from some peculiarly fanatical exaggeration of Marxist doctrine, but from Marxism itself. It was for failing literally to identify moral standards with the changing needs of a particular body of men that Proudhon and Hess, Herzen and Lassalle, were denounced as fools or knaves.

III

This may have led us far afield from Marxism as a movement in the
nineteenth century, and it is of course true that the full force of
Marx's philosophical ideas, rich and comprehensive but sophisticated and at times none too clear, was scarcely realised by the
majority of even his closest followers, not to speak of the founding
members of the First International. Such thoughts as those that I
have outlined were not likely to have been present in the minds of
Tolain or Jung, Odger or Cremer, or even the faithful Eccarius,[1]
who simply looked on Marx as a learned and implacably radical
German thinker, champion of the rights of the working classes,
thunderer against exploiters and bosses and their regime, a man
likely to have more arresting ideas and greater powers of exposition than they themselves, and a capacity for drafting a programme
for international consumption which they did not feel themselves
sufficiently competent to aspire to. Even Engels and Liebknecht
did not fully rise to the height of Marx's terrifying vision. Marxism
in their hands was modelled on the natural sciences as they were
conceived in the nineteenth century. Engels' expositions bear a
strong family resemblance to Comtean positivism: nature and man
obey inexorable laws, not invented by them, but which they
cannot alter, and it is as well to understand these laws, which
explain the past and predict the future, if one is to be effective in
action. In Engels Marxism became a materialist-positivist sociology, with laws different, indeed, from those proposed by Comte or
Buckle, but laws in the same sense; and generations of Marxists,
from Plekhanov onwards, adopted this simplified version, which
omitted the heart of the doctrine, that of the absolute unity of
theory and practice. They uttered the words, they spoke of
'dialectic'; indeed Plekhanov, as is well known, invented the term
'dialectical materialism'. But it would be idle to look into his works
or those of Lenin, or Kautsky, or Mehring, or Bernstein or Guesde
or Lafargue, for a satisfactory explanation of these terms or the
parts they played in Marxist thought. For that we have had to wait
for Marxists in our own century, who have given us a Marx very
different from the Darwin of the social sciences of Engels' sketch,
or the calm sociologist drawn by Kautsky or Plekhanov, or the
supreme political strategist, tactician and revolutionary of the later
Russian tradition. All this is so. Nevertheless, something of the real

[1] But see p. 116 above, note 2.

Marx did penetrate into the First and Second Internationals. It is this unique something, it seems to me, that gave them their unique characteristics.

To begin with the theory of class war: the attitude of 'we' or 'they'; above all, the doctrine of the impossibility of social compromise between one class and another. This is in principle different from the either/or positions of earlier extremists, leaders of religious or political movements and parties – Catholics or Calvinists, Babeuf or Maistre, Blanquists or radical anarchists. For these, while they proclaimed the total incompatibility of opposed doctrines, did hold out the possibility – indeed the prospect – of ultimate unity, of the salvation of the enemy by his conversion. In drafting the address to the First International Marx allowed the formula 'simple laws of morals and justice, which ought to govern the relations of private individuals, as the rules paramount of the intercourse of nations',[1] but in so doing he was all too conscious of making a purely tactical concession to the absurd notion of a universal morality, which foolish idealists who did not understand history, like Moses Hess or the still more foolish liberals, believed in. Marx wrote to Engels that he had been compelled to insert some phrases about rights and justice which 'can do no harm'[2] – and this was not, as it was sometimes interpreted, a mere revulsion against the clichés and commonplaces which every liberal and socialist group, every movement for the improvement of mankind, had automatically adopted and thereby deprived of all force and meaning – it was a genuine hostility to *their* morality, that is, to the notion of the existence of ultimate human ends, common to all men as such.

To Marx this was the most dangerous of all heresies, inasmuch as it held out the possibility of conciliation, collaboration with the enemy – not only temporary armistices, in which he believed, tactical retreats *pour mieux sauter*, in order to launch an even more

---

[1] References for quotations from Marx are given, by volume and page, to two editions, one in German, one in English: Karl Marx, Friedrich Engels, *Werke* (Berlin, 1956–83; hereafter MEW); Karl Marx, Frederick Engels, *Collected Works* (London, New York and Moscow, 1975–   ; hereafter CW). The translations from the German used by the author do not necessarily follow the English edition, which is cited for the convenience of English readers. If the passage was originally written in German, the MEW reference is given first; and vice versa. The reference for this passage is CW xx 13, MEW xvi 13.

[2] Letter from Marx to Engels, 4 November 1864: MEW xxxi 15, CW xlii 18.

effective attack, preferably (as Lenin afterwards insisted) from deep within the rear of that enemy, but genuine harmony of interests, peaceful liquidation of differences, not ending in the total elimination of one class by the other. For Marx any real concession to *them* would ruin the appeasers, for it would inevitably be condemned by the march of events – by the emergence of the new revolutionary men. This is why Lassalle, who had left nothing to be desired in the ferocity of his campaigns against the bourgeoisie, is damned nevertheless for supposing that the workers could use the State – always a class instrument with which to crush class resistance – as an instrument of progress for the workers, who would, gradually, by political action, grow to control it and would turn it to their own purposes.

Lassalle had already shown the cloven hoof in fearing a Franco-Prussian war because he held that it was a danger to the unity and advance of European culture, as if there were such a thing as a single European culture and not a class culture and a class State that must first be destroyed before anything else could possibly be built up. Plekhanov had plainly shown a similar attitude to Germany in 1914; he was a genuine internationalist – no one could accuse him of temporising with the tsarist regime – yet the victory of the Central Powers threatened the foundations of European civilisation, to which he was clearly committed, and from this he instinctively, for all his revolutionary words, recoiled, no less than Guesde, for whom the triumph of Marxism was bound up with those democratic and anti-clerical principles for which France stood, imperfectly it was true, but Germany and Austria did not stand at all.

I believe that Lenin was fundamentally right in supposing that Marx would have attacked such an attitude root and branch. He detested the entire structure; the kingdom of freedom could not be entered before the cities of the Philistines had been laid wholly waste. In his account of the civil wars in France Marx insists over and over again that the entire monstrous structure must be destroyed and nothing be kept, that what is shot through with the ideology of one class is useless to its conqueror and successor. That is why he insisted upon the importance of trade unions (which for Lassalle hampered the rational and centralising activities of the State), because, however reactionary or blind, they could one day be turned into representatives of a class interest, whereas the State was incurably national. The State must not be captured alive, it must be eliminated, not, of course, as the majority of the anarchists wanted, by opposition to political action and by terrorism, but by organised political action, which alone is effective in the world.

This became historically important. Wherever the respect for the State was part and parcel of the national tradition, wherever it was interwoven with the deepest and innermost strands of national culture and myth, as in France and Germany, the class content of Marx's doctrine became watered down. There were plenty of brave words: but it remained true that not only Jaurès and Vandervelde, Bernstein, David and Vollmar, but the orthodox and the intransigent – Kautsky and Bebel, Guesde and de Paepe – did not really hate the State and did not really find it impossible to communicate, and even cooperate in a limited way, with other classes. It was a different story in Poland and Russia, Asia and Africa, where the State was an external bureaucracy and had no emotional hold upon either workers or intellectuals. Georges Sorel caught this element in Marx and turned it to his own uses, but it remained correspondingly remote from Jaurès' generous, all-inclusive, democratic, unfanatical humanism.

Marx gnawed continually upon this bone. In the *Critique of the Gotha Programme* he does not merely attack the notion that there could be a 'free State' for workers[1] – for the State is much too free already, free to forward the interests of the bourgeoisie, and, since it is by nature a form of coercion, useless in a classless society – but he objects to the phrase 'brotherhood of nations'[2] on the ground that nations cannot be brothers, only workers can. All talk of ultimate principles and universal morality infuriated him. This comes out most sharply in the famous words used about rights – another trap for the unwary – which so delighted Lenin later, 'Right can never be higher than the economic structure and the cultural development which this determines', so that equal rights – defences against coercion or encroachment – will become unnecessary when the 'narrow horizon of bourgeois right' will be left behind;[3] only when class structure and warfare has been overcome, and co-operative, socialised endeavour has ensured the all-round development of every individual.

This position went a long way towards justifying ruthless

[1] MEW xix 27, CW xxiv 94.
[2] MEW xix 23–4, CW xxiv 89–90.
[3] MEW xix 21, CW xxiv 87.

political conduct that went counter to the normal moral principles of the average, decent German or French or Russian social democrat. Before the objective conditions which created the 'narrow horizon of bourgeois right' had been done away with – and who could say how long that would take? – there could be no absolute standards to appeal to, only the standards of class interest; and class interest was a matter for the class itself or its best representatives – the party, the strategists in charge of its campaigns – to determine. I have laid emphasis upon this aspect of Marxist thought because it is this formidable quality of cutting oneself off from the mass of respectable mankind into an organisation that openly defies political respectability, with a loyalty not to the present but to the future, that enabled the First International, despite all its internal conflicts, its Proudhonists and Bakuninists and its relative ineffectiveness and weakness, to make a powerful and somewhat terrifying impression on the imagination of Europe.

The concrete achievements of the First International were not great. It led workers' groups of one country to help strike action or agitation in other countries; it kept foreign strike-breakers from being shipped from one country to another; there was more co-operation than ever before between workers of different lands in pressing for social benefits and reforms. All these efforts were novel and not useless. It was also credited with plots, *émeutes* and disturbances with which it had little to do – culminating, of course, in the Paris Commune, in which Marx's followers played a small part compared to the neo-Jacobins and Blanquists. Nevertheless, the International, simply by existing, made a great impression, and not on the workers alone. Even Dostoevsky, in remote St Petersburg, saw it (particularly after the Paris Commune) as the great enemy, the great anti-Church, a world organisation openly based on the old detestable principles of the *philosophes* – materialism and the possibility of a paradise on earth created by unaided human hands – as serious a rival to true Christianity, as dangerous and universal and wicked, as the hated Roman Catholic Church herself.

Dostoevsky voiced sentiments which had earlier appeared in the Russian Press. The Congresses of Geneva in 1866, Brussels in 1868 and Basle in 1869 did not pass unnoticed. The liberal Press reported them with nervous objectivity; the right-wing organs were more hostile. After 1871 the censorship suppressed references to them. The International became a bogey to the police. When the

Spanish government demanded international action against the International, the Russians – and they alone – responded favourably. In 1871 a harmless English merchant was arrested in Odessa, suspected of being the *littérateur* Karl Marx in disguise. Rightly or wrongly the organisation was regarded as a force in Russia, as it was not, for example, in England. This much impact, then, the International did make upon Russia. It played a part in the history of Russian revolution too. Its specifically Marxist section was peopled by obscurities: Utin did make himself notorious then and later; but A. D. Trusov, E. L. Tomanovskaya, V. V. and E. G. Bartenev/a – these figures have been consigned to deep oblivion, perhaps not wholly undeserved. Marx himself represented the Russians in the General Council, and the populist hero Hermann Lopatin – a really doughty revolutionary, who was himself a member of the Council – although friendly to Marx, was no more Marxist than Lavrov, who represented Batignolles. Still, it was the First International that allowed the Russians to break through their own obsessive national problems and enter fully into the ecumenical movement; until 1914 no more genuinely internationalist body, nor one more loyal to the world movement, existed than the Russian members, Menshevik and Bolshevik equally. To this extent the First International Working Men's Association played a direct and crucial role in creating a tradition which had a decisive influence, if not on the social situation, at any rate on the men and the ideas by which the Russian Revolution was made.

The national sections of the International, it is true, mainly functioned as platforms from which Marx fought rival tendencies, and which occasionally displayed too much independence and factionalism for him. If Lassalle had not died in the very year of its creation and Proudhon shortly after, Marx might have had even more trouble; even as it was, Bakunin proved a hard nut to crack, and the Proudhonists and his own more naïve followers could make themselves unimpressed and obstructive. It is customary to attribute the quarrels by which the International was torn to Marx's own authoritarian and intolerant character. This does not seem to me a sufficient explanation, though it obviously did play a part in the final duel, and the death of the organisation. Marx never intended to create an organisation for short-term ends. He wished to make a world revolution. He wished, therefore, to train the cadres for it. He was convinced of one thing, as Lenin was convinced after him: that any serious movement, to be successful, must have a clear and solid theoretical base; that where there is no discipline in ideas there is no effectiveness in action; that while clear theoretical foundations are not enough, they are indispensable; that one of the reasons for the ineffectiveness of the communist clubs and sects from the 1830s to the 1860s, of Proudhon's or Blanqui's neo-Babouvists, of Mutualists after 1848, as of all the other socialist and radical groups which spoke their word and then disintegrated, was the absence of a philosophy based on a scientifically demonstrable theory of human history and human potentialities, without which no movement could be serious or lasting. Even Lassalle's splendidly organised German workers' party, Marx was convinced, was doomed to come to nothing so long as it rested on the rickety intellectual foundations on which Lassalle, who was no master of theory, had erected it. Hence the sacrifice of almost everything, including in the end the International itself, to the claims of orthodoxy. Better correct principles without a movement than a movement without correct principles; for on the strong foundation of correct principles a new movement can be built, but a movement resting on unsystematic expediency, opportunism, a tendency to conciliate enemies in order to attain short-term objectives, or still worse on a false doctrine, is built on shifting sands: it wastes men's substance and blood to no effect, and its inevitable defects weaken the resolution to victory.

Marx was implacably determined to establish the International on sound foundations or not to establish it at all. And he did succeed to this degree: he created an organisation with a clear and intransigent doctrine, which not merely excited intellectual assent or *de facto* co-operation, but, because of the controlled but passionate language, at once concrete and evocative, of which on occasions he was master, was capable of stimulating faith, mobilising what was non-rational as well as rational in men's minds. He and he alone did lay the foundations of a world-wide mass party of the left; and of a cause capable of being presented in simple, indeed often over-simple, language: and he provided concrete formulae, that is, formulae with specific indications of the type of action to which they were meant to lead, which could be used by propagandists and agitators who could be effective without reaching the mental level of the founders or leaders of the movement. Moreover, he welded some flesh-and-blood trade unionists to the movement, and did something to protect their status from the contempt of intellectuals and theorists, and therefore gave it a greater possibility not only of concerted industrial action, but of continuity after setbacks or government suppression, which movements composed of individual ideologists could seldom preserve. He established its central 'Bureau' in tolerant, uninterested but liberal England, in that London in which, as we have noted, by some peculiar quirk of fate, there took place two of the most important events affecting internal Russian history – the birth of the International in 1864 and of the Bolsheviks in 1903.

Marx was a man of war, and his own militant energy communicated to his organisation and its successors a revolutionary impetus which they never wholly lost. The essential thing was to identify the movement with organised class warfare. Hence Marx's comparative benevolence towards Blanqui, who was far from Marxist in doctrine. At least Blanqui fought, and fought fearlessly and intelligently and ruthlessly. Thus, too, he disapproved of the Paris Commune in the beginning – he had little to do with its establishment – but in the end, after its defeat, he annexed it. The Commune stressed loose federation and decentralisation, and free election of its central group; the last, by a species of intellectual acrobatics, was later represented as the embryo of the dictatorship of the proletariat. Yet the Jacobins were not committed to the proletarian cause; the Blanquists played scarcely any part in the International; none of it was Marxist in inspiration or substance; it accomplished very little in the way of social legislation; Marx charged it with not being tough enough, not violent enough to blackmail the forces of Versailles into some compromise. Yet it had the root of the matter in it: it was revolutionary, collectivist, egalitarian, anti-bourgeois; it was not afraid of pulling down by shedding blood; so he incorporated it boldly into the mythology of his party. No one else wanted to claim it: it was viewed with horror by European public opinion in general; even the radicals, Louis Blanc, Mazzini, Mill, could not swallow its acts of terrorism. Marx did not favour its tactics, but, like the workers who fell at the barricades in 1848, the Communards were martyrs, victims in an anti-capitalist war. Hence Marx firmly claimed it as a triumph, short-lived but the first in history, of the young but growing and menacing army of the new working class that would inherit the world. The Commune was full of anti-Marxist heretics; but after its death he magnetised its remnants into his orbit. This alone gave the International, on the one hand, notoriety as a band of terrorists, but, on the other, clothed it in the dignity of a great historic force, almost a European power with which governments must reckon. This was not the case. But the force of Marx's personality and of his strategic gifts created a myth and an illusion which played a decisive part in the moulding of the future.

The principles had been laid down; the movement could claim its saints and martyrs: the most serious danger came from subversion from within, from heresy or weakness. The war had been begun. Bakunin threatened to disrupt his party; Marx had no hesitation about burying it in hope of later resurrection. The German Marxists preserved the sacred flame. The men who, led by Wilhelm Liebknecht, met at Gotha were not a world movement, but they were equipped with realistic directives, strategic and tactical, and they had a bible: this was more than Proudhon or Bakunin, Blanqui or the left-wing Chartists left to their followers. The men of Gotha ended by swallowing the Lassalleans, who did possess organisation, but little theoretical equipment: the latter turned out to be historically more important than the pragmatists imagined. It is true that the Lassalleans under Becker had developed a strong tradition, and influenced their Marxist partners to a high degree: hence their tolerance towards the Prussian State, and a degree of *de facto* collaboration with the government on the part of the German social democrats far greater than could ever have been palatable to Marx. In 1880 Guesde duly created a Marxist party in France which, although it was never more than one among many branches of the French socialist movement, embodied the full orthodoxy of Marx's approach, and engaged in mass agitation. Marxism as a new political movement was launched before the death of the founder; by the time of Engels' death it was world-wide.

IV

Let me return for a moment to Marx's ideological achievement. What he succeeded in doing even in his lifetime (still more after his death) was to translate the sense of human atomisation, of the dehumanisation of which vast impersonal institutions, bureaucracies, factories, armies, political parties were at once a cause and a symptom, with a consequent feeling of mounting suffocation to which Nietzsche, Carlyle and Ibsen, Thoreau and Whitman, Tolstoy, Ruskin and Flaubert had, in their very different ways, given profound indignant poetical expression – he translated this horror of anthill life, not into Utopian dreams, like Fourier or

Cabet, or liberal protest, like Tocqueville or Mill, nor into attempts to save human freedom by loose co-operative textures, like the followers of Proudhon or Bakunin or Kropotkin (for approaches of this type he regarded as rearguard operations doomed to failure), but into an inevitable phase in human development, possessing its own powerfully creative aspects in the concentration and the rationalisation of human brain-power and energy. Capitalism is for him neither a wilful crime nor an impersonal disaster: it is rationally explicable and therefore unavoidable and (since history is a rational, though not a wholly self-conscious, process), in the end, beneficent. Like all other class-based institutions, it is engaged in digging its own grave; hence the intelligent historical student can extract from the process as a whole an eschatological assurance that from the bones of the old, new institutions would spring, made inevitable by their predecessors, free from the defects of all previous human establishments, with no seeds of death or mortality in them, destined to last for ever.

This was to prove irresistible to those who were disillusioned by the libertarian slogans of the pre-1848 period, which rested on moral ideals alone, and had been rendered bankrupt, in the eyes of the realists, by the failures of these revolutions. The disillusioned in all lands were now looking for the opposite: not for idealistic eloquence, however noble and moving, but drier light, realistic plans, an assessment, such as Machiavelli had provided in his day, of what the facts were, and what could be done by real men rather than angels. The very harshness of Marx's vision of history, its insistence upon the seamy side of the social process, upon the need for long, tedious, painful labour, the anti-heroic realism, the mordant, deflationary epigrams, the deliberate and ferocious anti-idealism of tone, themselves came as a welcome antidote to the huge emotional and intellectual inflation of the preceding period, particularly when, after the long reaction of the 1850s, opportunities for practical action once again seemed to present themselves, on however modest a scale.

When the Second International came to be founded in 1889, there was an attempt to preserve this same intentness upon brass tacks as against what were deemed to be syndicalist and anarchist fantasies of the French Possibilists and Allemanists, Anarchists and Syndicalists and various types of proto-Revisionism, which were already at work, particularly in Germany and England. It is usual to say that the Second International was a tame affair compared to its predecessor, that despite Engels' tutelage over its early years, it lacked bite, and leant heavily upon the splendidly organised and vote-getting German Social Democratic Party. Certainly it discussed all the burning issues, intelligently and clearly; it was genuinely internationalist; Germans and Frenchmen, Russians and Japanese acted as brothers here, and here alone; it even agreed to united action – a general strike, abstention from participation in the unthinkable case of war. But when 1914 came it collapsed ignominiously into its national sections, each of which patriotically voted war credits for its own respective government, and thereby discredited International Social Democracy for ever, leaving each country to grope its way back to its own peculiar forms of socialism.

There is, of course, much truth in this. Nevertheless, let the following also be remembered:

1. The International, because it contained actual representatives of trade unions, became the foster mother and nurse of socialist parties and labour parties in many lands. The German party might have progressed without it; but other parties owed a great many of their initial ideas to the sense of solidarity which it undoubtedly bred amongst its members.

2. It was the only international organisation in which anti-conservatives and anti-clericals, those who believed that social justice was unattainable in either an individualistically organised or a class-riven society, egalitarians and radicals of many kinds, found a common home.

3. Its internationalism was, despite all that has been said against this, perfectly sincere. The leaders knew, as many of them know now – behind the Iron Curtain[1] even more clearly than in our world – that national solidarity among their followers was stronger than their international allegiance. Whether this could have been otherwise, whether nationalism could, in practice, have been defeated by socialist internationalism, however it was organised, whatever its strategy, seems doubtful. (I return to this below.)

Let us remember the situation in 1914. It was one in which Victor Adler in 1914 knew clearly that the Austrian workers would

---

[1] This was written, I must remind the reader, in 1964.

simply not follow him if he declared himself against war, or even used its outbreak, as his son Friedrich wanted, as an opportunity for revolution. The German Social Democrats Scheidemann, Müller, Helphand could cite Marx's implacable opposition to the Tsarist Empire as the central reservoir of world reaction, and his defence of wars against it as at least not unjustified – more justified, in his judgement, than the war against Napoleon III (of which Marx, after all, had not exactly disapproved). This was a situation in which the French socialists saw themselves engaged in defence of the Republic, which, if not as democratic as they could wish, nevertheless held out higher hopes of this ideal, malleable as it was to workers' political pressure, than the cast-iron establishment in Germany, which, despite a splendid workers' party – the pride of International Labour – yielded not at all, conceded very little. Were they to sabotage a war (or make an effort to do this) which no one in France could doubt was a purely defensive war against all that was most reactionary and brutal in Europe? If such seasoned Marxists as Plekhanov or Vera Zasulich sincerely believed this, why not Guesde, still more Jaurès or Keir Hardie? What were these leaders to do? If they wished to save their souls they could do so only at the expense of their bodies, that is, the body of the political movement. Their fate, had they denounced the war or attempted to resist it, would most probably have been that of Herzen when he supported the Polish rising in 1863, something that does him undying moral credit, but cost him his influence in Russia, and split the opposition to tsarism. And he led no movement, and had no agonising practical problems to solve.

The First International partly owed its notoriety and impact to the fact that, in an age of conscription and mobilisable patriotism – when States depended for their power on national sentiment and not on mercenaries and professional armies – they boldly struck against this: but anti-patriotism was weakened exactly by the degree of success of Western labour movements in influencing and integrating themselves into national policies, as syndicalists and anarchists had always warned. Anti-patriotism was high only in lands whose socialists were persecuted.[1] The proposition that Jaurès and Kautsky, had they chosen to do so, could actually have averted war by affirming their anti-war resolutions of the year before seems highly unplausible; I know of no reputable historian

[1] Russia, Poland, the Balkans, Asia etc.

prepared to defend this proposition. I do not say that the socialist parties acted rightly, but Lenin's incredulity and Rosa Luxemburg's protests could in a sense come only from persons who were not at the head of mass movements playing an effective part – as advocated by Marxists against anarchists and syndicalists – in the day-to-day political life of their respective countries. Indeed, I should like to repeat that I still think that the internationalism of the International was perfectly genuine: not simply as an abstract dogma, but as a belief that played as effective a part in these men's actual conduct as, in the circumstances, could have been expected. When Jaurès 'surrendered' to the Germans in 1904, in order to preserve the unity of the movement, when Plekhanov, during the Russo-Japanese war, demonstratively shook hands with the Japanese socialist Katayama, these were not empty gestures. The fact that nationalism, in the event, proved stronger than socialism, that it proved victorious when in conflict with it – a remarkable but undeniable feature of the entire nineteenth and twentieth centuries – and the corollary of this, that socialism or communism later, for example in Africa and Asia, succeeded only when they marched in alliance with nationalism – this may be deplored or gloried in or dispassionately recorded: but it is not a fact for which the International can, as such, be held accountable or blamed.

What weakened the International from the point of view of the intransigents and the revolutionaries was neither the weakness of the leaders' characters nor their own or their followers' hankering after fleshpots, nor Bernstein's or the Fabians' demonstrations that Marx had been mistaken. It is true that Bernstein and others had argued convincingly that the wages of the workers, whether conceived in absolute or relative terms, were not declining as, according to the doctrine, they should have been, but, on the contrary, rising; that landowning was, even if Bernstein had exaggerated this process, not becoming concentrated in a few powerful hands to nearly the degree that the theory demanded; that the workers were obtaining more benefits by peaceful methods than by fighting the State every inch; that the gaps between the lower bourgeoisie and the upper ranks of skilled workers were gradually becoming obliterated; that, as Engels himself had remarked, workers in general were getting more by exploiting the legal system, now that Bismarck's laws had been lifted, than by fighting it. All this, together with arguments designed to point to the same 'revisionist' conclusions, was, indeed, urged by Fabians in England and, in part, by the 'economists' in Russia. But it is not this that was the main factor in taming the German socialists. Nor is there any need to resort to such doubtful expedients as national character. What lowered the militancy of German Social Democracy was its very success. Marx had advocated political action; a mass movement; not sects of fanatical conspirators, with a *politique du pire*, setting the masses on fire in the manner of Blanqui, or refusal of all political participation in the manner of the Syndicalists and Anarchists. Did not the 'General' himself – Friedrich Engels – make the following famous remarks in an essay written in the 1890s?

> The methods of 1848 have become obsolete ... The time has passed for sudden *émeutes*, revolutions made by a small conscious minority at the head of the unconscious masses. The task of totally transforming the social structure must engage the masses themselves, they themselves must understand the point of the struggle, what it is for which they shed their blood and give their lives. This is the lesson of the past fifty years.[1]

'The time has passed ...' – for whom? Engels did not specify the West; and Plekhanov and the Russian Marxists can scarcely be blamed if they regarded Lenin's turning of a blind eye to this particular directive as heretical: since then this formulation, whether regarded as a description or as a recommendation (a distinction in principle not recognised in Hegelian-Marxist doctrine) has been more honoured in the breach than in the observance.

The German party carried out this programme; but found it all too easy to do so compatibly with its non-violent, solidly democratic traditions. By using parliamentary methods for acquiring power, and by increasing its representation in the Reichstag from election to election, through the 1890s and into the early part of the twentieth century, it was inevitably brought into contact with the general political life of the State, in particular other parties. It was not merely a question of social security or educational policy. Its extraordinary achievement – for good or ill – was the creation of a world within a world, an independent almost self-contained society within the framework of the middle-class establishment.

[1] From Engels' introduction of 1895 to a new edition of Marx's *The Class Struggles in France 1848–1850*: MEW xxii 513, 523, CW xxvii 510, 520.

The members of the German Social Democratic Party lived largely within their own strongly built, all-providing welfare organisation, with their own schools and educational and sporting organisations; they attended their own lectures and picnics and concerts, and were provided with all else that a respectable German needs. Inevitably, this led to a certain degree of comfortable complacency; it was the price of the exercise of power, and therefore of responsibility. It was the German *Rechtsstaat* – a genuinely law-abiding society – that despite all its shortcomings made them peaceful, optimistic and believers in gradualist methods. In it they found themselves, without knowing it, a growing pillar of a developing society; it was not, therefore, altogether unreasonable for Bernstein to say (and for Kautsky to believe, though he did not admit it) that, if things went on like this, there might be a painless transition to socialism in a foreseeable period.

Marx had indeed conceded that the revolutions need not be violent; that in highly industrialised States a seizure of power could occur without terror and atrocities; what exactly 'the dictatorship of the proletariat' meant, after the early 1850s and the dreams and hopes of the ephemeral German 'Communist League', had never been made clear in circumstances where it did not seem likely to be actualised. Marx, after all, did not describe the Commune, either in his critique of the Gotha Programme or on any subsequent occasion, as embodying any such dictatorship; that was Lenin's gloss on Engels. What Marx would have attacked violently was not the Social Democrats' lack of interest in dictatorship, but the idea of a slow *embourgeoisement*, the gradual acquisition of all the attributes and enjoyments of a bourgeois life by the workers as part of their slowly increasing prosperity and political strength. Whatever else Marx wanted, he demanded a radical transformation: he was no less anxious than, say, his opponent Herzen to put an end to the world of sordid bourgeois values by some one great cleansing act. That is what he meant when he spoke of revolution as a necessary cataclysm through which a society must pass in order to wash off from itself the filth of the earlier, degraded period, the march through mud and blood which, for him, the rise of capitalism necessarily entails. This apocalyptic vision was totally lacking in the coherent, idealistic but not very revolutionary writings of Kautsky and his henchmen, still more in the moderate demands of Vollmar or David, or for that matter Jaurès and Viviani, or Vandervelde and Bebel, or John Burns or Daniel de

Leon, not to speak of Samuel Gompers or the average American labour leader of the time, with their essentially syndicalist and anti-political outlook.

But if that was Marx's true goal, it was not destined to be realised in the industrialised countries which he designated as the theatre of the revolution. For here a fatal dilemma raises its terrible horns: if it is only on the expanding base of increasingly efficient productivity that a rational socialist system can be built, as every social democrat, reasonably enough, insisted over and over again, it would neither need, nor be likely to issue from, a revolution; this was not the climate in which revolutionary forces throve. Marx believed that class war was likely to reach its highest point of exacerbation in industrial societies, because it was there that the embattled economic classes truly came face to face, as they could not do in less developed countries. He insisted that it was in conditions of mounting monopoly and concentration of the means of production, exchange and distribution that the explosion would occur, with fewer and fewer capitalists controlling vaster and vaster empires, their number reduced by constant internecine warfare, until the proletariat, trained by them, unintentionally but inevitably, into ruthless social and technological efficiency and unity, with a mere flick of its wrist removed them and took charge. We all know that this did not occur. Concentration and monopoly grew apace but, whatever their evil social consequences, they did not include the increasing alienation of the proletariat into a disciplined revolutionary force. In so far as both Internationals were built on these presumptions they rested upon a miscalculation. The nature of this error concerns the most fascinating and crucial issue of our time.

V

. . . the economical subjection of the man of labour to the monopoliser of the means of labour, that is, the sources of life, lies at the bottom of servitude in all its forms, of all social misery, mental degradation, and political dependence . . . the economical emancipation of the working classes is therefore the great end to which every political movement ought to be subordinate as a means . . .[1]

So ran the Provisional Rules of the International Working Men's

[1] CW xx 14, MEW xvi 14.

Association published in November 1864. In 1891 the united German Social Democratic Party spoke of 'an ever more enormous army of surplus workers, an ever sharper conflict between exploiters and exploited', and 'an increase in insecurity of livelihood, in misery, oppression, enslavement, debasement and exploitation'.[1] If it is industrial nations that are the subject of these propositions, then this represents a genuine triumph of doctrine over facts. Even in Germany it was absurd to speak, in 1891, of an actual growth in poverty, enslavement, insecurity and so on. There was no criterion in terms of which German workers were worse off economically or politically than in 1864; and by the end of the decade the growth of organisation, prosperity, security had increased very greatly. If there was 'debasement' it could be due only to the increasingly bureaucratic nature of the Party itself, to the general nature of industrial society in all its layers, and not to the specific activity of the oppressor class. The facts, as Bakunin prophesied, pointed to decrease, not increase, of tension in the great industrial nations of the West. Economically, and socially too, German Social Democracy, its institutions quietly woven into the texture of the German State system, had become the envy of working-class workers everywhere, and the scarcely criticised model of such incorruptibly orthodox socialists, free from all taint of liberalism, as Plekhanov, Lenin, Rosa Luxemburg, Jules Guesde. In England the Reform Bill of 1867 seems to have deflected the energies of British trade union leaders from the international scene towards self-improvement, a process only accelerated by their reluctance to be associated with the notorious Communards of 1871. It was trade union legislation of the late 1860s (roughly 1867–75), and the social legislation that followed, that must have been responsible for making Fabian proposals seem more plausible to labour leaders than Marxist recipes, to a greater extent than such factors – often blamed by disappointed radicals – as some deeply non-revolutionary element of the British national character, or the insularity of the workers, or their traditional loyalties, or the power of religious Non-Conformity.

In a sense it was Marxism, in these countries and at that period at least, that acted as its own grave-digger, rather than the capitalism

---

[1] In the 'Erfurt Programme' ('Programm der Sozialdemokratischen Partei Deutschlands beschlossen auf dem Parteitag zu Erfurt 1891'): p. 4 in *Protokoll über die Verhandlungen des Parteitages der Sozialdemokratischen Partei Deutschlands* (Berlin, 1891).

for which that role had been cast. The more effective the political organisation of the Western workers, the more concessions they were able to wring from the State, the more drawn they were into the path of peaceful reform, the more solidarity they inevitably felt with institutions which proved to be not the stone wall of reactionaries of the Marxist prognosis, condemned by history to resist, however blindly and uselessly and suicidally, but a far more flexible and concession-minded entity. Resistance stiffens, peaceful penetration softens, the discipline and theoretical fanaticism of militant parties. In France Millerand's acceptance of government office in a bourgeois administration was roundly condemned by the International; nevertheless, a situation in which this proved possible, in which bourgeois parties were prepared to buy off their opponents in this fashion, not only flattered their self-esteem, but provided concrete evidence of the growing power of the working-class opposition.

The twentieth century is beyond my ken: but the best account of its development *vis-à-vis* Marx's prophecies is contained in an analysis given by that very honest and intermittently intelligent thinker, the late John Strachey, who, in what was almost his last book,[1] dealt critically with Marx's basic supposition, namely that internal competition between capitalists would make it objectively impossible for them not to press wages down to the lowest level compatible with the workers' survival. This proved untrue: concessions were made; the tycoons and soldiers, who in Marx's predictions would never yield, proved apt pupils of Maynard Keynes, and successfully averted the final crisis which Marx believed to be so near. His own iron law of wages, different from Lassalle's, but at one with it at least in supposing that capitalists are compelled by objective forces to extract the maximum surplus value out of labour, proved erroneous. Marx had obviously gravely overestimated the inflexibility and stupidity, and perhaps the very power, of the military-industrial complex against which, from opposite ends of the political spectrum, Burckhardt and Wright Mills have warned us. Concessions to unions, radical social legislation carried through by Lloyd George in England and Franklin Roosevelt in the United States, progressive social policies in Scandinavia and Welfare-State England, Keynesian and post-Keynesian economic policies in general are not allowed for in any Marxist prognosis in

[1] *Contemporary Capitalism* (London and New York, 1956), chapter 5.

the pre-1914 period of which I speak. Many a mistake was made by the Soviet Union, owing to the faithful adherence of its leaders, not, as is commonly thought, to mere Machiavellianism or tough-minded opportunism, but to over-literal Marxist analyses of the economic aspects of the world situation, with consequent miscalculations about Germany in the 1930s, Europe in the later 1940s, and great tracts of Asia and Africa as well. It may be argued that, had Marxism not existed and become fundamental to the outlook of political parties, bourgeois democracies could not have reacted as imaginatively and effectively as they did, both by repulsion and attraction. If this is so, it is an unexpected twist of the dialectic, whereby Marxism has generated its own antibodies – an interesting topic for historical sociology.

The real triumphs of Marx's strategy occurred, as everyone knows, not in the highly industrialised societies but in their polar opposites, those economically backward lands which formed a field of exploitation for the advanced industrial countries – Russia, Spain and China, elsewhere in Asia, Africa, and then Cuba. It was none other than Bakunin, whom Marx held in such intellectual contempt, who took the view that the kind of revolution in which both he and Marx believed – one that would destroy the whole system completely and usher in a new world – could be made only by truly alienated, desperate men, not organically tied by strands of interest and sentiment to the world which they were committed to destroy. He therefore viewed Marx's conception of an orderly party as itself fatally bourgeois in spirit; for solid, serious, intelligent workers, with families and regular employment, organised into a tidy, efficiently functioning party machine under proper intellectual leadership (Bakunin's 'pedantocracy'), would surely think twice before they set out to destroy a society which, after all, had made it possible for them to attain to the level of education, organisation, prosperity and above all respectability which alone had made them politically effective. He therefore concluded that the only effective revolutionaries would be those who, for one reason or another, had no stake in existing society, had never had one, or had been robbed of it, and had nothing to gain from the development of their society along existing lines, and had therefore nothing to lose by the most extreme upheaval. Underdeveloped or backward societies, therefore, had far better prospects of revolution than hierarchically organised, industrial ones; oppressed, unorganised, dark, illiterate peasants, wherever they might be –

Russia, the Balkans, Italy, Spain – had really nothing to hope for from the State or the bourgeoisie or industrial development – they were a doomed class, as well as criminals, outlaws, rootless vagrants, sinking into greater and greater squalor, and resembled the proletariat, who had nothing to lose but their chains as described by Marx – a description based too much perhaps on the conditions of the 1830s and 1840s – more than the workers even of the late 1860s and 1870s.

History has to some degree borne this out. It is Marx's doctrines of 1840–50 which the Second International adopted, half-heartedly perhaps, and without any intention of implementing them, doctrines which Marx himself later quietly withdrew in favour of a more gradualist approach. Yet it was this earlier doctrine, the semi-Blanquist revolutionary tactics, that proved effective in the end, not indeed in the West, but in underdeveloped societies, in Russia and Asia, of which Marx in 1847–50 could scarcely have been thinking. This doctrine – preached to the Rhineland revolutionaries in 1849 and the small communist groups in the following year – is that in economically pre-industrial societies, those who wish to make a proletarian revolution must begin by collaborating with the bourgeoisie in turning out the economically backward, reactionary, semi-feudal regimes, and allow, indeed actively co-operate in bringing to birth, the bourgeois democratic republic in which alone working-class organisations can grow in relative freedom. The next step – after the bourgeois democracy is in being – is to harry their erstwhile allies mercilessly until the moment comes when they too can be turned out neck and crop. This is the policy of the gradually expanding Trojan horse – the policy of the proletarian cuckoo in the liberal-democratic nest. So long as the proletariat is too weak in numbers and in strength to seize power and to govern, it needs the only conditions in which it can peacefully grow to maturity, that is, a tolerant bourgeois democracy, in which it is nurtured to health and strength. This is to go on until the proletariat has become literally the majority of the population, when it can seize power, with or without violence, as circumstances dictate. The Erfurt Programme lost sight of all this, reasonably enough, since, as Engels said, no one could fail to note the difference between the Germany of 1891 and the Germany of 1849. Despite all its tough talk about revolution, there is nothing in this document about dictatorship of the proletariat, illegal methods, or denunciation of the State as such. The prospect of that head-on collision between the classes to which the whole Marxist strategy was hitherto directed became a good deal dimmer than even so mild a man as Kautsky, let alone Engels, can have supposed.

But in Russia a very different situation prevailed, and one far closer to the Germany with which Marx had been most intimately acquainted. There the regime was such that some kind of a revolution was objectively probable. The proletariat counted for little: the middle classes for rather more than Marxist historians allow. Political tension between the holders of real power – the middle classes on the one hand versus the nobility and the tsarist bureaucracy on the other – grew steadily. Sooner or later it would come into open collision. In the Russian Empire the ruling class – the landowners and the bureaucrats – really did behave as Marx mistakenly supposed capitalists would be bound to behave in the West: like men caught in their own system, who, even if they catch sight in a moment of terrible insight of the catastrophe for which the system is headed, cannot manage, can scarcely begin seriously to try, to extricate themselves from their predicament.

This is the situation in which concessions seem to the men in power to lead to a revolution as fatally as blind obstinacy, for this last might – who knows? – still manage to hold back the awful tide, at least for a while. This is how the monarchist ideologists – Leontiev, Pobedonostsev – actually talked. Here, by contrast with the West, there really existed a situation in which the ignorance and misery of the small but growing proletariat, but far more, of the vast, inert peasantry, was such that it made sense to speak of an intellectual élite of committed socialists guiding an amorphous mass, if not of proletarians, at least of 'the naked and hungry', towards a major revolution. Here there was a blindly reactionary government against which it was not difficult to mobilise liberal as well as working-class and peasant groups, in which deliberately treacherous alliances with the bourgeoisie seemed a rational and feasible stratagem. The Russian bourgeoisie itself was, if stronger than many suppose, yet by no means powerful; all parties were united in common fear and hatred of the government; it was not absurd to suppose that, if the proletariat was properly organised, it could, when the hour struck, make itself an embarrassing but indispensable ally of the liberal democrats, helping them into power only in order to oust them in a second revolution, which must be the last. This is perhaps why Plekhanov suppressed Marx's embarrassing letters to the Russian Narodniks,[1] in which, however grudgingly, he allowed the possibility of some non-social-democratic path to socialism. For here it became necessary to play down Marx's remorseless rejection of liberal slogans, of words like 'freedom', 'moral regeneration', 'altruism', 'human solidarity'; these stock terms may have seemed meaningless and even nauseating hypocrisy in the West; yet the Belgian Marxists, for example, in 1893, insisted on including them in their programme because they were not prepared to work for socialism on any other terms; and what was true in Belgium was far truer of Russia, where these phrases still expressed genuine human demands in a totally oppressive system, and did not ring false in the mouths of committed revolutionaries.

In an underdeveloped territory caught in a world of rapid growth, governed by men unwilling or unable to adjust themselves with sufficient rapidity to counteract the danger to their country's national integrity, or at any rate to its economic interests – a danger constituted by potentially predatory, fast-developing neighbours – a revolution is, as nearly as anything that can be predicted in this world, inevitable. When and how it will occur is another matter. This was the situation in Japan as well as Russia in the nineteenth century, in the Turkish Empire and in China, in Spain and Portugal and in the Balkan countries in the late nineteenth century, and in the early twentieth, and in our day in Africa and Latin America. Since, given this pattern of forces, the prospects of revolution are high, the frustrated middle class is bound to be its carrier, at any rate in part. It is to this 'conjuncture' that Marx's recipe of the 1848–51 period applies, and it was this, indeed, that Lenin adopted in 1917. Everyone knows how far he deviated from the path of rigid orthodoxy as expounded faultlessly by Plekhanov and Kautsky, but that is not my point. My point is that conditions in Russia in 1917, and in other underdeveloped countries at other corresponding moments, made the Marxist tactics of 1848–51 more applicable than the situation of industrial countries in, let us say, the late nineteenth century (or at any time) made the later Marxist formulae and tactics of the revised Marxism of Marx himself. The earlier formulae applied to the backward Russia: the later formulae

---

[1] e.g. Marx to the Editorial Board of *Otechestvennie zapiski*, November 1877 (not sent); Marx to Danielson, 10 April 1879 and 19 February 1881; Marx to Vera Zasulich, 8 March 1881.

applied neither to the Europe of the 1870s, nor during the half
century that followed. The fact that Marx's disciples recoiled from
seeing this, or at least from formulating it, recalls the cynical Ignaz
Auer's celebrated remark to Bernstein apropos of the latter's
critique of Marxism: 'One does not say such things; one simply
does them.'

VI

There is another factor, mentioned briefly above,[1] which cannot
be left out of account if the melancholy petering out of the Second
International is to be justly estimated: nationalism. All authors of
original theories tend to exaggerate. Perhaps it is impossible to
break through the orthodoxy and prevalent opinion of a given time
without such exaggeration. Most great thinkers have done so, and
Marx is no exception. No one will wish seriously to deny the
originality and critical importance of his great Saint-Simonian
insights – he and none other burnt into our consciousness the
theorem that socialised production is not compatible with individ-
ualised machinery of distribution; he foresaw the rise of Big
Business earlier than others. More than this, he translated into
concrete terms Saint-Simon's insight that men transform themselves and their lives, as well as their social and political organisation, by technological innovation. He made very clear the role
played by men's own past handiwork in hampering their own later
progress, the role of those 'fetters' upon productive forces that are
constituted by institutions or systems of belief or ways of behaviour which men have made but which delude later generations into
taking them as objectively valid and eternal; a delusion which can
be dispelled only by asking *cui bono*? – who are the groups or
classes whose power or survival is, whether they know it or not,
enhanced by these institutions, the more if they retain their
hallowed status? Marx and none other stressed the importance of
social organisation, not as a timeless, socially useful weapon, but as
something inevitably brought forth by the process of industrialisation itself. It was he too who inured us, to our doom as some
would say, to the need to break eggs, however sacred, for the sake
of various social omelettes, brutalities and massacres of innocents
from which many recoil, but which Marx not merely regarded as

---

[1] See p. 150 above.

inevitable, but at times came near to representing as positively desirable. Marx's particular doctrines of the relations of thought and action, of words and their real meanings and social role, as they are uttered now by this, now by that class or its representatives – all these are transforming notions which, even though some were pushed too far, and some are positive fallacies, have for good or ill altered our world. The Second International absorbed these ideas and somewhat tamed them, but never lost them entirely. Without Bebel and Kautsky and Plekhanov, the stress on orthodoxy and the expulsions of heretics, neither Lenin nor Mao nor the particular forms which the death throes of the old colonialism took would have emerged as they did. The tradition of Marxism, pure and undiluted, never died: yet what it gained from the intensity of its vision, its intellectual coherence and its drive for revolutionary unity and organisation it has paid for – very dearly – in terms of blindness to social realities. I have mentioned its underestimate of the elasticity and social inventiveness of intelligent capitalism, of the enterprise which the State itself can show, whether for social progress, as in Scandinavia or English-speaking lands, or for repression and war, as in Germany and Italy in the period before the great wars.

I return again to what seems to me to be the most powerful factor of all: nationalism. Even more than choice of security against liberty on the part of individuals and groups, even more than historical feeling or the power of tradition or inertia, which were systematically underestimated or explained away by dogmatic Marxists, nationalism grew to be a vast influence despite all the forces for international unification at work in the last hundred years. This is not the place to examine its roots. It is perhaps enough to recall what everyone knows – that, whatever shoots of liberal internationalism may have sprung up in Germany towards the end of the eighteenth and the beginning of the nineteenth century, they withered in the blast of anti-Napoleonic nationalism by 1815. The revolutions of 1848 were destroyed with its help. Without the collision of chauvinisms in Austria-Hungary, without wounded nationalism in France in 1870 (and there was a powerful dose of it even in the Commune of 1871), without the alliance of national and capitalist interests in the imperialism of 1864–1914, without the identification of the Revolution with the cause of Russia's national integrity in 1919, the history of our world would surely have been very different.

The history of European working-class organisation cannot be divorced from the fortunes of the party created by Lassalle, from the shape given it by a man whom Marx rightly suspected of tenderness towards the *Volksgeist*, and something very like romantic German nationalism. The workers were, in virtue of their very degree of economic and social progress, drawn into this tide, and could scarcely be expected to swim successfully against it. Lenin and Rosa Luxemburg sustained a profound shock when 1914 blew up the pretensions of the Second International. But this was, at least in part, because in the Russian Empire the workers were in a relatively pre-industrial stage, walled off from the rest of Western society and its nationalism, so that their nationalism was comparatively feebler, at any rate among Russian factory workers. Where it was deeper – for instance in Poland – it was equally impotent against the Russians, Austrians and Germans: if anything, it allied itself with Austrian Russophobia. We know that Lenin and Rosa Luxemburg and Martov were personally entirely free from this sentiment. For Lenin, no less than for Trotsky (despite false contrasts that have been drawn), the importance of the Revolution in Russia resided more in the fact that it was to be the snapping of the weakest link in the enemy's chain of command – the beginning of a world-wide revolution – than that it occurred in Russia. Socialism in one country was no part of the original design; Lenin was no more a Russian nationalist than Stalin was a Georgian one, or Martov a supporter of embryonic Jewish nationalism, which he fought in all its forms with particular ferocity. Yet the lesson of history thus far seems to me to be that social revolutions succeed best in situations where the social and the national enemy can be identified, where deprivation of political and human rights, poverty and injustice coincide with some degree of national humiliation: where these ills can be attributed to foreign exploiters as well as domestic tyrants. Perhaps the fact that Marxist movements seem weakest in Britain and the 'White Commonwealth', in Scandinavia and North America, is not unconnected with those historical factors which prevented a coincidence of mounting social injustice with inflammation of nationalist wounds in these uninvaded countries: a combination which seems almost invariably to lead to revolutionary transformation.

Thus by a curious paradox it was the doctrines of the Russian neo-Jacobin Tkachev, whom Engels denounced so harshly in 1875, that formulated a programme of action which Lenin, whether consciously or not, implemented in 1917; while it was the plans of the semi-Marxist, gradualist and democratic Lavrov, which Engels regarded with a benevolent eye, that proved impractical in Russia and, so far as they did prove practical in Western Europe, modified militant Marxism and turned it into relatively peaceful and semi-Fabian channels. If these are the dialectical turns of history they are scarcely those that Marx anticipated. No man spoke more often or with greater penetration of the unintended consequences of human acts; yet one may allow oneself to wonder what, despite his belief in the use of force, he would have made of the fact that his doctrines were destined to come into their own, thus far at least, in underdeveloped countries, by methods and in forms inevitably determined by the immaturity and barbarism surviving in such societies, when his own vision was one of a free society as the ripest fruit of human civilisation – the crown of the richest possible development of the most advanced productive techniques wielded by men rendered free and classless by rational control of their environment. It was the doctrines of 1848–50 that triumphed in Russia, in China, in the Balkans, where there were no masses in the Marxist sense, where the socialist leaders had no extensive social and political responsibilities, where there were no worlds resting upon their shoulders; where socialist parties could act on their own; where they were composed largely of intellectuals.

I should like to suggest, however tentatively, that it worked in Russia, in part at least, because men in prison, cut off from reality, believe more fiercely; their ideas are narrower, clearer and more intense, their faith is more genuine. That is how Blanqui believed; that is how Gramsci believed; this was the position of German revolutionaries in the 1840s and 1850s, and this was the position of Russian revolutionary socialists in the 1890s. By this date there were in Germany and France, in Austria-Hungary and Britain, in Belgium and Holland, masses indeed, but there were also nationalism and respected religious organisations, growing prosperity and hope of economic security, and consequent faith in gradualist methods. The walls between classes grew to be thinner than in theory they should have been, and the leaders felt responsibility for the day-to-day lives of hundreds of thousands of members of large, elaborately organised, peaceful, social-democratic or respectable labour party establishments. There the doctrine of no collaboration with the bourgeoisie, no reformism or gradualism – the workers must win solely by their own efforts or not at all – was not practicable; in underdeveloped countries it was, for obvious reasons, far more so. Despite the great relevance of the Marxist analysis in the 1880s, during the period of decline of free trade and of social mobility, the increase of protectionism, of bureaucratic State control, of military imperialism and interlocking power élites, including trade unions and nationalist associations – in spite, in other words, of a growth of centralism which Marx had analysed and predicted with skill and insight – these other factors proved countervailing. Labour leaders, even Marxists, were drawn, perhaps against their will and without their knowledge, into the peaceful arena in which interests were adjusted rather than driven into collision, and the notion of conciliation, pluralism, an imperfect but not intolerable *modus vivendi* with other classes, was more or less taken for granted. And so the faith in one group of human beings – the proletariat – as being representative of the whole of future mankind, as the chosen instrument of history, to obstruct whose real will (as interpreted by its leaders) was *lèse-humanité* – sin against the spirit of man – became weakened, and Marxism itself tended to be reduced to a kind of crudely materialistic positivism, a mere theory of history which did not claim to supply ultimate values and so could be attached – soldered on – to other moral systems: neo-Kantianism, Christianity, egalitarianism or nationalism. This is how the Second International petered out – slowly and dismally, not with a bang, even though the assassination of Jaurès was sometimes represented as precisely that.

Yet to the despised old Second International, more than to any other source, we owe the strongest formulation of the most agonising problems which are today more agonising than ever: such questions as the relations of freedom and centralised authority, forced upon us, whatever our professed theoretical allegiances, by industrialism itself (a relationship which is not made clearer or more tolerable by being called dialectical); the vitality of national versus international forces; the relations of trade unions and socialist parties; direct economic action versus the activities of political parties; the consequences of conspiratorial methods under repressive regimes; the conflict of new nationalisms (and racisms), born out of the struggle against imperialism, with the optimum utilisation, under centralised direction, of the resources of underdeveloped territories for all mankind; the part played by purely economic factors as against national or imperialist sentiments (not themselves directly created by economic forms) in causing wars and revolutions; the possibility of the prevention of wars by 'industrial action' – general strikes and other interventions by workers' organisations – not to speak of the many questions of social legislation, immigration policy, penal reform, the rights of women with which all those long congresses with their interminable speeches, in Paris and Brussels and London and Amsterdam, Stuttgart and Copenhagen and Basle, were occupied from 1889 to 1914.

In spite of all the vast transformation of Marxism since 1918, it is the case that in our part of the world these ancient problems are far from obsolete today. Is this because we lag behind the times, and are ourselves a huge, anomalous anachronism, the last prehistoric men, whose final disappearance will mark the birth of the new world? Or is it, perhaps, as I cannot help thinking, because Marx, like many pioneers of genius, wildly exaggerated, and overstressed the historical relativity and the transience of all social questions in the face not merely of the process of time and change, but of men's ability to end them once and for ever by finding a single final rational solution: whereupon our problems will be relegated to the museum of antiquities (to use Engels' phrase) and the vast act of revolutionary transformation will, if not today, then tomorrow, close for ever the great and terrible debate, and human history will begin at last? Since a good many of Marx's specific prophecies have not been fulfilled, perhaps the great all-embracing vision will, as I believe, prove no less delusive.

# THE ROMANTIC REVOLUTION

*A Crisis in the History of Modern Thought*

I

MY SUBJECT is a turning-point in the history of Western political thought, and indeed more widely, in the history of human thought and behaviour in Europe. By a turning-point I mean a transformation of outlook. This is something different from the kind of change that occurs when a discovery, even one of crucial importance, solves even the most central and tormenting questions. A solution to a question, set in terms of that question, does not necessarily alter the categories and concepts in terms of which the question presented itself; if anything it gives these categories added authority and life. Newton's discoveries did not subvert the foundations of the physics of Kepler and Galileo. The economic ideas and methods of Keynes did not break the continuity of the subject created by Adam Smith and Ricardo. By a turning-point I mean something different: a radical change in the entire conceptual framework within which the questions had been posed; new ideas, new words, new relationships in terms of which the old problems are not so much solved as made to look remote, obsolete and, at times, unintelligible, so that the agonising problems and doubts of the past seem queer ways of thought, or confusions that belong to a world which has gone.

In the history of Western political thought there have occurred at least (it seems to me) three major turning-points of this type. One is usually placed in the short but mysterious period between the death of Aristotle and the rise of Stoicism, when, in less than two decades, the dominant philosophical schools of Athens ceased to conceive of individuals as intelligible only in the context of social life, ceased to discuss the questions connected with public and political life that had preoccupied the Academy and the Lyceum, as if these questions were no longer central, or even significant, and suddenly spoke of men purely in terms of inner experience and individual salvation, as insulated entities whose virtue consisted in their capacity to insulate themselves still further. This great transvaluation of all values – from the public to the private, the outer to the inner, the political to the ethical, the city to the individual, from social order to unpolitical anarchism, and the corresponding change in ideas and language, could scarcely have taken place only in the fifteen or twenty years after the death of Alexander allotted to it by historians of thought. We do not know, and perhaps shall never know, how much systematic opposition to the outlook embodied in the ideas of Plato and Aristotle existed during the preceding hundred years. We know too little about the thought of the early Cynics, Sceptics and Sophists who looked on public affairs as insusceptible to objective reason. All we know about these predecessors and opponents of Plato and Aristotle, or nearly all, is learned from the writing of their enemies; it is as if all we knew about the doctrines of Bertrand Russell came from Soviet textbooks, or of the Middle Ages from the doctrines of Bertrand Russell. However that may be, this was certainly one major turning-point in the history of human thought, after which nothing was the same.

An overturn of equal dimensions seems to me to have been inaugurated by Machiavelli. The sharp division between the natural and the moral virtues, the assumption that political values not merely are different from, but may in principle be incompatible with, Christian ethics, the utilitarian view of religion, the discrediting of theology, and of metaphysical and theological justification, of the very notion of an ideal commonwealth as a logical contradiction in theory and necessarily disastrous in practice – all this was something new and startling. Men had not previously been openly called upon to choose between irreconcilable sets of values, private and public, in a world without purpose, and told in advance that there could in principle exist no ultimate, objective criterion for this choice, since the two paths often led in opposite directions, which had little in common. I will not here enlarge upon the vast consequences of this dagger plunged into the body of the European tradition, as Meinecke has called it.

The third great turning-point – it seems to me the greatest yet, since nothing so revolutionary has happened since – occurred towards the end of the eighteenth century, principally in Germany; and although it is well enough known under the name of 'romanticism', its full meaning and importance have not been appreciated even now. I should like to state my thesis in its simplest form – too simple to be altogether accurate or just. It is this: that the eighteenth century saw the destruction of the notion of truth and validity in ethics and politics, not merely objective or absolute truth, but subjective and relative truth also – truth and validity as such – with vast and indeed incalculable results. The movement we call romanticism transformed modern ethics and politics in a far more serious way than has been realised.

## II

During the entire span of the central tradition of Western thought it had been assumed that all general questions were of the same logical type: they were questions of fact. Therefore they were answerable by those who were in a position to know the relevant data and to interpret them correctly. The belief that if a question is not in principle answerable it is not a genuine question at all, that somewhere there exists a solution for every problem, though it may be concealed and difficult of access, like hidden treasure (which was taken for granted by positivism in the age of Enlightenment and in the nineteenth century, and also in our day), is the major assumption that is presupposed in the whole of Western thought up to the point of which I speak. Moral and political questions, in this respect, did not differ from others. Such questions as 'What is the best life for men?', 'Why should I obey you or other persons?' (perhaps the most central question of political philosophy), 'What are rights?', 'What is freedom and why seek it?', 'What are obligations, power, justice, equality?' and the like were regarded as being in principle answerable in the same way as more obviously factual questions such as 'What is water composed of?', 'How many stars are there?', 'When did Julius Caesar die?', 'Which foot did he put first when crossing the Rubicon?', 'Why did Hitler exterminate so many human beings?', 'Does God exist?' I may not myself be able to tell how far Lisbon is from Constantinople, or whether the patient will die of this disease, but I know in what region to look for an answer, what to do, what authorities to consult. I know what kinds of propositions could, and what could not, be answers to my question. That is what I mean by saying that I know that the true answer must be discoverable in principle, although I may not know it, and, indeed, nobody – save an omniscient being – may know it.

There were violent disputes among the rival claimants to such knowledge. Some looked for the truth in individual revelation, or dogmatic faith, or sacred books; or in the pronouncements of the expert interpreters of such truth – witch-doctors, priests, Churches, prophets, men in touch with unseen forces. All the Churches might not always return the same answer, but it was assumed that some such answers must be discoverable: if not the pronouncements of this sect or religion, then of another one. Some men looked for the answer to the insights of metaphysicians, or of the individual conscience, or to the immemorial wisdom of the tribe or culture, or the uncorrupted heart of the simple good man; some listened to the voice of the people met in assembly, some to the divine king or leader. Some thought the truth was timeless, others that it evolved historically; it was searched for in the past or in the future, in this life or the next, in the pronouncements of reason or of mystics and other irrational sources, in theology, in the application of mathematical methods to the data of experience, in the conclusions of common sense, or the laboratories of the natural scientists. Wars of extermination were fought over rival claims to be able to answer these questions truly. It could not be otherwise when the reward was the solution of questions of life and death, personal salvation, living according to the truth. This is the faith of Platonists and Stoics, Christians and Jews, thinkers and men of action, believers and unbelievers of every shade, to our day.

In spite of the vast differences that separated these outlooks, one great presupposition underlies them all, or rather three branches of one presupposition. The first is that there is such an entity as a human nature, natural or supernatural, which can be understood by the relevant experts; the second is that to have a specific nature is to pursue certain specific goals imposed on it or built into it by God or an impersonal nature of things, and that to pursue these goals is alone what makes men human; the third is that these goals, and the corresponding interests and values (which it is the business of theology or philosophy or science to discover and formulate), cannot possibly conflict with one another – indeed, that they must form a harmonious whole.

The greatest embodiment of these assumptions is the conception of natural law, classical, medieval and modern. They were accepted by everyone: they were not questioned even by some of the sharpest critics of natural law – sceptics, empiricists, subjectivists, or believers in organic or historical evolution. An ancient Sophist, according to Aristotle, had indeed observed that fire burned both in Athens and in Persia, whereas social and moral views changed before our very eyes.[1] Similarly Montesquieu had said that, when Montezuma told Cortez that the Christian religion might be best for Spaniards, but the Aztec religion was best for his people, what he was saying was not absurd.[2] This was thought scandalous by all who believed that moral or religious or political truths were valid for everyone, everywhere, at all times; that is to say, both by the Christian Churches and by dogmatic materialists and positivists such as Helvétius and Condillac and their friends. But even the relativists and the sceptics said no more than that individuals and societies had different needs in accordance with different geographical or climatic conditions, or different systems of law and education, or general outlooks and patterns of life – all that Montesquieu had called the spirit of the laws. Nevertheless objective answers to such questions were, of course, discoverable: you needed only to know the conditions in which men lived. Given these, you could say, with a claim to eternal objective truth, that since the needs of the Persians were different from those of the Parisians, what was good in Persia might be bad in Paris. But the answers were still objective, the truth of the prescription for Persia did not contradict the prescription for Paris. I beat my wife in Bukhara, I do not beat her in Birmingham: different circumstances dictate different methods, although the goals are much the same; or differ according to differing stimuli.

This remained equally true even for so thoroughgoing a sceptic as Hume: to find out the right way of life it is of no use to look for innate ideas or a priori truths. The former do not exist; the latter give no information about the world, only about the way we use our words and symbols. But is there nowhere to look? Indeed there is. Values are what men seek: they seek satisfaction of their needs. The science of empirical psychology will tell you what men want, what they approve and disapprove, and sociology or social anthropology will tell you about the differences and similarities between the needs and the moral and political values of (and within) different nations, groups, classes, civilisations. Even the German historical school, which denounced most fiercely of all the notion of immutable, universal principles, substituted for them a

---

[1] Aristotle, *Nicomachean Ethics*, 1134$^b$26.
[2] *De l'esprit des lois*, book 24, chapter 24.

sense of the continuity of a specific 'organic' entity – a particular nation, or tribe, or tradition, but, at any rate in the early doctrines of this school, in the writings of Herder, Savigny, Niebuhr (and indeed, in England, Burke), did not say or imply that these various patterns of development were hostile to one another, or not elements in one grand universal whole, a vast unity in difference. The paths might be necessarily different; but the goal was one for all men: it combined peace, justice, virtue, happiness, harmonious coexistence. That is the heart of Lessing's famous parable of the three rings, which spoke for the entire Enlightenment.

Holbach said that man was a thing in nature like other three-dimensional entities: that ethics was a science which discovered, firstly, what human nature was, then what it needed, and finally how to satisfy these needs; and politics was this science applied to groups – morality and politics are the sciences of breeding and satisfying human animals, or, to change the metaphor, the agriculture of the mind, as Helvétius said. Le Mercier de la Rivière declared that human ends are given: given by the constitution of human nature. We cannot alter them, only understand their laws and act accordingly. Politics is navigation – it requires knowledge of seas and winds and rocks and the ports which one cannot but wish to reach: that is what being rational means. 'The despotism of the laws and the personal despotism of the lawgiver are one and the same: that of the irresistible power of evidence,' said Le Mercier.[1] The legislator is merely the builder: the plan has been laid down by nature. Helvétius said he did not care whether men were virtuous or vicious; it is necessary only that they be intelligent – for if they are intelligent they will in fact pursue happiness by the most effective means, whether they realise this or not, whatever their interpretation of their own conduct may be. Montesquieu thought that the ways of achieving such ends as happiness or justice or stability, which were common to all men, would differ in different circumstances; Hume that these ends were subjective and not demonstrable a priori; Herder that they were not universal or fully rational, and depended upon the stage in the organic development reached by a given society pursuing its own peculiar, unique path. But if the ends, subjective or objective, uniform or variable, are given, by God, by reason, by tradition, then the only genuine

[1] *L'Ordre naturel et essentiel des sociétés politiques* (London, 1767), vol. 1, p. 311.

questions left are those of means. Political questions turn out to be pure questions of technology.

Again, there might be differences on another plane. Some, following Plato, believed that these ends could be discovered only by specially trained experts: sages, or divinely inspired seers, or *philosophes*, or scientists, or historians. Condorcet saw no reason why progress should not be made in human affairs by a government of experts in the sciences of man, if only the same methods were applied to men as had been applied to societies of bees and beavers. Herder disagreed profoundly, because human societies develop and transform themselves by pursuing spiritual goals, whereas those of bees and beavers do not. But he said nothing that went against Condorcet's proposition that 'Nature binds by an unbreakable chain truth, happiness and virtue';[1] for otherwise there was no cosmos. If you could show that truth, for example, might not be compatible with happiness, or happiness with virtue, then, if all three were regarded as absolute values (and this in the eighteenth century, as at most other times, was a truism), it followed that no objectively demonstrable answer could in principle be given to the questions 'What goal shall we pursue?', 'Which is the best way of life?' Yet unless these questions can in principle be answered, what precisely was it that we were asking? Kant and Rousseau broke away from Plato in asserting that answers to questions of value were not matters of expertise at all, since every rational man (and any man could be rational) could discover the answer to these fundamental moral questions; and moreover that the answers of all rational men would of necessity coincide. Indeed, their belief in democracy rests upon this doctrine.

The point I wish to make, and it seems to me a crucial one, is that all these diverse schools agreed that questions of value were a species of questions of fact. Since one truth – say the answer to the question 'Should I pursue justice?' – cannot be incompatible with another truth – say the answer to 'Should I practise mercy?' (for one true proposition cannot logically contradict another) – an ideal state of affairs embodying the correct solutions of all the central problems of social life could be worked out, at least in principle. Any obstacles to its realisation must be empirical or contingent. All

---

[1] *Esquisse d'un tableau historique des progrès de l'esprit humain*, ed. O. H. Prior and Yvon Belaval (Paris, 1970), p. 228.

human weakness, error, idleness, corruption, misery, all conflict and therefore all evil and all tragedy, are due to ignorance and error. If men knew, they would not err; if they did not err, they could – and, being rational, would – pursue the satisfaction of their true interests by the most efficient methods. These activities, being based on reason, could never collide; for there is nothing in the nature of men or the world which makes tragedy unavoidable. Sin, crime, suffering are forms of maladjustment due to blindness. Knowledge, whether it is conceived as scientific or mystical, empirical or theological, on earth or in heaven, creates beauty, harmony and happiness. There are no incongruities in the world of saints or angels.

## III

Virtue is knowledge. This central, Western faith, with all its ramifications, which survived the breakdown of classical Greek philosophy, the rise of Christianity, which survived the barbarians and the medieval Church, the Renaissance and the Reformation, and indeed shaped them all in one form or another, this strongest pillar of European rationalism, the central leg of the great tripod, was undermined, or at least cracked, by the romantic movement. It seems to me, first, that certain among the romantics cut the deepest of all the roots of the classical outlook – namely the belief that values, the answers to questions of action and choice, could be discovered at all – and maintained that there were no answers to some of these questions, either subjective or objective, either empirical or a priori. Secondly, there was for them no guarantee that values did not, in principle, conflict with one another, or, if they did, that there was a way out; and they held, like Machiavelli, that to deny this was a form of self-deception, naïve, or shallow, pathetic and always disastrous. Thirdly, my thesis is that by their positive doctrine the romantics introduced a new set of values, not reconcilable with the old, and that most Europeans are today the heirs of both opposing traditions. We accept both outlooks, and shift from one foot to the other in a fashion that we cannot avoid if we are honest with ourselves, but which is not intellectually coherent. To trace this momentous shift in outlook could be a life's work. Here I can make only a few excessively oversimplified points to indicate the contour of this revolutionary phenomenon.

IV

The destructive element – the earliest tremor of the coming earthquake – is first traceable in the innocent pages of Rousseau and Kant. Everyone knows that, according to both Rousseau and Kant, to discover what I ought to do I have to listen to an inner voice. This voice issues commands: it orders. Rousseau calls it reason. Kant also calls it rational, and indeed offers criteria whereby its injunctions can be discriminated from those of other, rival voices – those of the emotions, for example, or self-interest. Yet both these thinkers, despite their deep disagreements with certain aspects of the philosophy of the Enlightenment, largely still belong to it, in that whatever the inner voice of reason commands is for them objective, universal, timeless, true for all men, in all places, at all times, as the tradition of natural law had taught. Yet, in Kant's teaching, this voice acquires certain peculiar characteristics. His central concept is that of individual responsibility. The very formulation of the question, concerning what a man should do (and by a natural transference – which he was politically too timorous to stress – also the community), implies that a man or group can always act in one way or another; in other words, can choose. A man's choice, to be properly so called, must be free; if he is determined to act by forces over which he has no control, whether they be physical, as some seventeenth-century philosophers had maintained, or psychological – desires, fears, hopes – as well as physiological and biological, as the eighteenth-century materialists had taught, then the notion of choice is, for Kant, vacuous, and no significance can be attached to such words as 'should', 'goal', 'duty' and so on. Rousseau, too, looks on the individual as embodying the essence of his freedom – to curtail a man's freedom, however benevolently, in his own putative interest, as recommended to the enlightened despot by the eighteenth-century reformers, is to kill the individual's humanity, to turn him into an animal or an object. To be truly free, a man, for Kant, must be free to go to the bad as well as to the good; otherwise there is no merit in (rationally) choosing the good, and the notion of desert becomes empty. To be free is to be self-directed. If I am determined by something over which I have no control I am not free. But the craving for happiness can be an external controlling factor of this type: I may be unable to control it. Moreover happiness is something which I may or may not achieve: it depends upon too many circumstances over which I have no power. If it is my goal, or duty, to perform a particular action, I must be able to do it; I cannot be blamed for not doing what is beyond my powers. Only if I am able to choose freely can I (or, so it follows, my culture or nation) be regarded as having obligations or responsibilities, indeed as a moral agent at all. If the source of moral or political rules is external to me, I am not free, not capable of rational choice.

The values of rational creatures must, therefore, according to this line of thought, be enjoined upon me by myself, for if they issue from some outside source, I depend upon that source, and am not free. This is what Kant means by saying that autonomy is the basis of all morality: to be at the mercy of some outside force, whether blind nature or some transcendent power, God or nature, that orders me as it wills, is heteronomy, a form of dependence on something that I do not control, slavery. I, and I alone, must be the author of my own values. I must indeed obey rules, but I am free, as Rousseau taught, because the rules are of my own making. Extraneous commands degrade men; indeed it is because men, and they alone, are the authors of values, that they are themselves supremely valuable; to use men for ends that are not their own, hence to exploit human beings, degrade them, humiliate them, is to deny their human essence, to deny that they are men; and this is the most heinous of all sins. To justify coercing or enslaving or crushing a creature I must plead that I do so in the name of a value higher than the creature whose freedom I violate. But if *ex hypothesi* there can be no such values – for all values are created by free (rational) human choice – then to perpetrate this is to trample on the highest value of all – the ultimate ends that human reason proposes for itself: reason and rational choice are the essence of men's humanity, of their dignity as human beings, of their difference, as free beings, from things and beasts. It is this that causes so violent a revulsion in us, whoever we are, when we see creatures like ourselves manipulated, trampled on, dehumanised, treated as, or turned into, brutes.

Kant speaks as if these rules were the commands of reason, and therefore if they hold for me they must hold for every other rational creature, for it is the essence of reason, whether theoretical or practical, in the sciences and in life, to be universally valid. Whether in a religious or a humanistic guise, this and this alone is the basis of our notion of moral rights and moral rules, of the liberty, equality and dignity of all men as such. He calls these rules categorical imperatives.

Perhaps Kant did not, like Hume, consciously intend to draw a sharp distinction between imperatives and statements of fact: but in any case his formulation had revolutionary consequences. Commands or imperatives are not factual statements; they are not descriptions; they are not true or false. Commands may be right or wrong, they may be corrupt or disinterested; they may be intelligible or obscure; they may be trivial or important; but they do not describe anything: they order, they direct, they terrify, they generate action. Similarly a goal or a value is something that a man sets himself to aim at, it is not an independent entity that can be stumbled upon. Values are not natural growths that a science, say psychology or sociology, can study, but are made by men, are forms of free action or creation.

Kant does not indeed move towards this conclusion; indeed it goes counter to all that he believed – that is, the universality of reason, the possibility of rational demonstration of moral values. But some of Kant's romantic successors drew out the full consequences of the view that values are commands, and that they are created, not discovered. The old analogy between moral (or political) and scientific or metaphysical or theological knowledge is broken. Morality – and politics so far as it is social morality – is a creative process: the new romantic model is that of art.

What does the artist do? He creates something, he expresses himself; he does not copy, imitate, transcribe (that is mere craftsmanship). He acts, makes, invents; he does not discover, calculate, deduce, reason. To create is, in a certain sense, to depend solely on one's own self. One invents both the goal and the path towards it. Where, asked Herzen, is the song before the composer has conceived it? Where is the dance before it has been danced, where is the poem before the poet has uttered it? They are not there – in some external sphere – to be discovered, whether by experts or by the common man. All creation is in some sense creation out of nothing. It is the only fully autonomous activity of man. It is self-liberation from causal laws, from the mechanism of the external world, from tyrants, or environmental influences, or the passions, which govern me – factors in relation to which I am as much an object in nature as trees, or stones, or animals.

If the essence of man is self-mastery – the conscious choice of his own ends and form of life – this constitutes a radical break with the older model that dominated the notion of man's place in the cosmos. The notion of natural laws as flowing from the need for harmony with nature, the functional conception of man as fulfilled by finding his place in the universal orchestra – the unquestioned foundation of European moral and spiritual cosmology from the pre-Socratics to Rousseau – is destroyed; for to seek to adjust one's self to something that obeys its own laws, whether it is conceived as static or dynamic, as an unchangeable reality beneath the flux of experience or as a purposive process realised in nature or history, is tantamount to obeying something that one cannot determine, laws that dictate from without; or if they speak from within as well, at any rate not created, nor freely alterable by individuals or societies. If to be free is the condition of being human, and to be free is to issue laws to myself, then it is not authority from without, no matter how sublime the source, that constitutes the validity and truth of principles of action, but the fact that it is ordained by a free agent.

This is a reversal of the notion of truth as correspondence, or at any rate a fixed relation to the *rerum natura* that is given and eternal, which is the basis of natural law. The traditional view of the world is transformed. Art is not imitation, nor representation, but *expression*; I am most truly myself when I create – that, and not capacity for reasoning, is the divine spark within me; that is the sense in which I am made in God's image (*sicut Deus*). Nature is no longer Dame Nature or Mistress Nature, neither the despot of the materialists nor the governess of the deists, nor Hume's kindly housekeeper, nor Shaftesbury's *natura naturans*, 'All-loving and All-lovely, All-divine!',[1] but, in whatever guise I meet her, she is the counterpart of act or spirit, the matter upon which I work my will, that which I mould.

This image haunts the German romantics, Wackenroder, Tieck, Jacobi, Schiller, Novalis, the Schlegels, Schelling. Its most original, and perhaps most vivid, expression is in the early writings of Fichte, who developed the notion of the categorical imperative beyond and against Kant. I become aware of my own self, said Fichte, not as an element in some larger pattern, but in the clash with the not-self, the *Anstoss*, the violent impact of collision with dead matter, which I resist and which I must subjugate to my free

[1] *The Moralists: A Philosophical Rhapsody* (London, 1709), part 3, section 1, p. 158.

creative design. The self is activity, effort, self-direction. It wills, alters, carves up the world, both in thought and in action, in accordance with its own concepts and categories. In Kant this was a preconscious activity of the imagination. In Fichte it is a conscious creative activity. 'I do not accept anything because I must,' said Fichte (as previous thinkers, say Descartes or Locke, had said), 'I believe it because I will','[1] and again, 'If man allows laws to be made for him by the will of others, he thereby makes himself into a beast, that is, he injures his inborn human dignity.'[2] I am a member of two worlds, that is to say, of the material, ruled by cause and effect, and of the spiritual,[3] where 'I am wholly my own creation.'[4] Josiah Royce, summarising this aspect of Fichte's views, wrote: 'The world is the poem . . . dreamed out by the inner life.'[5] Our worlds are literally different if we differ spiritually. To be a poet, a soldier, a banker is to create different worlds. My philosophy depends on the kind of man I am, not vice versa. In some sense my world must depend on my free choice. The material – dead nature (including my body and its functions) – is given. What I make of it is not: if it were, I too should go through the repetitive cycles – cause, effect, cause – that govern inanimate matter, or the evolutionary pattern that determines organic nature, plants, animals, my own body, my sensuous self, all that I cannot control freely.

This is stated in the great rhetorical climax of Fichte's famous speeches to the German nation (delivered in his later phase), the basic text of all German nationalism:

> Either you believe in the original principle in man – a freedom, a perfectibility . . . or you do not . . . All those who have within them a creative quickening of life, or else, assuming that such a gift has been withheld from them, at least reject what is but vanity, and await the moment when they are caught up in the current of original life, or even, if they are not yet at this point, at any rate have some confused presentiment of freedom – have towards it not hatred nor fear but a

[1] *Johann Gottlieb Fichte's Sämmtliche Werke*, ed. I. H. Fichte (Berlin, 1845–6) (hereafter SW), vol. 2, p. 256. Subsequent references to Fichte are to this edition, by volume and page, thus: SW ii 256.
[2] SW vi 82.
[3] e.g. SW ii 282, 288.
[4] SW ii 256.
[5] Josiah Royce, *The Spirit of Modern Philosophy* (Boston and New York, 1892), p. 162.

feeling of love – these are a part of primal humanity . . . All those who, on the other hand, have resigned themselves to represent only a derivative, second-hand product, who are but the annexe to life . . . considered as people they are strangers, outsiders . . . All those who believe in freedom of the spirit . . . they are with us . . . All those who believe in the arrested being or retrogression, or putting inanimate nature at the helm of the world . . . they are strangers to us.[1]

Fichte's attempt to show that the Germans are creative and the French are dead does not concern us here: what matters is his thesis that values are made, not found. In his early, politically radical, writings, while Rousseau was his master, he thought that values are created by the rational individual, and because reason is identical in all men, the laws and values of the life of reason are binding on them all. In his later works the self is successively identified with the transcendental demiurge, the great creative spirit, of which we are all aspects or fragments, that is to say, God; then with man in general; then with the German people, or any 'creative' group or community, through which alone the individual can fulfil his true, inner, timeless, creative self. 'The individual does not exist,' Fichte declared, 'he should not count for anything, but must vanish completely; the group alone exists.'[2] 'The life of reason consists in this, that the individual forget himself in the species – to risk his life for the life of all and sacrifice his life to theirs.'[3] The function of freedom is to realise 'complete freedom, complete independence of everything which is not ourselves, our pure ego'.[4] If this ego is identified with 'the people', then the people has the moral right to realise its destiny by every weapon of cunning and of force.

I am not drawing attention to this strand in Fichte's thought in order to indicate one of the sources of mystical nationalism, or to demonstrate the perversion of his earlier individualism, but to show how the essence of man is now identified, not with reason, which must be one in all men, but with the source of action, the will; the wills of men can conflict as the products of reason – true descriptive statements – logically cannot. I have cited only Fichte, but there is scarcely a romantic writer who does not abound in passages of this type: the break with the objective classical world –

[1] SW vii 374–5.
[2] SW vii 37–8.
[3] SW vii 35.
[4] SW vi 86–7.

the image of the world common to Plato, Aquinas and Voltaire – is very dramatic.

Many corollaries that are new politically, as well as aesthetically and philosophically, issue from this. Fichte's 'pure ego', identical in all the scattered earthly selves, gives way to the bold, unbridled individual artist or creative personality, who conceives his own values and lives and dies for them because they are *his* values – for there is no other source from which they can arise. The free, anarchic spirit, worshipped in Friedrich Schlegel's novel *Lucinde* and in Tieck's *William Lovell*, leads in its socialised form to the notion of autarky – the closed, centrally planned society of Fichte and of Friedrich List, and that of many socialists, which insulates itself against outside interference in order to be independent and express its own inner personality without interference by other men. This self-insulation – concentration on the inner life, on that which alone I can control, together with the definition of my self or my community in terms of something not subject to external influences – is, no doubt, historically connected with the defeats and devastation inflicted upon the Germans by Richelieu and Louis XIV, and the consequent emotional need on the part of the humiliated nation to restore its respect for itself by withdrawal into an inner citadel that could not be taken from it by the conqueror – its inner life, the spiritual realm that no tyrant could seize, no natural disaster destroy. In the twentieth century the selfsame need, caused by defeat in war, led to a much more violent manifestation of these defensive-aggressive symptoms, and in due course to the spread of the disease itself, which has had the appalling consequences known to all. However that may be, whether or not it was the ambition of Richelieu (or Alexander or Julius Caesar), with the consequent sense of impotence of the average German (or Athenian or Roman) citizen (especially of the intellectuals among them), that led to the substitution of personal, aesthetic or metaphysical issues for social or political ones, this process, which began almost imperceptibly among the pietists in the despotically ruled German States towards the end of the seventeenth century, led to the greatest spiritual upheaval of modern times. To set such phenomena in their historical context is, of course, important; but their influence upon our own age is more radical than any historical account of them would lead one to suppose.

Individual character, will, activity – these are everything. Work ceases to be conceived as a painful necessity, and becomes (in

Fichte) the sacred task of man, for only thereby can he impress his unique, creative personality upon the dead stuff that is nature. This leads to the concepts of the dignity of labour and the right to work, sanctified by man and not by the service of God. The true nature of man is not passive receptivity – leisure, contemplation – but activity. Creators are contrasted with mere collaborators in the creative process, still more with those whom Fichte described as asleep, or who are adrift with the current of things. *Das Gegebene* – the given – is now contrasted with *das Aufgegebene* – the task that I set before me – sacred because it issues from my own untrammelled 'rational' will. The concept of vocation – *Beruf* – which is central to Lutheran social teaching, is retained and exalted in the romantic philosophy, save that the source of authority is now not God or nature, but the individual's concern for his freedom to choose his end, the end which alone fulfils the demands of his moral, or aesthetic, or philosophical, or political, nature. 'Man shall be and do something.'[1] To know something to be my mission (or that of my nation or culture or Church) is not to know facts or contemplate hypotheses in a scientific or philosophical spirit, nor merely to be moved by emotion (emotion is not the heart of romanticism: that is an egregious error made by a great many historians and critics), but is more akin to the state of the artist in his hour of inspiration, of personal truth, when he knows what he must do to realise his inner vision, at once part of himself and an objective command – issued by himself to himself – to act or live in a certain fashion. This knowledge is one that all creative personalities possess: whether they be artists, thinkers, men of action, whether they create in isolation or collectively. To know my true goal is not to know the truth as conceived in the thought of the Enlightenment, according to which you first discover the truth, then apply it; rather your very action expresses – is one with – your convictions. Morality and politics are not a set of propositions: they are action, self-dedication to goals made concrete. To be a man is not to understand or reason but to act; to act, to make, to create, to be free are identical: this is the difference between the animals and man. The artist creates; he does not transcribe or discover. But, as Herder had taught, the individual is plunged in the native stream of his society; the life of a society is not the mere sum of the lives of its members. Communities, true

[1] SW vi 383.

communities, create collectively. And so the aesthetic model is translated into the social and political terms that were destined to play so fateful a part in the history of modern Europe. Fichte says this much more explicitly than Herder or Burke. The path leads directly from him to the romantic chauvinism of German historians of the last century.

v

A particular variant of this attitude is Friedrich Schiller's attempt to find the field of freedom in art, conceived as a kind of play. The material world is a field of cause and effect which imprisons our bodies, in which our behaviour is determined in the manner that the natural sciences describe and explain. What then distinguishes us from the rest of nature? Not that we are determined less rigorously than the rest of nature, though perhaps in a somewhat different fashion, which is the answer of older theorists; but that we have the power of abstracting our spirit from ('rising above') the world of nature, and constructing one in which different laws and rules obtain, free, because invented by us. When we are at play, we ourselves construct the universe and its laws. Children who play at being Red Indians *are* Red Indians: nothing obstructs them; the ordinary laws – social, psychological, even physical – have been suspended; we can alter anything, even, perhaps, the laws of logic, as our imagination chooses. This 'noumenal' world is one in which our imagination and reason have full scope. In this world virtue is rewarded, goodness, beauty, truth celebrated, vice punished, as they are not, all too self-evidently, in the so-called real world. Art is literally a game, invention, creation out of nothing, in which both the contents of the world and the rules that it obeys are fashioned in accordance with our own free, untrammelled wishes. Into this we may escape, whenever we please, and find liberation from the treadmill of physical life. This is the world of art, morality, reason. The values of it are not discovered but created, and the relation of these values are what we please to make them. So, too, Schelling conceives the world as the continuous creative activity of the Absolute Spirit, and the degrees of insight or understanding of men according to their creative capacity. Among these, as Bergson did later, he includes philosophers, artists, poets, historians, statesmen, as possessing a far deeper insight into the history of men and all the processes of their life, biological, physiological, psychological, than that of reasoners who attempt to apply inappropriate models, drawn from the 'dead' sciences of chemistry or mathematics, to the 'living' flow of life. More than any other thinker of this time, Schelling conceived of values and myths, so far from being self-delusion on the part of early peoples, or deliberate mystifications by priests or poets, as concrete embodiments of the human impulse to create which man shared with all nature. Echoing Vico, he maintained that men understood only what they saw from within, as actors, not from without, as observers. This served to divide the dead from the living among the students of nature, history and art alike. As a metaphysical doctrine Schelling's teaching remained obscure and esoteric; but it had sufficient influence to feed the already swollen torrent of romantic politics, especially the notion of the goals of social life as created by inspired men of genius who proceeded not by careful reasoning but by flashes of revelation, huge irrational leaps, and carried the rest of mankind with them in a great creative drive forward, which released the hidden forces within it.

VI

The political consequences of this are highly novel. If we alone are the authors of the values, then what matters is our inner state – motive, not consequence. For we cannot guarantee consequences: they are part of the natural world, the world of cause and effect, of necessity, not of the world of freedom. We can be responsible only for what is in our power. Hence a transformed scale of moral and political values, something altogether new in the European consciousness. What matters now is motive, integrity, sincerity, fidelity in principle, purity of heart, spontaneity; not happiness or strength or wisdom or success, or natural beauty, or other natural values, which are outside the realm of moral freedom, since they depend on external factors that are largely beyond our control. The sage, the specialist, the man who knows, who achieves happiness, or virtue, or wisdom, by means of understanding, or action founded upon understanding, is replaced by the tragic hero who seeks to realise himself at whatever cost, against whatever odds, with no matter what consequences; and whether, in a worldly sense, he succeeds or does not succeed is immaterial.

All three of the fundamental presuppositions of the old outlook are destroyed by this reversal of values. In the first place, man has no identifiable nature, whether static or dynamic, for he creates himself: he creates his own values, and thereby transforms himself, and the transformed self creates new values, so that we cannot *ex hypothesi* ever tell what the upshot will be of his attempt to realise them; for he can only attempt – he cannot be answerable for the consequences, or know whether he will succeed or not. In the second place, since his values are not discovered but created, no system of propositions can be constructed to describe them, for they are not facts, not entities in the world; they are not there to be identified and labelled by a science of ethics or politics, whether empirically or a priori. Finally, there is no guarantee that the values of different civilisations, or nations, or individuals, will necessarily harmonise. There may also be clashes between the values of one individual at different times, or even at the same time. Who shall say whether knowledge is at all times compatible with happiness? To know the world may plunge one into misery; justice may preclude mercy; equality may bridle liberty; efficiency may kill spontaneity; virtue may drive out pleasure, or power, or knowledge. Knowledge may not be a moral value at all, even though no philosopher after Plato made this denial. For it is possible to know all that is knowable, and yet to embrace evil if one is so minded: if man were not free to choose evil, he would not be truly free, creation would become a quasi-mechanical self-propulsion along the tramlines of infallible omniscience, harmonious and frictionless, but not consistent with choice or freedom. When a man pursues his own values, what we have learnt to admire in him is his spiritual attitude – the sincerity, the intensity, the dedication with which he seeks to follow the light within himself. We cannot tell whether he will succeed in creating a work of art, a form of life, a political movement, a philosophical system. All that is within his power is to make the effort. There is only one totally unforgivable act – to betray what one believes in. This creed may take the form of unbridled fanaticism, and lead to appalling results.

The heroic image of the nineteenth century is that of Beethoven: a man may be ignorant, boorish, self-absorbed, barbarous, at war with society or himself, but provided he serves his ideal, obeys the voice within him, he is saved, he is autonomous. Only if he denies himself, or sells himself for money or position, or comfort, or power, or pleasure – the goods of the external world – does he commit the ultimate sin by turning himself into a thing, something heteronomous, a natural object. Only the motive, the *état d'âme*, counts. If I believe in one form of life and you in another and these come into conflict, it is far better that we fight, and one or both of us are killed, than that there should be a compromise which betrays what is sacred to each of us. The very concept of idealism as a noble attribute is novel. To praise someone as an idealist is to say that he is prepared to lay down his life for ends in which he believes for their own sake. The question of whether these ends are correct is no longer intelligible, because all men – and, for those for whom the creative power is not the individual, but a culture, a nation, a Church, a tradition, all these – live by their own unique, particular vision.

This is novel, since it could not have been understood before the mid-eighteenth century. No doubt it had always been right for a Christian to die for his faith; but that was because it was the true faith, and only by it could a man be saved, and therefore it constituted the highest value in his scale, and not in his alone, but in that of all mankind. If a Christian killed a Moslem in a crusade, or a Catholic a Protestant in one of the wars of religion, he would not, if he was a compassionate man, spit upon his dead adversary's tomb: he might feel regret that men so brave, perhaps so kind, could die for a false faith. The fact that they held this faith sincerely, and gave their lives for it, so far from mitigating their sin, only made it worse. If the faith was false or wicked, then the more pure, intense, passionate, 'authentic' the enemy's addiction to his belief or heresy, the more evil he was, the less entitled to admiration.

The romantic attitude is the complete reverse of this. In the early nineteenth century there is deep admiration for martyrs, minorities, those who fight against overwhelming odds, those who, for the sake of their ideals, court certain destruction. There is a high premium on defiance for its own sake, on defeat and failure, as against compromise and worldly success. A man who devotes all his energies to the expression of what is within him, even if he fails, and produces not a masterpiece, but, like Balzac's mad painter, a chaos of colours, has succeeded in preserving his human semblance and saved his soul, as the fashionable painter who has prostituted his gifts has not. This would have meant little to Aristotle, who considered only achievement admirable; and equally little to a sixteenth-century Christian, who cared only for the truth – public, objective, universal truth. In the mid-eighteenth century, in Lessing's *Minna von Barnhelm*, the idealist, Major Tellheim, is a

touching and high-minded – honourably proud – but absurd
figure: twenty-five years later he is the tragic hero, like Karl Moor
in Schiller's *The Robbers*, and later all the Don Juans, Fausts,
Medeas and other rebellious and satanic heroines and heroes.

This subjectivism leads to a reversal of values: worship of
integrity and purity as against effectiveness or capacity for discovery and knowledge; freedom against happiness; conflict, war, self-
immolation against compromise, adjustment, toleration; the wild
genius, the outcast, the suffering hero, Byron's Giaours, Laras,
Cains against the tame, civilised, respectable or philistine society
shocked by the rebel's claims and standards. It is the morality of
commitment, self-surrender and self-assertion against that of pru-
dence, calculation, realism. It is at this time that the very word
'realism' becomes pejorative and acquires the overtones of ruthlessness, cynicism, shabby compromise with inferior values. 'Give all
thou canst,' exclaims Wordsworth; 'high Heaven rejects the lore /
Of nicely-calculated less or more'.[1] High heaven accepts those
whom men reject: Schiller's heroes, the lonely thinkers and doers
of Ibsen's plays, as well as the more violent individualists of Kleist
or Stendhal and Balzac – the Prince of Homburg, Julien Sorel,
Rastignac, Carlyle's heroic makers of nations, Steerforth, Dostoevsky's diabolic characters.

If the new aesthetic ideal of romanticism is socially relatively
innocuous, the worship of political individualism can take a more
sinister form. The counterpart of Beethoven is Napoleon. Napoleon was represented by his romantic admirers as doing with
human beings what Beethoven did with sounds, or Shakespeare
with words. Men are either endowed with creative powers or they
are not, and if they are not, if they are 'asleep or passive', they must
serve the ends of the creators, and achieve their fulfilment by being
moulded by them; and though they may be violated, tortured and
destroyed in the process, yet they are thereby lifted to a higher
level than that to which they could have risen by their own efforts.
Their agony contributes to a great work of art. Napoleon's Empire
is conceived as the counterpart of a symphony, an epic – a vast
creation of a free human spirit. So Hugo and Vigny and Tieck. This
is the doctrine that has underlain nationalism, Fascism, and every
movement that rests on a morality in which the model of freedom
derived from artistic creation, or from self-realising, vital drives,

[1] 'Tax not the royal Saint', *Ecclesiastical Sonnets* 3. 43.

has been substituted for the older model of science or rational happiness or knowledge; and which conceives freedom as making free with all that resists me.

This is a vast revolution of ideas. The subjectivism upon which it is founded still works in us and our political ideas. A counter-revolution against it was indeed attempted, both by Hegel and by Karl Marx – an attempt to restore objective values, not indeed drawn from a concept of immutable natural law, but from that of the objective forces embodied in the historical self-transformation of society and nation, State or class. These thinkers taught in their very different fashions that the notion of a natural harmony of interests was shallow, that conflict, whether conceived as springing from metaphysical necessity or from the pattern of social development, was intrinsic to the individual and society. They maintained that to resist that which is bound to win because its victory was entailed by the development of 'reason' itself – for example, the growth of the State or the interests of a given class – was wicked as well as foolish because the principle on which such resistance was founded was anti-rational. The history of institutions was the history of the growth of human reason, and to try to arrest or retard this movement was to lean on principles and methods rendered obsolete by the process of history itself; to cling to what is obsolete is against morality – indeed, immoral, if morality evolves with the evolving needs and trends of a humanity pursuing rational goals. Kant, who first among secular thinkers dug the great unbridgeable gulf between duty and interest, was sufficiently a child of the Enlightenment to believe that the just would be rewarded. This could not be rationally demonstrated: but a world in which the upright suffered was a bad world, and this possibility he rejected by an act of faith in the ultimate goodness of God. Lessing, Chateaubriand, the young Kleist, the middle-aged Schiller founded their belief in a world order on the same precarious – Quixotic, non-rational – foundations. For Kleist they crumbled: like Joseph de Maistre, he saw no rational or personal escape from the spectacle of life rendered meaningless by increasing and unexplained violence, cruelty and frustration. Hegel boldly accepted history as the history of mounting conflict – as the 'slaughter-bench'[1] of humanity – and with great ingenuity and daring tried to represent this battlefield as an objective process which, being the

[1] *Sämtliche Werke*, ed. Hermann Glockner, vol. 11 (Stuttgart, 1928), p. 49.

growth of self-understanding by man, could be represented as the fulfilment of man as a rational being, a demand of reason – which is ultimately identical in men and in the external world, and seeks to achieve an ultimate harmony – and hence as the true realm of self-direction, of human freedom. Progress – the process of self-awareness, of self-liberation from whatever hinders the march of the spirit – must culminate in the triumph of reason, when all will be clear, real, harmonious. Marx translated this agonised ascent into material – social-economic – terms: there is in his doctrine too a golden age, in which mankind, integrated, liberated from illusions and the servitude of which these are the symptoms, will be happy for ever. We are back with Plato and natural law and the *philosophia perennis*: unless we create the conditions necessary for understanding – and understand, and act accordingly – reality will go on dividing and destroying us.

This attempt to restore objective standards was not altogether successful; it won no decisive victory. The subjective morality of the romantic movement entered the European consciousness too deeply. Men were prepared to revolt, and indeed die, for principles which they regarded neither as local nor as temporary, nor as the interests of a given group or civilisation, but as being at the same time absolute and personal, that is, guaranteed by none of the objective criteria which verified factual statements or rendered universal truths universal, objective and binding on all men.

Indeed, it is some such outlook that has revived in modern days in the form of existentialism, particularly in its atheistic variety. Values for these thinkers are not facts, the world is *wertfrei*, free of values, pursues no goals, entails no evaluative propositions, neither ethical nor aesthetic nor political. It faces man as a bleak set of facts in which he can discern patterns, towards which he can have attitudes, but which itself dictates nothing. To deduce that this or that moral order or political establishment is better, or more desirable, or more rational, because of the structure of things in general, is, for thinkers of this type, mere self-deception – issuing from a pathetic desire to find support for one's views in the nature of things. For things have in this sense no nature; their properties have no logical or spiritual relation to human purposes or action. The freedom which for existentialists, as for the romantics, distinguishes men from objects in nature consists precisely in commitment to this or that course of action, this or that form of life, which cannot be justified outside themselves. It is mere cowardice – an attempt to take oneself or others in – to look for an alibi outside the human will in some external authority: natural, historical, social, moral. Moreover it is a contradiction in terms. Authority, justification, purpose – these are concepts which arise only in the course of decisions by individuals to live or act in this or that way; the transference of them to external agencies, divine or natural, can spring only from weakness, fear of admitting that we, and we alone, are responsible for what we do in the area allotted to us, for which we can give no reason save that that is what we aim at, that these are the goals that are ours because we have chosen them – for there is and can be nothing else that we can appeal to, only, as Benjamin Constant once observed, the echo of our own prayers, wishes, laments, that come back to us from the brazen dome of an impersonal world as if they were voices from without. This is not far from the position of emotive ethics – all that was permitted by rigorous modern positivism – whereby, also, our political and moral judgements, so far as they involve values, describe nothing, although they may express, convey, incarnate attitudes of the most crucial importance to us, but not in the form of propositions, for these must be true or false; while ethical attitudes, political beliefs and allegiances, do not describe anything. Therefore they are not true or false, are only what they are, forms of life, intentions, choices, forms of vision, policies, states of mind or feeling or will – individual or collective, determined or free.


VII

In conclusion, there is this to be said: the new romantic transvaluation of values substituted the morality of motive for that of consequence, that of the inner life for that of effectiveness in the external world. What effect has this had upon the ideas of the man in the street, the unphilosophical members of Western societies? Profound, transforming, but not decisive. For it seems to me that the older morality, which judged the acts of men as did Aristotle, or the Utilitarians, or all the schools of objective morality (including such antinomians as the followers of Hume and Montesquieu, and Herder too), that is to say, to a large degree in terms of their consequences – this morality did not go under before this revolutionary wave. Upon what are our own political judgements founded? Do we truly believe that value judgements are not judgements at all, but arbitrary acts of self-commitment? Do we believe that the sciences of man are irrelevant to political purposes, that anthropology, psychology, sociology can instruct us only about means, about techniques? In Lenin's phrase, 'Who whom?'[1] Who gets what, where, when, how? Do we believe that since values collide there are no reasons for choosing one rather than another, so that if men, or groups of men, are possessed by different outlooks, that is the end of the matter, so that war between them is a more honourable proceeding (for those who believe in honour) than attempts to find an intermediate solution that fully satisfies the true beliefs of neither side?

The answer to this seems to me both yes and no. Kant once truly remarked (in an aside) that out of the crooked timber of humanity no straight thing was ever made.[2] We contrive to believe both in the morality of motive and in that of consequence. We admire effectiveness, beauty, intelligence, the natural virtues: like the Aristotelians, Utilitarians, Marxists, we think well of those who have, in fact, benefited mankind in terms of values that the great majority of men, for very long periods of time and in a great many places, have adopted as their own, and we admire them whatever their motive. But also, like liberals and existentialists (and I fear I must add nationalists and even Fascists), we admire the morality of motive too, we admire those who, whatever the anticipated consequences of their acts, are moved by ends that we and they value for their own sakes, without thinking of the consequences.

We admire men stirred by the lust for power or jealousy of others, or monomaniacal vanity – even though we may detest these characteristics – if they have brought about what we regard as benefits to mankind. We admire Peter the Great, Frederick the Great, or Napoleon, and, however morally low we rate their motives, we call them great, we study their lives and acts. Our view of human potentiality is profoundly affected by such study. We regard the views of those who, like Tolstoy, desire to minimise the part that they have played, or of those who, like H. G. Wells, wish to denigrate them because they were moved by ignoble motives, or followed inferior ends, as being eccentric, irrelevant, subjective, unhistorical. At the same time we view inquisitors and exterminators – Torquemada, John of Leiden or Lenin – even if we abhor

[1] V. I. Lenin, *Polnoe sobranie sochinenii*, vol. 44 (Moscow, 1964), p. 161.
[2] 'Idee zu einer allgemeinen Geschichte in weltbürgerlicher Absicht' (1784): *Kant's gesammelte Schriften* (Berlin, 1900– ) (hereafter KGS), vol. 8, p. 23, line 22.

their views, not merely as human agents of this or that degree of importance in causing historical change, but as human beings to whom we assign a positive moral (and political) value in virtue of the sincerity and intelligibility of their motives. We do not regard them merely as evil because they have caused widespread undeserved suffering, as the Utilitarians – James Mill or Bentham – would certainly have had us do, and as their disciples would today.

This is clearly not consistent; but it is the case. We are heirs to two traditions. The later of these has to a degree subverted the older; with the consequence that, in the face of those who stubbornly continue the older tradition, whether in the shape of Marxism, for example, or of the Roman Church, those who do not accept such doctrines complain of too much moral indifference to suffering caused by men to one another, too ruthless an objectivity. The majority of the civilised members of Western societies continue in attitudes that cause more logical than moral discomfort: we shift uneasily from one foot to the other, from motive to consequence, from estimate of character to estimate of achievement. For the development of this logically unsatisfactory but historically and psychologically enriched capacity for understanding men and societies, we have to thank the last great revolution in values and standards. No movement in human opinion has had a similar sweep and effect. It still awaits its historians: for unless it is grasped, no modern political movement appears to me wholly intelligible. This alone seems to me sufficient reason for paying attention to this extraordinary, at times sinister, phenomenon.

# ARTISTIC COMMITMENT

## A Russian Legacy

MY PURPOSE is twofold: first, to provide an illustration of a phenomenon in modern cultural history which seems to me interesting and important, but not often emphasised, perhaps because it is too self-evident; second, to offer a defence of some of the founding fathers of the Russian liberal intelligentsia against the false charge, too often made against them, that, however unwittingly, they forged some of the chains in which Soviet artists, particularly writers, were bound in our century. Let me begin with the first of these theses.

## I

More than one Russian critic in the nineteenth century observed that every idea of any consequence in Russian thought outside the natural sciences and other specialised disciplines – every general idea – came from abroad; that not a single philosophical or historical, social or artistic doctrine or outlook that had any life in it was born on Russian soil. This, I think, is broadly true: but what is more interesting, it seems to me, is that all these ideas, whatever their origin, fell in Russia upon a spiritual soil so welcoming, so fertile, that upon it they swiftly grew to vast, luxuriant shapes; and were thereby transformed.

The historical reasons for this are familiar enough. Because the number of educated Russians in the first half of the nineteenth century was small and culturally isolated from the mass of the population, and therefore forced to look for spiritual sustenance elsewhere, this, in its turn, generated a hunger for ideas – any ideas – on the part of this minority, an eagerness increased by many factors: by the slow but steady spread of education, until it reached socially discontented groups; by contact with Western liberal ideas through books and *salons*, but still more through visits to the West, especially since the march of the conquering armies to Paris in 1814–15; by the search for faith and ideologies to fill the vacuum left by the erosion of religion and the growing inadequacy of a naked medieval absolutism in a 'developing' country; and especially by the painful quest for a solution of the 'social question' – the wound created by the existence of the vast gulf that divided the privileged and the literate from the great mass of their oppressed, poverty-stricken and illiterate brothers, whose condition moved the human beings among them to a sense of indignation and intolerable personal guilt.

All this is familiar enough. What I wish to stress, however, is that the passionate, and often uncritical, enthusiasm with which new ideas are at times received in culturally backward regions infuses them with such emotion, hope and faith that in this new, more intensified, over-simplified state they grow more formidable than they were in their beginnings in their native land, where they jostled and collided with other doctrines and theories, forming a climate of ideas in which no single trend or tendency was dominant and irresistible. Transformed and vitalised by contact with the unexhausted Russian imagination – by being taken seriously by men resolved to practise what they believed – some of these ideas returned to the West, and made a vast impact upon it. They left it as secular, theoretical, abstract doctrines; they returned as fiery, sectarian, quasi-religious faiths. It was so, for example, with populism, which derived from Herder and the Germans, but in its Russian guise travelled far beyond central Europe, and has today become an explosive, world-wide movement; it was so with historicism, particularly in its Marxist form; it was so, even more, with the conception of the Communist Party, which, however closely deduced from principles enunciated by Marx or Engels, was turned by Lenin into an instrument not dreamt of by the founding fathers.

I should like to call this the 'rebound' or 'boomerang effect'. I do not know whether there is any significant parallel for it in the past: Greek Stoicism, transformed by the Romans, did not return to transform the world of the Eastern Mediterranean whence it came; nor can it be plausibly maintained that America's influence outside her borders has led to a second conquest of Europe by the ideas of Locke or Montesquieu or Puritanism or the common law. It seems, rather, that the interplay between Russia and the West has something *sui generis* in it, despite the fact that the effect of

Western ideas, when they impinge on culturally backward countries, is itself neither unique nor unfamiliar. It is one of these
boomerang effects that I should like to discuss, namely the
phenomenon of artistic, and in particular literary, commitment, or
*engagement* as it came to be called, which has dominated so much
of Russian thought and art, and through this medium has had so
profound an effect everywhere in the world, although by now its
influence may have passed beyond its peak.

Of course, the doctrine that the artist is socially responsible –
responsible to society – for what he does is very ancient. Plato,
who is, I suppose, the first European writer to raise the issue (as he
was the first to raise most issues of permanent interest in the West),
took this for granted. In the *Ion* the poet is the inspired visionary
who knows the truth and speaks it under supernatural influence. In
the *Republic* he is a gifted liar who does damage. In either case, his
social importance is not denied. Nor, so far as I know, did anyone
explicitly deny or minimise the artist's power and responsibility in
the later classical world or the Middle Ages. The writer, or indeed
any artist, must be either a teacher of virtue or of a skill, or a
glorifier of a custom or a regime, or a provider of pleasure, or an
inspired seer, or, at the very least, a craftsman who provides useful
knowledge or utters useful words. Even in the Renaissance, which
was not inclined towards utilitarian doctrines, the artist at his
highest is semi-divine, *sicut deus*, because he creates a world
alongside that of God, because he informs his work of art with his
own creative soul, as God informs the real world; and so creation is
marvellous, because it is a form of being at one with the *anima
mundi*, the spirit that for Neoplatonic Christianity informs and
moves the universe. Dante, Tasso, Milton were seen by their
admirers, and perhaps saw themselves, as divinely inspired seers;
others were conceived as providers of delight – Boccaccio, Rabe-
lais, Shakespeare probably saw themselves in this way. All art has a
purpose beyond itself: to tell the truth, to instruct, to please, to
heal, to transfigure men; or to serve God by embellishing his
universe and by moving men's minds and hearts to fulfil his (or
nature's) purposes.

The doctrine of art for art's sake, and the corresponding denial
of the social responsibility or function of the artist, the doctrine
that the artist creates as the bird sings on the bough, as the lily
bursts into flower, to all appearance for no ulterior purpose, and
that the artist is consequently a child of nature, entitled to be

oblivious, if he so chooses, of the precarious constructions of men that surround him – the notion, that is, that the justification of art is art itself – is a late doctrine, a reaction to the older, traditional view grown oppressive or, at any rate, no longer convincing. The very notion of ends in themselves – of a goal pursued solely and purely for its own sake – is not to be found, so far as I know, in the classical world or, outside it, in the great religions of the West. The universe and man's activity in it are seen as part of some single unitary pattern, however it is conceived: a static harmony outside time and space, or a cosmic drama moving towards some apocalyptic or transcendent climax; or in more humanistic and less teleological terms, as the search for happiness or truth, or knowledge or justice or love, or the realisation of man's creative capacities – some great monistic scheme of total self-fulfilment. The notion of an end to be pursued for its own sake, irrespective of the consequences, no matter whether or not such pursuit accords with other activities, or the course of nature, or the structure of the world – that springs from a strain in Protestantism (and, it may be, Hebraism) first made fully explicit in Germany in the eighteenth century, perhaps even before Kant. Once the principle of duty for duty's sake had been enunciated, the spell of unity was broken, and acceptance of a plurality of independent, perhaps even incompatible, goals became a possible ideology. Beauty for beauty's sake, power for power's sake, pleasure, glory, knowledge, the expression of the individual's unique personality and temperament – all these (or their opposites) could be conceived as ends in themselves, independent of one another; to be pursued not because they were objectively recognised as indispensable ingredients in some universally accepted human purpose, but because they were one's own – the individual's, or those of a nation, a Church, a culture, a race. The rise of self-expression as the dominant category, whether individual or collective, as against the quest for objective truth to which the seeker must submit, is at the heart alike of romanticism, nationalism, élitism, anarchism, populism.

This is the soil from which, in due course, there sprang the doctrine of art for art's sake. It was born as a protest of the artist against attempts to harness him to some extraneous purpose he found alien or constricting or degrading. This is the position of Kant, Goethe, Schelling, the Schlegels. It is anti-utilitarian and anti-philistine, it is directed against efforts on the part of Jacobins, or the *Directoire*, or Napoleon, to mobilise artists, and, particularly during the Restoration, to curb subversive ideas and direct thought and art into politically or religiously desirable channels. After 1830 it takes the form of a vehement outcry against the commercialisation of art, the domination of the bourgeois consumer, the conception of the artist as a purveyor for a mass market, the rejection of the hardly veiled demand that he sell his integrity, his gifts and his independence for gain or fame or popularity or official favour. The romantic revolt against uniformity, laws, discipline, conformity to any rules not freely self-imposed (or, better still, spontaneously generated for his own ends by the creative artist) becomes fused with the denunciation of the brutal levelling processes of industrialism, and its effects – the regimentation, degradation and dehumanisation of men. The heroic images in the mythology of protest are those of the lonely artist whose real life is within him, in his art, of Chatterton, Lenz, Beethoven, Byron, men contemptuous or defiant in the face of the solid ranks of the enemies of art and culture – the corrupt and philistine public, the barbarian mob, the Churches, the police, the military jackboot. Even such lions of romanticism as Scott, Balzac, Hugo are denounced by the more extreme wing of the 'pure' for betraying their sacred calling, prostituting their art to the taste of the masses, writing for money or for fame, like Dumas or Eugène Sue.

The philosophical basis for this is provided by critics and professors under the spell of Kant's proclamation of disinterestedness as a condition of all ultimate values – truth, rightness, beauty. This is the message of the Parisian lawgivers, Sacy, Quatremère de Quincy, and later of Cousin and Jouffroy and, indeed, of Benjamin Constant, who looked on the Jacobin Terror and the regimentation of the individual as a nightmare, and spoke of 'art for art's sake' as early as 1804. If, in the beginning, the enemy of the free artist was the establishment – the State, the Church, the market, tradition – it was not long before a second front was opened against him from the Left: from the early collectivist movement, inspired by Saint-Simon and Fourier, which from its attack on the irresponsibility of the frivolous, hedonistic eighteenth century moved on to attack its nineteenth-century emulators. Schiller had said that in a divided society, where men have wandered from their true, integral souls that once were whole and harmonious, it was the function of art to avenge insulted nature, and seek to restore men and societies to themselves. Only art, only the imagination, can salve the wounds inflicted by the division of labour, the specialisation of function, by the growth of mass society, the increasing mechanisation of man.

The function of art, therefore, becomes therapeutic, the recreation of unbroken men. Even Goethe, with all his hatred of anything faintly utilitarian, tends towards this Rousseau-ish view, the idea of art as *Bildung* – the formation of integral human character. Saint-Simon went further. Stupidity, ignorance, irresponsibility, idleness caused the great disaster of the Jacobin Revolution – the destruction, by the brutal mob, of intellect and genius, the triumph of the forces of darkness. Common sense, even genius, is not enough. Society must be rebuilt on new, 'adamantine', rational foundations provided by social experts – men who understand the nature and goals of social processes: artists have an essential part to play in the peaceful reconstruction of society. For an artist to participate in the creation of a new rational society is not to divert his art towards some alien goal.

The Saint-Simonians were the first group of thinkers to develop something like a coherent doctrine or an all-embracing ideology: art, they taught, is nothing if it is not communication; it is intended to express a man's consciousness of his needs and his ideals, conditioned by those of the class to which he belongs, which are in their turn determined by the particular stage of the technological development of the society to which it belongs. Since all expression in words or other media is inevitably an attempt to act, to convince, exhort, denounce, expose, warn, to put forward a particular vision, this must be rendered conscious, and used to serve a coherent ideal of life founded on true, that is, scientific, understanding of the historical process. Such understanding alone can determine the true goals of a given society and the proper parts to be played by this or that individual or body of men if they are to avoid illusions, unmask false prophets, and so fulfil their potentialities to the fullest degree, in the social context in which they cannot, in any case, help living and acting. This is the doctrine later adapted, developed and codified by the Marxist schools. Naturally enough those of Saint-Simon's disciples who discussed the function of art, especially Buchez, Pierre Leroux and their allies, looked on remoteness from, or neutrality about, social problems not merely as frivolity or egoism, but as being itself a moral attitude and a vicious one – as disdain for values which the artist ignores or rejects either because he is blind to them, or too weak or cowardly or morally distorted to face the social reality of his time, and act in the light of what he sees.[1]

This is the faith of European radicals of the 1830s. Hence the attacks on eighteenth-century literature, of which Carlyle's denunciations were only the most violent and notorious. Young France, Young Germany, Young Italy, even Wordsworth and Coleridge in England, and of course Shelley, were steeped in the religion of art as a form of salvation, personal and political, public and private. Art is the sacred function of spiritually gifted beings – poets, thinkers, seers – who possess, as Schelling taught, a deeper insight into reality than scientists or politicians or ordinary, bourgeois philistines. The idea of social responsibility which this conferred is the substance of the left-wing attack of the 1830s upon the doctrine which held that the artist was either wholly independent or he was nothing, that he must be dedicated to the light within him and to nothing else, whether or not it is recognised by others, or has social, or moral, or religious, or political implications, as conceived by the expounders of the traditional outlook.

It is against this Saint-Simonian conception of the artist as a priest of a social religion, as well as against cruder pressure for social conformity, that the famous diatribe of the most eloquent defender of the new doctrine of art for art's sake, the poet and novelist Théophile Gautier, is directed. It is to be found in the famous Preface to his novel *Mademoiselle de Maupin*:

No, imbeciles! No! Fools and cretins, a book will not make a plate of soup; a novel is not a pair of boots; a sonnet is not a syringe; a drama is not a railway – those forms of civilisation which have caused humanity to march on the road to progress.

By all the bowels of all the popes, past, present and future, no! Ten thousand times no!

[1] 'The artists of present-day society', wrote X. Joncières in *Le Globe* (8 April 1832), '... have never understood the alliance of poetry and society. We, on the other hand, wish to link everything to politics in its broadest sense ... We are quickly relating all to it which comes into our hands. Literature is there and it must obtain citizenship rights and occupy a place in our political life.' Compare this from another contributor to *Le Globe* (10 March 1831): 'The function of art, understood in its sacred sense, is to accompany, anticipate and incite mankind ceaselessly in its march to a more and more beautiful destiny sometimes with harmonious music, at others with a rough and strict voice.' These passages are cited and translated in George G. Iggers, *The Cult of Authority* (The Hague, 1958), p. 173.

You cannot make a hat out of a metonymy, and you cannot make a simile in the form of a bedroom slipper, and you cannot use an antithesis as an umbrella ... An ode is, I have a feeling, too light a garment for the winter ...[1]

Gautier's philippic, directed though it may have been against all forms of positivism, utilitarianism, socialism, and in particular against what in his day was called 'realism', and later 'naturalism', was merely the loudest salvo in a controversy which has from that day never ceased. The insistence that art was not art unless it was useless; that the beautiful was an end in itself, and so too was the ugly, the monstrous, anything but the *juste milieu* of the July monarchy, the world of bankers, manufacturers, swindlers, careerists, or the stupid or corrupt conformist majority; that to use art as a social or political instrument for ends external to it was to prostitute it – this view was echoed by Musset, by Mérimée, and in his later days by Heine, who, despite his Saint-Simonian phase and the political radicalism of his young days, reserved some of his bitterest gibes for those who advocated the conscription of art to the service of political purposes. Flaubert and Baudelaire, Maupassant and the Goncourts, Parnassians and aesthetes fought under this banner against the advocates of social concern – preachers and prophets, naturalists, socialists, moralists, nationalists, clericals, romantic Utopians. But the most passionate and, in the event, the most influential counter-attack on the doctrine of pure art came from the latecomers to the feast, the untutored barbarians beyond the Eastern marches – Russian writers and Russian critics – still, at that period, almost totally unknown in the West.

## II

Russia had, in her day, fallen under the spell of the doctrine of art for art's sake. Pushkin in 1830, in his marvellous poem 'To the Poet', says: 'You are King: live alone. Take the free road wherever your free spirit takes you.'[2] 'The purpose of poetry is poetry,' he declares, 'as Delvig says (if he did not steal it from someone else).

---

[1] The novel was published in 1835, the Preface dated 1834. This passage appears on p. 19 in the edition published in Paris in 1880.

[2] A. S. Pushkin, *Sobranie sochinenii*, 10 vols (Moscow, 1974–8) (hereafter SS), ii 225.

Ryleev's *Meditations* always have an aim and always miss.'[1] This attitude (of which the most celebrated expression is, of course, the credo of the poet in his 'The Poet and the Mob') holds not of Pushkin alone, but of the brilliant group of aristocratic amateurs, his companions, born and largely rooted in the eighteenth century. Their sympathies for the Decembrist movement did not, for the most part, in spite of Ryleev and perhaps Küchelbecker, entail the ideal of a civic art. Contrast with this the words written a few years after Pushkin's death by Belinsky, who, whatever else may be thought of him, spoke for an entire stratum of Russian society when he said:

> No one save men of limited vision, or men who are spiritually un-grown-up, can order the poet to be obliged to sing hymns to virtue or punish sin by writing a satire; but every intelligent man has the right to demand that a poet's poetry either give him answers to the questions of the time or at least be filled with the sorrow of these weighty, insoluble questions.[2]

This is the opening shot in a controversy which raises profound issues and whose day is anything but over. Turgenev in his memoirs gives a touching and amusing description of Belinsky pacing up and down as he read Pushkin's disdainful lines, addressed by the poet to the mob: 'The kitchen pot is dearer to you / Because in it you cook your food.'[3] 'Yes,' says Belinsky, glaring and striding rapidly from corner to corner – 'yes, I do cook my food in it, and my family's food and another pauper's food. I must feed my family and myself before I prostrate myself in front of stone effigies, even if they are carved by some marvellous super-Phidias: and let all your indignant gentryfolk and versifiers go hang, one and all!'[4] His violent anti-aestheticism in the 1840s represented, as so often, a complete and painful repudiation of his own earlier views. He had once believed with (as he supposed) Fichte, and before and after that with Schelling, that art constituted self-liberation, the escape of the spirit from empirical reality into a

[1] ibid. ix 146.

[2] V. G. Belinsky, *Polnoe sobranie sochinenii*, 13 vols (Moscow, 1953–9) (hereafter PSS), vii 345.

[3] Pushkin, SS ii 167.

[4] I. S. Turgenev, *Polnoe sobranie sochinenii i pisem*, 28 vols (Moscow/Leningrad, 1960–8) (hereafter PSSP), *Sochineniya* xiv 45–6.

pure sphere of spiritual freedom in which the human soul could contemplate the ideal which even the basest creature reflected in its soul. Capacity to rise to this vision, beyond the spectacle of chaos, ugliness, conflict – the accidents of the everyday world, of the senses – was the attribute of an élite of free spirits, able to contemplate true reality.

Belinsky's writings are, in the late 1830s, filled with passionate, fanatical, Neoplatonic aestheticism, as refracted through Schelling, and preached to Belinsky (who had little German) by his mentors, Stankevich and Bakunin. Nor did his conversion to Hegelian quietism in 1839 or 1840, which he maintained with so much agony of spirit, greatly modify his view of the independence, the self-justifying character, of all true art. If 'the real is the rational'; if (as Hegel's anticipator, Pope, held) all evil is but good misunderstood; if to understand something is to grasp its rational necessity, and therefore its justification; if reality is intelligible as an all-embracing pattern of the progress of the spirit, so that what on a short view seems brutal, ugly, unjust, repulsive will be seen, if viewed from a higher standpoint, to be an indispensable element in a more inclusive harmony achieved by the moral spirit in its dialectical ascent (that is, the unending effort of the spirit to understand both itself and the external world, which is but its own true self split off, alienated, from itself) – if all this is so, then all protests against the social order, all attempts to direct art towards the immediate improvement of the human lot, are vulgar, short-sighted, premature, ineffective, un-grown-up, a misconception of the deepest interests of the human spirit. Hence his sharp denunciations of the Schiller of the early plays, of Victor Hugo (who after the suppression of his *Le Roi s'amuse* swung back from the Right to the Left opposition), George Sand, Leroux and the whole school of social criticism and social art in France. In a similar (somewhat Burkean) spirit, he denounced Griboedov and other Russian critics and carpers who failed to rise to a height whence rational spirit can perceive why what is must be as it is, why it is irrational to wish to alter it overnight to suit childishly Utopian, capricious, subjective whims. The contents of true poetry, he says in 1840, 'are the problems not of the day, but of the ages; not of a country, but of the world; not of a party, but of mankind'.[1] And in the same essay

[1] PSS iii 399.

he writes that art 'serves a society by expressing its own consciousness – it serves it not as something that exists by and for itself – its
purpose, its reason, lies in itself'.[1] There is nothing here that
Gautier or Flaubert would have found amiss. This was the view, at
this date, not only of Belinsky, but of the philosophical circle
round Stankevich (whose last year of life this was), of Turgenev no
less than of Bakunin; of Katkov, Botkin, Panaev, of the Slavophils
no less than the Westerners: all but the Saint-Simonian hotheads
like Herzen and Ogarev.

Yet it is not to be wondered at if a man of Belinsky's
temperament and, perhaps, origins did not long remain indifferent
to the claims of social criticism. He did violently reject Hegelian
acceptance of a morally intolerable reality – 'reconciliation' to a
world of oppression, injustice, brutality and human misery, in the
name of a harmonious reality, beyond the stars, in which all things
are seen to be rationally necessary, and, to the wise, wholly
intelligible. Whatever offers a man no comfort when he is in
torment, gives no answer to those who cry for justice, is for him,
now, a deception and a mockery. Even while he was forcing
himself to stifle his doubts during his Hegelian moment, he could
not swallow the view of art that the master expounded in his
lectures on aesthetics. 'The art of our time', he wrote in 1843, 'is . . .
the realisation in aesthetic form of modern consciousness, of
modern thought about the meaning and purpose of life, the path of
mankind, the eternal truths of existence.'[2] Yet only 'professional
art lovers' can be satisfied by art for art's sake.[3] 'Like truth and
goodness, beauty is its own end';[4] 'To miss this moment is never
to know what art is. But to stay in this position is to have a one-
sided notion of it.'[5] He goes further: 'Our age is especially hostile
to this tendency in art. It resolutely denies art for art's sake, beauty
for beauty's sake.'[6]

These quotations directly echo the 'committed' Saint-Simonian
position in the great controversy which then divided the Paris
journals. They show that by 1843, in the essay on Nikitenko's
'Address on Criticism' – what he calls his vigorous philippic

[1] ibid. 397.
[2] PSS vi 280.
[3] ibid. 277.
[4] PSS iv 497.
[5] PSS vi 276.
[6] ibid. 277.

against the aesthetes – the die is cast: 'Reality is the first and last word of our time.'[1] George Sand, whom he had once rejected with Hugo and Schiller and Griboedov as a shallow protester, blind to the majestic vision of the slow unfolding of rational reality, is now declared to be 'surely the Joan of Arc of our time, star of salvation, prophetess of a magnificent future'.[2] He became a devoted, uncritical admirer of her art and her lyrical socialist populism; and not he alone. Herzen's novel *Who is to Blame?* was written under her direct influence. There was a time when Turgenev, Saltykov, even Dostoevsky, regarded her as a towering genius. Pisemsky got into trouble with the censor for dangerous views evidently inspired by George Sand's *Jacques*; even the 'pure aesthete' Druzhinin owed her a debt in his novel *Polin'ka Saks*; the whole of Young Russia in the Moscow and Petersburg of Nicholas I appears to have been at her feet. Yet this did not lead to capitulation to some species of proto-Marxism, or even to proto-Zolaism. In 1843 Belinsky – then at the height of his infatuation with the Paris socialists – declared that art gains nothing from being told that it is intelligent, truthful, profound, but unpoetical, and again, that the ideal is 'not an exaggeration, a lie, a childish fantasy; it is a fact of reality as it is, but a fact not copied from reality, but passed through the poet's fantasy, illuminated by the light of very general (not isolated, particular and contingent) significance, *"raised to a pearl of creation"*[3] and therefore more like itself, more faithful to itself than the most slavish copy of reality is to its original'.[4] Art for art's sake may be a fallacy, but if a work of art is not art if it does not pass the aesthetic test, and no amount of morally worthy sentiment or intellectual acuteness will save it.

This conviction he never abandoned. Four years later, during one of his most radical periods, he compares Herzen's novel *Who is to Blame?* with one of Goncharov's novels published at the same time. Herzen 'is first and foremost a philosopher,' Belinsky says, 'and only a little bit of a poet'.[5] In this respect, the most complete contrast with him is offered by Goncharov, the author of *An Ordinary Story*. The latter is a poet and an artist and no more. He

[1] PSS vi 268.
[2] PSS xii 115.
[3] An image from Gogol's *Dead Souls*, chapter 7.
[4] PSS vi 526.
[5] PSS x 326.

feels neither love nor hatred for the characters he creates; they do not amuse or irritate him; he offers no moral lessons either to them or to the reader. His attitude is this: 'if they are in trouble, that is their look-out – no concern of mine'.[1]

> Of all contemporary writers he alone, only he alone approaches the ideal of pure art, while all the others have departed from it immeasurably – and in so doing prosper. All contemporary writers have something over and above talent, and this something is more important than talent, and constitutes its strength; Mr Goncharov possesses nothing but talent; he much more than anyone today is an artist-poet. His talent is not of the first order, but it is powerful and remarkable.[2]

And again:

> In Iskander's [that is, Herzen's] case what dominates is always the idea – he knows in advance what and why he is writing – he depicts a scene from reality with marvellous fidelity only in order to say his own word about it, to pronounce some kind of judgement. Mr Goncharov paints his figures, characters, scenes in the first place to satisfy his own inner demands, to extract pleasure from his own capacity for painting; to discuss, judge, draw moral consequences – that he must leave to his readers. Iskander's pictures ... are remarkable not so much for the fidelity of his painting, for the skill of his brush, as for the depth of his understanding of the reality he depicts; they are remarkable for their realism more than for their poetical truth. What makes them attractive is a style which is not so much poetic as executed with intelligence, thought, humour, wit, which are always arresting because of their originality and novelty ... For Goncharov, poetry is the primary and only factor.[3]

Goncharov tells us in his reminiscences that Belinsky sometimes attacked him for showing no anger, no irritation, no subjective feeling:

> 'For you it is all one, a scoundrel, a fool, a monster or a decent kindly character – you paint them all the same: neither love nor hate for anybody!' He used to say this with a kind of good-natured fury, and one day put his hands affectionately on my shoulders and added,

[1] ibid.
[2] ibid. 326–7.
[3] ibid. 343–4.

almost in a whisper, 'and this is good, this is necessary, this is the sign of an artist' – as if afraid that he might be overheard and accused of sympathy with an uncommitted writer.[1]

Perhaps Belinsky preferred Herzen, but Goncharov was, in his view, an artist and Herzen, in the end, was not.

Belinsky's position is crystal clear: 'No matter how beautiful the ideas in a poem, how powerfully it echoes the problems of the hour, if it lacks poetry, there can be no beautiful thought in it, and no problems either, and all that one may say about it is that it is a fine intention badly executed.'[2] This is so because the artist's commitment 'must be not only in the head, but above all in the heart, in the blood of the writer ... An idea ... which has not passed through one's own nature, has not received the stamp of one's personality, is dead capital not only for poetry, but for any literary activity.'[3] But he cannot rest in this. We have already noted his declaration in his essay of 1844 on Pushkin: 'every intelligent man has the right to demand that a poet's poetry either give him answers to the questions of the time or at least be filled with the sorrow of these weighty, insoluble questions'.[4] This is only a little less extreme than the notorious verdict of 1845: 'In our age art is not a master, but a slave. It serves interests outside itself.'[5] Even though he adds that this applies only to 'critical' ages – the Saint-Simonian name for transitional periods when the old is grown intolerable, and is undermined and doomed, and the new is not yet – it is nevertheless a genuine *cri de coeur*. It is only a violent version of his words in 1843: 'our time craves for convictions, it is tormented by hunger for the truth'[6] and 'our age is all questioning, all questing, all a search and yearning for the truth'.[7]

This is the earliest and most poignant formulation of the disquiet and, at times, agonised self-questioning that tormented the Russian intelligentsia for ever after. Henceforth no Russian writer could feel entirely free from this moral attitude: even if he rejected the demand, he felt obliged to come to terms, to settle his account,

---

[1] I. A. Goncharov, *Sobranie sochinenii*, 6 vols (Moscow, 1972), vi 427.
[2] PSS x 303.
[3] PSS x 312.
[4] loc. cit. (p. 202 above, note 2).
[5] PSS ix 78.
[6] PSS vi 267.
[7] ibid. 269.

with it. Yet in 1846 Belinsky tells us apropos of Pushkin's 'The Stone Guest' that it is a marvellous masterpiece, that to true art lovers it must seem 'artistically the best and highest creation of Pushkin', 'the pearl of Pushkin's creations, the richest and most magnificent diamond in his poetic crown', and adds that this kind of art cannot be popular, it is made for the few, but these few will love it with 'passion' and 'enthusiasm', and he counts himself among these few.[1] Those contradictions, or what appear to be such, multiply towards the end of his life. In the review of Russian literature of 1847, from which I have already quoted – a stupendous essay which is in a sense his swan song – appear the most famous lines of all:

> To take away from art the right to serve the public interest is not to elevate it but to debase it, because it means to deprive it of its most vital force – of thought – to transform it into the object of some kind of sybaritic enjoyment, the plaything of lazy idlers. It even means to kill it, as the sorry condition of painting in our time bears witness. This art, as if it did not notice the life that is seething around it, has closed its eyes to everything that is alive, contemporary, actual, and looks for inspiration only to the lifeless past, seeks ready-made ideals from it, ideals to which people long ago became indifferent, which interest no one any longer, which do not warm, do not inspire living sympathy in any one.[2]

But a little further on he observes, in a passage part of which I have already quoted:

> A good many people are fascinated now by the magic word 'commitment' [napravlenie], people think that is all that matters, and do not understand that in the sphere of art, in the first place, no commitment is worth anything at all unless there is talent, and in the second place, that commitment itself must be not only in the head, but above all in the heart, in the blood of the writer, it must above all be a feeling, an instinct, and only then perhaps a conscious idea – this commitment itself must be born, just as art itself must be. An idea that one has read in a book or heard, even if one has understood it quite correctly, but which has not passed through one's own nature, has not received the stamp of one's personality, is dead capital ... if you have no poetic

[1] PSS vii 569.
[2] PSS x 311.

talent ... your ideas and purposes will remain rhetorical common-places.[1]

The images or words of a true writer which have 'passed through his own nature and received the stamp of his personality' – even the most formalist critic would not be required to deny the claim of these to being works of art, even if they treat the 'accursed questions' – the *proklyatye voprosy* – of the day.[2] But Belinsky appears to go further. He asserts that social conditions impose specific obligations upon the writer: that in such times he is not free to compose purely for his own enjoyment – that hedonism is not enough, that the reader has the right to demand that burning social questions be discussed. And even though Belinsky may have said this only once, there is his fatal pronouncement that in terrible days like ours art must be a servant, serve outside purposes – the very enormity which drove the defenders of pure art in France to such violent and surely merited counter-attacks. And yet Belinsky is clear that Goethe's art is even for him art *par excellence*: like all great art it reflects the deepest tendencies of its time. But it has no *napravlenie*; nor has 'The Stone Guest', the 'pearl' of Pushkin's creation. As for *Onegin* – the 'encyclopaedia of Russian life'[3] – its 'direction' is, if anything, mistaken: Pushkin is denounced for making Tatiana continue with a loveless marriage to her husband, for preaching conformity to the false values of her society, much as Anna Ahkmatova once complained that Tolstoy killed Anna Karenina to satisfy not his own moral code – for he knew better – but that of his Moscow aunts. Yet Belinsky does not dream for a moment of denying the supreme genius of Pushkin's purest, least

[1] ibid. 312. Cf. PSS vii 311: 'With the man who is not a poet by nature, the idea he conceives may be profound, true, even holy, but all the same his work will turn out petty, sham, false, distorted, dead.'

[2] Although 'voprosy' was widely used by the 1830s to refer to the social questions that preoccupied the Russian intelligentsia, it seems that the specific phrase 'proklyatye voprosy' was coined in 1858 by Mikhail L. Mikhailov when he used it to render 'die verdammten Fragen' in his translation of Heine's poem 'Zum Lazarus' (1853/4): see 'Stikhotvoreniya Geine', *Sovremennik* 1858 No 3, p. 125; and p. 225 in *Heinrich Heines Sämtliche Werke*, ed. Oskar Walzel, vol. 3 (Leipzig, 1913). Alternatively, Mikhailov may have been capitalising on the fact that an existing Russian expression fitted Heine's words like a glove, but I have not yet seen an earlier published use of it. Ed.

[3] PSS vii 503.

socially 'directed' poetry; he does not complain of Pushkin's aestheticism.

What then is he saying? Is he the muddled, over-excitable, half-educated student, expelled from the university for lack of mental capacity, a mere bundle of burning but uncoordinated, undisciplined emotions, a living proof that sincerity and vehemence are not enough, the pathetic autodidact that later critics – Volynsky, Aikhenvald, Chizhevsky – have represented him as being? Such critics say that he received his ideas ready-made from others, that he poured them out without thought or restraint or organisation, as they came, helter-skelter; that he was a man who should, perhaps, be forgiven because he had to work in desperate haste to earn his daily bread, though his views do not thereby become entitled to serious respect; a decent, even noble, soul, but not an authority, not even an original figure; at most a symptom of the intellectually half-baked, anxiety-ridden youth of his time, a critic not fit to touch the hem of Schlegel's or Sainte-Beuve's or even Gershenzon's garment. So, too, in our own day he has, at times, been charged with originating, or at any rate creating conditions for, the dreary utilitarian or didactic criticism, or the crude and violent onslaughts on the theory and practice of art as an end in itself, which came pouring out from his epigoni and ended in the government inspectors of the Soviet literature of our own time.

This is, in effect, the view of the contemporary American critic who, in my view, has written the most perceptive and original work on this subject, Rufus Mathewson, whose *The Positive Hero in Russian Literature*[1] strikes me, even when I disagree with it, as a masterpiece of critical penetration. Yet I do not think that Mathewson's verdict that Belinsky was neither authoritarian nor a totalitarian, but that he was indispensable to the emergence of both, is just.[2] What Belinsky was doing, in effect, was not to deny, even at his most violent and anti-aesthetic, that art was art, to be judged by aesthetic criteria. The contrast he draws between Goncharov and Herzen seems to me, in this respect, crucial. He is moved by Herzen, he accepts his *napravlenie* with all his heart, he has no particular sympathy for Goncharov's point of view; but it is Goncharov who is declared to be the artist, and not Herzen. And

[1] Rufus W. Mathewson, *The Positive Hero in Russian Literature*, 2nd ed. (Stanford, 1975).

[2] ibid., p. 42.

his decisive service to Russian literature – the crowning of Pushkin, the celebration of Gogol, the discovery of Dostoevsky, Goncharov, Turgenev, the final sweeping out of the way of the Kukolniks, Marlinskys, Zagoskins, Senkovskys – this famous and literally epoch-making operation was conducted without reference to the social concerns of these writers, without use, conscious or unconscious, of the criterion which Mathewson brilliantly formulates for distinguishing the radical position from the liberal: the former viewing the writer as a function of his ideology, as opposed to the latter – the view of ideology as a function of the individual temperament and personality of the writer.[1]

Of course Belinsky was socially concerned, no one more so; and he doubtless did want the best artists of his time to respond morally to the social reality of which they were necessarily more conscious, to which they were more sensitive, than others. He may have preferred Goncharov not to be so cool and detached an observer of the moral and social attributes of his characters, and supposed, rightly or wrongly, that profound moral concern does not necessarily restrict artistic achievement. He knew, and he said, that Grigorovich was an inferior artist, even while he praised him for revealing the horrors of the life of the peasant; he would have preferred Pushkin to have broken from what he regarded as the conventional morality of his class and rank and education. All this is so. But he is never, it seems to me, betrayed by these concerns – which I admit I do not find wholly unsympathetic – into denying or misrepresenting the artistic quality of the writers whom he analyses, some of whom he did, after all, discover before anyone else.

Belinsky's mistakes seem to me to be mainly errors of taste rather than expressions of social or political or moral bias; he does not artificially promote progressives at the expense of reactionaries, conservatives, vacillating liberals or uncommitted neutrals. Goethe's *Faust* is for him the expression of the spirit of its age and society because it is a great work of art: it is not a great work of art because its author has given it a conscious social direction. Belinsky felt profound contempt for Goethe's chilly character and his conformist, timid, conservative life, but this did not for a moment cause him to doubt Goethe's genius in contrast to the inferior gifts of such socially committed writers, concerned with the insulted

[1] ibid., pp. 94–5.

and the oppressed, as, say, Hugo or Eugène Sue or Grigorovich, even if he did, like everyone else, vastly overestimate the gifts of George Sand. Mathewson rightly supposes that the doctrine of social commitment is artistically repressive, if only because it works against problematic, ambivalent art. He quotes Chekhov to the effect that the business of the artist is to state the problem fairly before the reader, not to provide solutions[1] – precisely what Belinsky supposed Goncharov to be doing. In the last analysis Belinsky does not demand of the artist anything save the gift of creation and authenticity, the investigation and expression in images of whatever is most real in his own experience. He condemns only what seems to him falsification: for example the substitution for this reality of idylls, fantasies, pseudo-classical pastiche, inflation, extravagance, archaism – all evasions of anything that has not been 'lived through' by the writer. Hence the occasional furies against romantic antiquarianism, enthusiasm for regional cultures – for him these are desperate expeditions to remote or exotic corners of life, anything to avoid self-knowledge. And this does entail a morality of art, the notion of the artist as in some sense responsible – as being on oath to tell the truth. But this is not tantamount to tolerating, let alone inviting, social or political control or even state patronage of art, even to the degree that Sainte-Beuve, of all people, pressed it on Napoleon III.

Let me go further: Belinsky's view does commit him to the belief that art is a voice speaking, a form of communication between one human being and another, or between anonymous groups of men who created the Eddas or the temples of Angkor Vat. This genuinely contradicts the rival view, of which perhaps Gautier is as good a spokesman as any, that the whole purpose of the artist is to make a beautiful object, whether it be an epic poem or a silver box, and that the artist's personality, his motives, his life, his concerns, his character, the social or psychological courses which shape him, are altogether irrelevant to the work of art itself; for, as T. S. Eliot believed, it lives by its own radiance. This is certainly what the classical critics of the seventeenth or eighteenth century believed, a doctrine which, in various forms, Baudelaire and Flaubert, Mallarmé and Eliot, Pater and Proust, and indeed Goethe himself consistently defended. It does not lack for defenders today.

[1] ibid., p. 93: the passage is from a letter of Chekhov to A. S. Suvorin, 27 October 1888 (Mathewson gives the wrong date).

This to Belinsky was a disastrous fallacy: but not for the reasons that animate Freudians, or Marxists, or cognate schools today. Belinsky believed that man is one, and not compounded of compartments or roles. If what a man says in one capacity is incompatible with what he says in another, then there is something that has been falsified or, at any rate, trivialised; turned into a mechanical or conventional gesture. If what a man says, it does not matter in what capacity – as an artist, a judge, a soldier, a chimney-sweep – would be rendered false or insincere if he uttered it in some other capacity – as a father, a revolutionary, a lover – then it is false or shallow in its original context. There is no region in which a man is exempt from responsibility as a man because he is merely exercising a function or a *métier* or performing a part. If you choose to suppress the truth, to substitute fantasies, to adulterate your material, to play on human responses like an instrument, if you choose to excite, amuse, frighten, attract, you are turning your gifts into a means for the acquisition of power or pleasure or profit, and this is a betrayal of your humanity to politics – politics in some base and odious sense – an unscrupulous trampling on, or at least evasion of, what you and all men know to be the true goals of mankind.

Art is not journalism and it is not moral instruction. But the fact that it is art does not absolve it, or rather the artist, from accountability. Nor is artistic activity a set of garments which one can don and doff at will: it is the expression of an undivided nature, or it is nothing. To be a creative genius and a philistine is not impossible – the morality of *Hermann and Dorothea*, or of *The Elective Affinities*, have demonstrated this in Goethe's case, and so did Hegel's personal character and life. What alone matters is what the work of art expresses, whether it is the fruit of conscious organisation or of a dark instinct: for the work *is* its creator, his truest voice, himself. Shakespeare, Milton, Dickens, Raphael, Gogol are to him their works; their private lives do not directly concern him: only the vision of life that they carry, their depth, their validity, their relation to the central problems that have agonised men at all times.

This position, which after 1842–3 he never again abandons, derives from Saint-Simon or his disciples rather than from Feuerbach. Its ultimate source is Schiller's conception of the artist as the avenger of insulted nature, the restorer of the integral human being whom convention has distorted or destroyed – that, and August

Wilhelm Schlegel's image of him as a kind of burning-glass in which the deepest and most characteristic tendencies of his society and age are collected, crystallised, and translated into an intense and quintessential expression of reality, which the reproduction of the scattered fragments of daily experience cannot approach. The historian of Russian literature will find here the beginning of a line that leads to Turgenev and Tolstoy, to some of the best critical writings of both Mikhailovsky and Plekhanov – at the opposite end of the scale to the men of the '60s and the reductive materialism of Chernyshevsky, the ideological radicalism of Dobrolyubov, the scientism and exaggerated contempt for artistic aims in Pisarev, not to speak of the mechanical patter of official Soviet formulae. This central current in Russian thought and writing, with its incalculable influence on the West during the last hundred years, springs, I believe, directly from the Saint-Simonian polemic with the champions of art for art's sake. The social roots and implications of this fateful confrontation is another story.

III

Yet there is something more to say. Belinsky's cry, isolated as it is, that 'In our age art is not a master, but a slave',[1] or that 'pure art is impossible in our age',[2] is not identical with saying that the artist and therefore his art are necessarily rooted in a particular social situation, and cannot be torn from it without withering or turning it into mere entertainment. It goes much further – far beyond the French originals – and does lend credence to the claim of, at any rate, Dobrolyubov to be descended from Belinsky. The truth is, I think, that, to use Turgenev's image, Belinsky was Don Quixote, passionate, single-minded, ready to die for his ideas, but at the same time a Quixote torn by an inner conflict which cannot be resolved. On the one hand he adored literature: he possessed a marvellous instinctive sense of what was literature and what was not; it has stood the test of time; and made him the most original, influential, and (despite several stupendous failures of taste) the most just and penetrating Russian critic of the century. Literature is the first and last love of his entire life: the need to enter wholly into the world of the writer, to live through his experience,

[1] loc. cit. (p. 207 above, note 5).
[2] ibid. 77.

surrender totally to his vision, is personal and subjective, a capacity for psychological, aesthetic absorption, an exercise of what Herder called *Hineinfühlen*,[1] free from the demands of the social situation and the historically changing needs of men. At the same time he sought for an all-embracing and indestructibly valid ideology; the *golod istiny* is a universal phenomenon in his time; no one was more deeply agonised by the injustice, the misery, the brutal arbitrariness of Russian life, which his letters convey as well as they have ever been conveyed by any human being. Consequently he was obsessed by the search for answers to the questions of what man should be, how life should be lived; and he hoped and wished that every human faculty, but especially literature, which was his life, should concern itself with these questions and offer help to the seekers after these truths. He is ready to sacrifice himself to his vision, he is ready to fight to the death against the enemies of the doctrine which he has won with so much torment. He knows this in himself: he knows that he is liable to overestimate the purely social significance of a piece of writing, that if the work has no artistic merit, then, however laudable its purposes, it may be something, but it is not a work of literature. He reiterates this until his dying day. But he confesses to an inner predilection. In a celebrated letter to Vasily Botkin he says that even if a story lacks art and poetry, then, unless it actively 'smacks of a dissertation' or 'falls into allegory', if it has any substance in it at all, 'I do not simply read, I devour it ... The main thing is that it should raise problems, make a moral impact on society.'[2] He admits that even an inferior piece of *belles-lettres*, if it is socially important, if it contains ideas, raises problems, may at times engage him personally more deeply than a work of art. My point is that he does not confuse these genres: art remains art, whether or not it is socially relevant, and retains its immortal value whatever its social worth; while no degree of concern with social problems, no matter how intelligent and sincere the writer, can by itself make a work of art. Schiller is nobler and more sympathetic than Goethe, but Goethe is the greater artist. Belinsky has no doubt about that.

These agonised discussions affected his contemporaries profoundly. Belinsky was not read abroad; but the great novelists,

[1] *Herder's sämmtliche Werke*, ed. Bernhard Suphan (Berlin, 1877–1913), vol. 5, p. 503.
[2] PSS xii 445.

who were formed during these years, and later the social preachers, did in due course affect thought in the West. This is a case of what I have called the 'boomerang effect'; to ignore it is to leave the cultural history of the West incomplete.


IV


The fortunes of the Saint-Simonian movement in France are well known: some of the master's most immediate disciples, inspired by the vision of planned centralised industrialisation, became highly successful railway kings and bankers, and organised the digging of the Suez and Panama canals. The doctrine developed into the positivism of Saint-Simon's disciple Auguste Comte, deeply affected Marxism, but also permeated the more moderate socialist and radical doctrines of the second half of the century. Saint-Simonian ideas, radiating from this source, took their place along-side other currents of thought, conservative, liberal, monarchist, Marxist, clerical, anti-clerical, with which they entered into various combinations to form the social, economic and intellectual history of the Second Empire and the Third Republic.

In Russia the effect was less obvious but deeper and more revolutionary. It was the first coherent ideology discovered by an intellectual and morally sensitive minority in search of a set of principles to guide action, particularly as expounded in the writings of the Saint-Simonian Left – the socialist tracts and articles of Pierre Leroux and his collaborators in the *Revue Indépendante*, the indignant denunciation of capitalism by their devoted disciple Lamennais, but above all the socialist novels of George Sand. The moral idealism of this movement affected Herzen, Belinsky and their friends during their most impressionable years, and, no matter how much they changed their specific views, this humane and civilised radicalism, with its genuine hatred of social inequality and the brutal exploitation of the weak by the strong, dominated them to the end. It was this concern, in its institutionalised, organised forms – Marxist or positivist – that Dostoevsky, who had in his youth been under the similar influence of the narrower but socially even more radical doctrines of Fourier, later mocked and denounced.

I do not mean to imply that if Herzen and his friends had not read Saint-Simon, or if Belinsky and Turgenev had not read George Sand when they did, or if tracts by Pierre Leroux or Louis

Blanc, or, for that matter, Fourier or Feuerbach, had not been smuggled into Russia, there would have been no movement of social protest, no repentant gentry in the 1840s, no conspiracies or repression or beginnings of an organised revolutionary movement in the 1860s. This would be an absurd thesis. I wish to assert no more than that Russian literature and thought took the forms that they did largely because of the impact that these French doctrines and the controversy over them, especially in the field of art, made on that particular milieu in Russia in the 1830s and 1840s. I do not know whether this should be called a cause or a mere occasion of what occurred: at any rate the Saint-Simonian ferment and the opposition to it are what set Herzen and Belinsky off in a direction which neither ever abandoned. The process which planted this particular seed in the exceptionally fertile soil of young Russian intellectuals in search of the ideal played, I should like to maintain, a more decisive role in the growth of both Russian liberalism and of Russian radicalism, moderate and revolutionary, than is commonly allowed; with the corollary that it did so through its transforming effect on the central figure of this period – the purest case anywhere to be found of a morally concerned writer – Belinsky, the power of whose influence, by both attraction and repulsion, on both thought and action in his native land, and thereby on the rest of the world, seems to me still underestimated.

This is one thesis. To this I wish to add a second one, namely that neither Belinsky nor any of his friends was ever betrayed into the view, by now familiar enough, of supposing that art, and in particular literature, fails as art unless it performs a direct social function – is a weapon in the achievement of the goals of the progressive section of mankind. No matter how near Belinsky occasionally came to demanding that art abandon its proper end and tend to other needs, he never confused it with morality, still less with propaganda, of whatever kind. In this respect Chernyshevsky and Dobrolyubov, Plekhanov and the Soviet commentators, who took from him only what they needed, distorted his image.

Perhaps an even more instructive case is that of his friend and, in some degree, disciple Ivan Turgenev. Of all Russian prose writers, Turgenev came nearest, perhaps, to the Western ideal of the pure artist. If he held any consistent belief in his life, it was that the highest art is not the vehicle of the artist's conscious convictions, that art is a form of 'negative capability', as it is in Shakespeare, of whom Schiller spoke as a god concealed by his works, fulfilling himself in them as an end in itself. The mainspring of Turgenev's dislike for Chernyshevsky (apart from his disdainful contempt for him as a man and critic) was the latter's utilitarian insistence that art must be subordinated to politics, to science, to ethics, because the primary purpose of art is action – transformation of society, the creation of the new socialist man. When Turgenev makes Rudin say 'I repeat, if a man has no firm principles in which he believes, no ground on which he is firmly based, how can he determine the needs, the significance, the future of his people? How can he know what he must do himself, if . . . '[1] it is Bakunin, or some other typical Russian radical of the 1840s, who is speaking, not the author; this is not his voice. The most essential Turgenev seems to me to speak in a letter to Pauline Viardot of 1848, in which he says:

> life, reality, its whims, its accidents, its habits, its evanescent beauty . . .
> I adore all that. I am rooted in the earth. I would rather look at the
> hurried movements of a duck, as it stands at the edge of a puddle and
> scratches the back of its neck with its moist foot; or at the long,
> gleaming drops of water as they fall slowly from the jaws of a cow,
> knee-deep in water, motionless, after it has drunk its fill – I prefer all
> this to anything that the Cherubim . . . can see in the sky . . . [2]

Why is this? Because the sky is not the earth, because it is 'eternal, limitless emptiness',[3] universal, abstract, unparticularised, unrelated to the terrestrial world of things and persons, sensations, feelings and ideas, colours, scents, actions, birth and death – the world of nature, which, however evanescent and coldly indifferent to the joys and sorrows of human beings, is all there is; the rest is mere talk, mere smoke.

Yet he lived when he did, and the impact of the social sermons from the West had done their work on him and his contemporaries. With Belinsky's eye upon him, both in the 1840s when they were close, and after Belinsky's death, the 'accursed' social questions are at the heart of all his novels. I need not enlarge on this: *On the Eve*, *Virgin Soil* and above all, of course, *Fathers and Sons* are far from irrelevant today – *Fathers and Sons* has perhaps fully come into its own only in our day. At the same time Turgenev

---

[1] PSSP, *Sochineniya* vi 263.
[2] PSSP, *Pis'ma* i 297–8. (The letter was written in French.)
[3] ibid. 297.

insists that he takes up no position – he is merely a creator; he knows that when the author, rightly, does not express his own sympathies, the reader, abandoned to his own devices, without direction, without a *napravlenie*, is puzzled; what is he to think? To be left to arrive at his own conclusions irritates him: reality – the chaos of reality, its unevennesses – exasperates the reader, since he wants a guiding hand, positive heroes.

Turgenev proudly refuses to provide this; writers who, like Shakespeare, or like Gogol, create characters who detach themselves from their authors and live their own independent lives seem to him to belong to a higher order than those whose characters are not self-propelled, whose bonds with the author are patent; these latter convey more warmth, more heart, more sincerity, more personal but less objective truth, possess less mastery, less art.[1] Yet, in 1855, seven years after Belinsky's death, he writes to Botkin, by this time a passionate defender of art for art's sake, 'There are epochs where literature cannot be *merely* art – there are interests higher than poetry', and he declares that moments of self-knowledge, of self-criticism, are just as necessary in national as in personal life.[2] So, too, he tells Tolstoy in 1858 that it is not 'lyrical twittering' that the times call for, not 'birds singing on boughs'.[3] He declines to take part in a journal dedicated to pure art, free from contamination by social issues, which Tolstoy at this time was meditating: 'You loathe all this political mess: true, it is a dirty, dusty, vulgar business. But then there is dirt and dust in the streets, and yet we cannot, after all, do without towns.'[4] Finally there is the celebrated passage about *Fathers and Sons* in the letter to Saltykov: 'I am ready to admit that ... I had no right to give our reactionary riff-raff the chance of seizing on a nickname, a name; the writer in me should have made this sacrifice to the citizen.'[5]

Even if this was written, as has been suggested, because Turgenev wished to justify himself to the stern Saltykov, it is still a sign, a symptom, of the long conflict between the claims of art as they all understood it – they did not disagree about its essence, these writers of the 1850s and '60s (save perhaps Nekrasov, who never comes wholly clean about this) – and the claims of personal

[1] PSSP, *Sochineniya* v 368.
[2] PSSP, *Pis'ma* ii 282.
[3] ibid. iii 188.
[4] ibid. 210.
[5] ibid. xi 191. The 'nickname' Turgenev refers to is 'nihilist'.

morality or political conviction. The conflict was not so much between the 'aesthetes' and the 'naturalists' – although this did, of course, take place – as within the individual writers themselves: Tolstoy, Turgenev, Goncharov, Pisemsky were all torn by it, peacefully or with torment, according to temperament. This had little enough to do with the critics of the radical *Sovremennik* ('Contemporary'). What respect had they left, by the late 1860s, for Chernyshevsky or Dobrolyubov, or Antonovich, or even Nekrasov? Herzen did not take it upon himself to guide, from London or Geneva, the literary conscience of Russian writers, even of those who were most intimate with him. It is surely the ghost of Belinsky, that terrible, incorruptible presence, that haunts them – it is he who once and for all, for better and for worse, set the moral tone of socially conscious literature, and the debate about its nature and its value, in Russia in the second half of the century and, in a sense, until our own day.

This was a genuine crisis, a *crise de foi*, not a mere dispute, a series of partisan assertions and counter-assertions. Even the young Chernyshevsky is not totally deaf to the claims of art: when reviewing Tolstoy's *Childhood and Adolescence* and his *Military Tales* in 1856, he says:

> We want novellas to describe social life as much as anyone does. But one must still understand that not every poetic idea permits social questions to be introduced into the work. One must not forget that the first rule of artistry is the unity of the work, and that consequently in depicting 'childhood' it is precisely childhood that one must describe, not something else, not social questions, nor military scenes, nor Peter the Great, nor Faust, nor Indiana, nor Rudin, but the child with his feelings and his concepts. And people who express such narrow demands talk about the freedom of creative art! It is amazing that they do not seek Macbeth in the *Iliad*, Dickens in Walter Scott, Gogol in Pushkin! One should understand that a poetic idea is destroyed when elements foreign to the work are introduced into it, and that if Pushkin, for example, had thought of depicting Russian landowners or his sympathy with Peter the Great in his 'The Stone Guest', 'The Stone Guest' would have turned out to have been an absurd work, so far as art is concerned. Everything has its proper place: scenes of southern love in 'The Stone Guest', scenes of Russian life in *Onegin*, Peter the Great in *The Bronze Horseman*. Thus, too, in *Childhood* or in *Adolescence*, only those elements that are characteristic of that age are appropriate, while patriotism, heroism, military life have their

place in the *Military Tales*, a terrible moral drama in *The Notes of a Billiard Marker*, the portrayal of a woman in *Two Hussars*. Do you remember that marvellous figure of the girl sitting by the window at night? Do you remember how her heart beats, how sweetly her breast is overcome with the premonitions of love?[1]

Then he goes on to praise Tolstoy for introducing nothing irrelevant into his work. Tolstoy is a poet, a master of real beauty and real poetry. But despite the commonplace sentiments and more than commonplace style, all this is still compatible with Belinsky's, Turgenev's, even Grigoriev's criteria.

This did not last, however. It is when we get to the notorious essay on Turgenev's *Asya* that we meet the classical Chernyshevsky of 'Forget about them, these erotic questions! The reader of our time cannot be bothered with them, occupied as he is with problems of administrative and judiciary improvements, of financial reforms, or the emancipation of the serfs',[2] or the famous passage which states that the chief value of marine paintings is that they will afford the inhabitants of our interior provinces a sight of the sea which they might otherwise never obtain.[3] It is such monstrosities on the part of honourable but aesthetically ungifted critics – martyrs to Russian socialism – together with Dobrolyubov's conception of criticism as concerned with the assessment of literature solely as a weapon of sociological analysis, leading to promotion of revolutionary remedies, that opened the path which led to Plekhanov, Lenin and all that followed. If Belinsky is the ancestor of this trend, so too are Turgenev, Tolstoy, Saltykov, even Apollon Grigoriev if one takes into account his ecstatic pages about the supreme genius of George Sand.

Let me repeat once again: the critical turning-point seems to me to have occurred in the early 1840s when the Saint-Simonian doctrines, having secured a response in the heart and blood of the agonised, unceasingly responsive critic Belinsky, radically influenced other major writers, not always sympathetic to his views. What Belinsky seems to me to have imprinted upon his successors was a genuine hatred of self-protective fantasies, of anything that falls between the writer and his object, that leads him away from

---

[1] N. G. Chernyshevsky, *Polnoe sobranie sochinenii*, 16 vols (Moscow, 1939–53), iii 429–30.

[2] ibid. v 166.

[3] ibid. ii 77.

the vision of what is most immediately real to him. Hence his furious rejection of archaism, sentimental regionalism, and romanticism about exotic and remote cultures in general, and the idyllic Slav past in particular, and, as part of this, his passionate emphasis on authenticity, on the fact that only two things are required of a writer: that he possess artistic talent – however this comes about, perhaps as a gift from heaven – and that he does not sin against the truth, that the work should be generated by an *Erlebniss* of the writer, or have been lived through by him in reality or in imagination. From this follows a corresponding disparagement of mere skill, craftsmanship, of the intrusion of the discursive intellect, inimical as it is to the free play of the creative imagination; and finally a demand that the author should recognise the moral centre of the situation that he is describing – grasp its universal significance for human beings as such as against its transient significance for readers whose ephemeral desires and circumstances will soon be over. The influence of these canons on Turgenev is evident enough. But he possessed another, more formidable, although indirect and certainly unconscious disciple.

Tolstoy was a notorious victim of his artistic genius and his social conscience. There was a time when his passion for pure art and his hatred of politics, encouraged by Fet and Botkin, were at their height. In 1858 he says:

> The majority of the public began to think that the task of all literature consisted only in denouncing evil and discussing and correcting it . . . that the days of the story and of verse have gone for ever, and that the time is coming when Pushkin will be forgotten and will no longer be read, that pure art is impossible, that literature is only a tool for the civic development of society and so forth. One could hear, it is true, during that time, the voices of Fet, Turgenev, Ostrovsky muffled by the political uproar . . . but society knew what it was doing, continued to sympathise with political literature alone, and considered it alone as literature. This enthusiasm was noble, necessary, even temporarily just. In order to have the strength to make these enormous strides forward which our society has made in recent times, it had to be one-sided, it had to get carried away beyond the goal in order to reach it, it had to see that single goal ahead. And actually how could one think about poetry when for the first time a picture of the evil surrounding us was being unveiled before one's eyes, and when the possibility of putting an end to it was being presented to us? How could we think about the beautiful, as we fell ill? It is not for us who make use of the

fruits of this enthusiasm to reproach people for it ... But however high-minded and wholesome this one-sided enthusiasm might have been, like any enthusiasm it could not endure. The literature of a people is its full, many-sided consciousness, in which must be reflected equally the national contemplation of beauty in a given epoch of development, and also the national love for goodness and truth.[1]

Nevertheless, and this belief he never abandoned, in addition to 'political literature' there is another kind of literature 'which reflects eternal, universally human interests, the most precious heartfelt consciousness of the people, a literature accessible to men of every nation, of every epoch, a literature without which no people possessing strength and richness has ever developed'.[2] Seven years later he said in a letter to Boborykin:

> If I were told that I could write a novel whereby I could establish beyond any possible doubt what I consider to be the correct view of all social questions, I should not devote even two hours to such a novel; whereas if I were told that what I write would be read by today's children in about twenty years time, that they would cry and laugh over it, and love life, I should give to this all my life and all my powers.[3]

In spite of all that followed – his condemnation of all art, which does not help to heal the moral wounds of men, as vanity and corruption – his artistic impulse cannot be suppressed. When, later in life, he had written *Khadzhi-Murat*, someone asked him how he came to do this – what was the moral or spiritual message of this work? He replied very coldly that he kept his artistic work distinct from his moral exhortation. He did not demand moral sermons from Chekhov; and, on the other hand, despite the fact that Bernard Shaw could not be accused of a lack of clarity or directness, or of avoiding social problems, or of lacking positive convictions, he would have none of him. Shaw wrote to him in admiration: after all, he had attacked some of the same enemies as those denounced by Tolstoy. But the old man refused to regard Shaw's writings as anything but vulgar, superficial, above all profoundly inartistic. His efforts to achieve a single and coherent

[1] L. N. Tolstoy, *Polnoe sobranie sochinenii*, 90 vols (Moscow/Leningrad, 1928–58; index 1964), v 271–2.
[2] ibid. 272.
[3] ibid. lxi 100.

philosophy of life founded upon infallible truths were even more
heroic and did more violence to his own instincts and cravings and
insight than the similar efforts of Belinsky or Turgenev, and he
ended in a correspondingly more terrifying failure. This same
dilemma – this attempt to square the circle – forms the substance of
Blok's late essays on 'The Intelligentsia and the People' and 'The
Shipwreck of Humanism'. The problem is, if anything, even more
agonising in *Dr Zhivago* and the published, and perhaps unpublished and, it may be, unwritten, works of Sinyavsky and his
companions.

To return to Tolstoy's peculiar relation to Belinsky. In 1856
Tolstoy was, with difficulty, induced to read him by Druzhinin,
who abhorred him, and Turgenev, who admired him. He declared
that he had one night dreamt that Belinsky had maintained that
social doctrines were true only if they were 'pushed to the end',[1]
and that he accepted this. He was delighted by Belinsky's articles
on Pushkin, and particularly by the idea that if one is to
understand a writer, one must immerse oneself in him completely –
and see only him and nothing else. On 2 January 1857 he notes in
his diary, 'Read Belinsky in the morning, and I am beginning to
like him';[2] and although in later years he thought him a tedious
and ungifted writer, the principles which he had enunciated entered
Tolstoy's outlook for good. It seems to me no accident that
Tolstoy carried out Belinsky's critical behests with such singular, if
unacknowledged and perhaps unconscious, fidelity. No word is
more pejorative in Tolstoy's critical vocabulary than 'contrived';
only directness, only simplicity, only clarity – if the writer is quite
clear about what it is that he wishes to say, and if his vision is
unimpeded, the result will *eo ipso* be art. This goes further than
Belinsky at his most extreme was prepared to go; Belinsky never
abandoned the view that artistic genius was something wholly *sui
generis*, and therefore that authenticity – the fact that a man's
vision is his own and no one else's and that he expresses what he
sees clearly and directly – is not by itself a sufficient condition for
the creation of a work of art. Tolstoy's view is, as so often, a
simplification and exaggeration of an already simple thesis.

The insistence on authenticity, the charges of what in our day,
under neo-Hegelian and existentialist influence, is spoken of as

[1] ibid. xlvii 198.
[2] ibid. 108.

false consciousness and bad faith, occur most frequently in Tolstoy's devastating criticisms of other – especially nineteenth-century – writers. Thus Goethe, for example, is condemned for viewing his creations from too remote a standpoint; hence his novels and his dramatic works, because they have not been 'lived through', however exquisitely composed these may be, however absolute the author's mastery over himself and his material, remain unconvincing – magnificent but cold and withdrawn, unable to achieve the direct communication of feeling which, for Tolstoy, is the primary idea, the sole purpose of art. This charge of complacent and disdainful self-sufficiency, the ironical references to Goethe's Olympian calm in the midst of social upheavals, his frigid self-satisfaction, his caution, his determined invulnerability, echo Belinsky; they are repeated by Turgenev, despite his admiration for Goethe's genius, both in the essay on *Faust* and elsewhere. No Russian writer wrote better about Goethe than Turgenev: nor was he by temperament as unsympathetic to him as, say, Herzen or Tolstoy. But the Saint-Simonian potion had done its work: he preferred Schiller, Byron, George Sand, and proclaimed this. In similar vein, with typical irony, Tolstoy says that he asks himself whether Flaubert – Flaubert who has described so exquisitely how St Julian the Hospitaller embraced the leper, the leper who was Christ – would have behaved similarly in this situation; this doubt undermines his confidence in the writer, the belief in his genuineness which, for him, was the basis of all true art.

This approach, whether one thinks it acceptable or absurd, is the kind of moralism in Belinsky which his followers admired, and his opponents detested. So too, when Tolstoy wishes to pillory the shortcomings of some of the most respected writers of his time, the poisoned arrows that he aims so unerringly are drawn from Belinsky's quiver. He undertakes to judge them in terms of three *desiderata*: seriousness of the problem; moral sincerity; and artistic capacity. Thus he informs us that Turgenev has certainly 'lived through', suffered in his innermost person, the experiences which he describes so vividly and artistically. But are these sad reflections and feelings of members of the decaying Russian gentry, as they sit in their country houses and brood, and discuss their personal relationships with other landowners as decadent, as unrepresentative of humanity in general as themselves – are these of sufficient worth to occupy the thoughts of a serious, 'healthy' being, a peasant, a decent worker, a morally 'sound' man or woman?

As for Nekrasov, who can deny that he is a writer endowed with immense artistic skill? The problems with which he deals – the misery, the oppression of the peasants, the violence and injustice to which they are exposed – who can deny the importance or human significance of this terrible topic? But sincerity? Has Nekrasov truly lived through these experiences in reality or in imagination? Does he convey to the reader the feeling that he is personally involved? Are the poems not merely genre pictures, by a skilful but detached painter, in fact an owner of serfs, whom he shows no sign of wishing to liberate, whose private life and real, personal concerns lie far from the sufferings of the victims, from the social and moral squalor of the life which he is so good at turning into verse, without any real personal, self-identifying *engagement* on his part? The dismissal of Nekrasov as insincere because he is insufficiently committed again goes beyond Belinsky's view of, for example, Goncharov. Tolstoy pushes the point further than Belinsky, with his scrupulous desire to know the truth, however complex, ever went, even on the rare occasions when his social conscience carried him away.

Finally, there is one of Tolstoy's verdicts on Dostoevsky: he is acknowledged to be dealing with problems of the greatest spiritual importance; his attitude, Tolstoy concedes, is profoundly sincere; but alas, he does not pass his (and Belinsky's) primary criterion, the possession of artistic gifts, that is, the capacity to express an individual vision simply and clearly. After all his characters have been paraded on the stage, the rest (Tolstoy declares) is a mere working out of the mechanism of the plot: for pages and pages it is all predictable, tedious, inartistic; Dostoevsky has a great deal to say, but he cannot write or compose.

V

I have cited these instances from both Turgenev and Tolstoy because these authors are not commonly thought to stand in the tradition of social criticism initiated by Belinsky – and my thesis is that the collision between the claims of art and the claims of society did not, in Belinsky's case, simply end in the victory of the latter, and so originate the clear, radical tradition of Chernyshevsky, Pisarev, Plekhanov and their Marxist epigoni; but, on the contrary, remained unresolved; and initiated the dilemma in which Russian writers and artists were caught from his time onwards, and which henceforth deeply affected the entire movement of Russian thought and art, and indeed of action too, and tormented liberals and conservatives, 'progressives' and those who, like Tolstoy or the populists, or the 'decadents' of the turn of the century whom he loathed and despised, condemned political activity and sought salvation elsewhere.

Perhaps the clearest statement of Belinsky's final position is to be found in his essay on criticism of 1843: 'We may be asked: how can one and the same piece of criticism organically combine two different points of view – historical and artistic? Or how can one demand of a poet that he freely follow his inspiration and, at the same time, serve the spirit of his time, not venturing to step out of its magic circle?'[1] Belinsky declared that this question is easily soluble, both theoretically and historically:

Every man, and consequently the poet too, undergoes the inevitable influence of time and place. He imbibes with his mother's milk the principles and the sum of concepts by which his society lives. This is what makes him a Frenchman, a German, a Russian and so forth; this is why, if he is born for example in the twelfth century, he is piously convinced that it is a sacred duty to burn alive men who do not think as others do, while if he is born in the nineteenth century he religiously believes that nobody must be burnt or slaughtered, that the business of society is not to avenge the victims of a crime, but the correction of the criminal through punishment, by means of which the society that has been injured will be satisfied and the holy law of Christian love and brotherhood will be fulfilled. But mankind has not suddenly leapt from the twelfth to the nineteenth century: it has had to live through a whole six centuries, in the course of which its conception of truth developed in its various stages, and in each of these six centuries this conception took on a particular form. It is this form that philosophy calls a *stage* of development of universal truth; and it is this *stage* that must be the pulse of the poet's creations, their prevailing passion (pathos), their main motif, the basic chord of their harmony. One cannot live in the past and through the past with one's eyes closed to the present: there would be something unnatural, false and dead in this. Why did European painters in the Middle Ages paint only Madonnas and saints? Because the Christian religion was the dominant element in the life of Europe at that time. After Luther all efforts to restore religious art in Europe would have been in vain. 'But', we shall be told, 'if one cannot get out of one's own time, there

cannot be any poets who do not belong to the spirit of their time, and
therefore there is no need to take up arms against something that
cannot occur.' 'No,' we reply, 'not only can occur, but does so,
especially in our own time.' The cause of this phenomenon lies in
societies whose conceptions are diametrically opposed to their reality,
which teach their children in schools a morality for which people now
laugh at them when they have left school. This is a state of irreligion,
decay, fragmentation, individuality and – its inevitable consequence –
egoism: unfortunately features of our age which are all too pronounced! When societies are in this state and live by old traditions
which are no longer believed in and which are contradicted by the new
truths discovered by science, truths which are brought about by the
movements of history; when societies are in such a state it is
sometimes the case that the noblest and most gifted personalities feel
themselves cut off from society, feel themselves solitary and the
weaker brethren among them drift off amiably into becoming the
priests and preachers of egoism and of all the social vices, in the belief
that evidently this has to be, that it cannot be otherwise, that it did not,
they say, begin with us, and will not end with us either. Others – and
these, alas, are sometimes the best men of their time – escape into
themselves and turn their backs in despair upon this reality which has
insulted all feeling and all reason. But this is a false and selfish means
of salvation. When there is a fire in our street one must run towards it,
not away from it, in order to find the means, together with others, for
putting it out; we must work like brothers to extinguish it. But many,
on the contrary, have elevated this egoistic and craven feeling into a
principle, a doctrine, a rule of life, and in the end into the dogma of the
highest wisdom. They are proud of it, they look with contempt upon a
world which, they ask you, please, to see, is not worth their suffering
and their joy. Ensconcing themselves in the embellished tower of the
castle of their imagination, and looking out through its many-coloured
glass, they sing like birds ... My God! *Man* becomes a *bird*! What a
truly Ovidian metamorphosis! And this is reinforced by the fascination of German artistic doctrines which, despite much depth, truth,
and light, are also exceedingly German, philistine, ascetic, anti-social.
What is bound to come of this? The death of talents who, given
another direction, would have left vivid traces of their existence in
society and who might have developed, gone forward, and reached
manhood. Hence the proliferation of microscopic geniuses, tiny great
men, who do indeed display much talent and power, but who will
make a bit of noise and then fall silent and soon die even before their
death, often in full bloom and at the height of their powers and
activity. Freedom of creation is easily reconciled with serving contemporary needs: but to do this it is not necessary to force oneself to write

on ready-made themes or do violence to one's fantasy; one needs only to be a citizen, the son of one's society and one's time, to identify oneself with its interests, make its needs one's own; one needs sympathy, love, a healthy, practical sense of truth, which does not divorce belief from action, a work of art from life. What has entered and gone deeply into the soul will emerge of its own accord.[1]

This is not, and could not be, Belinsky's final position. In the very same year, 1843, he began the essays on Pushkin; in the fifth of these he develops the thesis which moved Tolstoy so deeply – that truly to read a writer one must see only him, to the exclusion of the rest of the world. This, then, is how one must see 'The Stone Guest', or 'The Gypsies', which have as little to do with the deepest interests of the nation as the glacial masterpieces of Goethe or, at a lower level, Goncharov's An Ordinary Story. Yet he knew these to be true works of art by men who did not run when there was a fire in their street. I have quoted the passage from the essay of 1843 at such length because it seems to me the nearest that Belinsky ever came to saying, not indeed what art was or could or should be, but what he and those who thought like him wished it to be: what warmed their hearts, even though they knew that this position was not absolute, but, in the end, subjective, historically conditioned, likely to be shaken by events, by counter-examples, by wider sympathies.

Still, this statement, which like the famous letter to Gogol is a profession de foi, is, however it is interpreted, not Chernyshevsky's demand for serving the immediate needs of society; it is equidistant from both formalism and Marxism. Doubtless it would have been rejected indignantly by Flaubert or Baudelaire or Maupassant. It would have meant little to Stendhal or Jane Austen or Trollope, or even to James Joyce, despite his early socialism. It could not be accepted without heavy qualifications by Marxists; it was not cited by the men of the '60s. But when Korolenko said that his 'native land was above all else Russian literature'[2] (not Russia herself), this was a remark that any Russian writer could have made at any time in the last hundred years. And this, it seems to me, derives ultimately from the impact of the Saint-Simonian controversy about the functions of the artist upon Belinsky and his circle: it is

[1] ibid. 284–6.
[2] Istoriya moego sovremennika, chapter 27: vol. 4, p. 270 in V. G. Korolenko, Sobranie sochinenii v pyati tomakh (Leningrad, 1989–91).

due to this impact more than to any other single cause. If some contemporary of Korolenko in England, let us say Arnold Bennett, had said that his country was not England, it was English literature, what could this possibly have meant? How could he have said it? If even so socially conscious a writer as, say, Upton Sinclair or Henri Barbusse had said: 'My native land is American literature' – 'French literature' – this would have been obscure to the point of unintelligibility.

This is the difference that was made by the Russian doctrine of commitment of the 1840s, Russian because it entered the hearts and blood of its defenders, more deeply than those of its original begetters in Paris or elsewhere. This sentiment is perfectly intelligible today in Asia or Africa and nearer home, and is what the intelligentsia – and I use the word in an entirely laudatory sense – everywhere has always been concerned with, whether it is liberal and reformist or radical and revolutionary. The reader, said Goethe as cited by Belinsky, *should forget me, himself, the whole world, and live only in my book*'. Belinsky comments: 'Given the German's apathetic tolerance of everything that is and is done in the wide world, given his impersonal universality which by acknowledging *everything* can itself become *nothing*, the thought enunciated by Goethe makes art an end in itself and thereby frees it from any connection with *life*, which is always higher than *art*, because art is only one of the innumerable manifestations of life.'[1] This position can be accepted or rejected, doubted or debated, but it is not obscure. It seems to me that the centre of the conflict lies between this affirmation and that which Belinsky, with many a sideways glance at art which is free from anxiety, remote from the pressures that belong to the 'critical' periods of history, sought to defend; a position of which his 'manifesto' of 1843 seems to me the fullest statement. This is where the battle-lines have been drawn now for many decades: here, and not between the wooden directives with which a later generation of Russian positivists and Marxists tried not so much to solve as to dissolve the issue.

The two positions that I have tried to outline are to be found both between the 'pure' and the 'socially committed' Russian critics and artists, and within them. The major writers – Turgenev, Tolstoy, Herzen, Belinsky – were involved in this conflict and

---

[1] PSS vii 305. The editor of PSS cannot establish the source of the quotation from Goethe.

never achieved a resolution of the issue. This, in part, is what gives their theoretical discussions vitality, when the arguments of many of their Western contemporaries, Leroux and Chasles, even Taine and Renan, seem dead. For it is an issue which is central to modern society's social conflicts, but acute only in relatively backward communities, without the discipline of a rich and strong traditional culture, driven forcibly to adjust themselves to an alien pattern, while they are still free, at any rate as yet, from the exercise of total control over their life and art.

# KANT AS AN UNFAMILIAR
# SOURCE OF NATIONALISM

Beings who have received the gift of freedom are not content with the
enjoyment of comfort granted by others.

Immanuel Kant, *The Quarrel Between the Faculties* (1798)[1]

I

AT FIRST SIGHT nothing would seem more disparate than the idea
of nationality and the sane, rational, liberal internationalism of the
great Königsberg philosopher. Of all the influential thinkers of his
day, Kant seems the most remote from the rise of nationalism.
Nationalism, even in its mildest version, the consciousness of
national unity, is surely rooted in a sharp sense of the differences
between one human society and another, the uniqueness of
particular traditions, languages, customs – of occupation, over a
long period, of a particular piece of soil on which intense collective
feeling is concentrated. It stresses the peculiar links of kinship that
unite the members of one national community with each other, and
it emphasises the differences between them and that which obtains
elsewhere. In its pathological forms, it proclaims the supreme value
of the nation's own culture, history, race, spirit, institutions, even
of its physical attributes, and their superiority to those of others,
usually of its neighbours. But even in its moderate forms, nationalism springs from feeling rather than reason, from an intuitive
recognition that one belongs to a particular political or social or
cultural texture, indeed, to all three in one – to a pattern of life that
cannot be dissected into separate constituents, or looked at through
some intellectual microscope; something which can only be felt and
lived, not contemplated, analysed, taken to pieces, proved or

[1] KGS, vol. 7, p. 87, line 19 (for 'KGS' see p. 192 above, note 2).

disproved. The language used to describe it is usually romantic or, in extreme cases, violent, irrational, aggressive; and, especially in our own century, liable to end in cruel and destructive oppression, and, in the end, hideous slaughter.

Immanuel Kant stands for the exact opposite: calm, rational thought, hatred of all exclusiveness and privilege founded on mere immemorial tradition or on obscurantist political dogmatism, or anything that cannot be brought into the clear light of day and examined by rational men in a rational and systematic fashion. He defends nothing so firmly as the timeless, unchanging rights of the individual, whoever he may be, whatever his time, whatever his place, his society, his personal attributes, provided he is a man, the possessor of reason, and, as such, obliged to respect reason in all other men, as they respect it in him. Kant detested emotionalism, disordered enthusiasm, what he called *Schwärmerei*; it is indeed this kind of sentimental rhetoric, as it seemed to him, that in his view marred the outpourings of his contemporary and fellow Prussian Johann Gottfried Herder, the father of cultural (and ultimately every kind of) nationalism in Europe. Herder's constant talk about the uniqueness of each national tradition, of the strength that a man draws from being a member of an organic community, from being the child and carrier of its national spirit, its national style, Herder's hatred of cosmopolitanism, universalism, anything which flattened out differences between one community and another in favour of universal principles, which seemed to him nothing but huge straitjackets – all this seemed to Kant confused, uncritical, the substitution of emotion for reason, un-grown-up. Kant is a man of the Enlightenment, of its universalism, its belief in the dry light of reason and science, which transcends local and national boundaries, something the conclusions of which any sensible man can verify for himself, without benefit of a particular language or soil or blood in his veins. He hated inequality, he hated hierarchies, oligarchies, paternalism, no matter how benevolent. Many in Germany had welcomed the French Revolution. Kant never abandoned his faith in it, and its proclamation of the universal rights of man and citizen, even when it degenerated into terrorism and bloodshed, which Kant condemned, and which made most of its original liberal-minded supporters in many lands shy away from it in horror. His strictly political writings are celebrated models of liberal rationalism: thus, the ground of my obeying the law is that it orders, or should order, what any rational man, in my situation, would command himself to do or not do; States should devote their resources to education, culture, the moral improvement of their citizens, and not to increasing their material power and conquest; he elaborated a famous project for a league of nations, and for perpetual peace among them.

What greater contrast can there be, it might well be asked, than that between, on the one hand, the deep, dark, non-rational forces, fired by fanatical religious separatism and, perhaps, by the German sense of national humiliation in the face of the far grander, more powerful, enlightened and magnificent French, and, on the other, Kant's unswervingly rational universalism, with its deep suspicion of mystical or poetical language, of metaphorical talk, of insights and visions?

And yet, wildly paradoxical as this may seem, there is indeed a connection between Kant's view and the rise of romantic nationalism: a traceable line of influence, and, in my view, an important and central one. The fact that Kant would have abhorred the very idea of so disreputable a connection does not, I am afraid, make it less real. Ideas do, at times, develop lives and powers of their own and, like Frankenstein's monster, act in ways wholly unforeseen by their begetters, and, it may be, directed against their will, and sometimes turn on them to destroy them. Men, least of all thinkers, cannot be held responsible for the unintended and improbable consequences of their ideas, for plants that grow from seeds that fall on propitious soil, and bloom, sometimes hideously, in a favouring climate which the sower never knew, or could never imagine. Many complicated, even accidental, factors conspire to generate a single movement; even orthodox Marxism did not grow out of Marx's doctrines alone. It would be absurd to charge Hegel, for instance, with the sinister shapes into which some of his notions have turned in our day. So, too, I wish to suggest, it has been with the greatest of modern philosophers. It is the odd career of one of Kant's noblest and most humane doctrines in the turbulent nineteenth century, its influence on the modern world and on our own lives – a career that would have horrified Kant himself – that I should like to discuss.

II

As everyone knows, Kant's moral philosophy (which probably produced a deeper immediate impact than even his theory of knowledge or of the nature of human experience) is founded upon the conviction that the most important distinguishing characteristic of human beings is their freedom to act, to choose between, at the very least, two courses of action, two alternatives. Unless a man can be said to be the true author of his own acts, he cannot be described as being responsible for them, and where there is no responsibility, there is, for Kant, no morality at all. Morality, for him, largely consists in the recognition of rational, that is, universal rules, binding upon every rational being, according to which men have an obligation to perform particular acts, and an obligation to refrain from contrary ones. But you cannot tell anyone save a free being that he is obliged to act thus or thus: things, plants, animals are not obliged, because they are not choosers, they are determined to behave as they do by causal forces outside their control. The same applies to human beings who are unable to control their bodies or their minds: infants or idiots or men put into an abnormal state by the influence of drugs or hypnotism or sleep, or whatever cause prevents the agent from being able to make rational choices. The very notion of an agent entails, for Kant, freedom of the will to act rightly or wrongly, virtuously or viciously. And he goes further than most defenders of free will in maintaining that it is not only 'external' factors – physical, chemical, biological, physiological, geographical, ecological – that can prevent or destroy freedom, but 'internal' psychological ones, too. If a man says that he could not act otherwise than as he did because he was overcome by passion, because of irresistible emotional drives, because his upbringing or his character, being what they are, caused or determined him to act as he did, he is proclaiming himself to be unfree: a mere 'turnspit',[1] to use Kant's term, at the mercy of causal forces, external or internal, physical or mental, a mere object in space, or at least in time, not, in the end, different in this respect from plants or animals, or, indeed, inanimate objects; part of a cosmic causal mechanism in which he is at best a mere cog or wheel. Nor would the latest scientific categories, which abolish precisely determinable causal sequences in favour of functions of probabilities, or statistical predictions, have made any difference to Kant. He would have dismissed as so much irrelevance the mountain of loose metaphysical talk which has been built on a crude misunderstanding of the implications of indeterminism in

[1] KGS, vol. 5, p. 97, line 15.

physics, or quantum mechanics. Like other attempted compromises with determinism, he would have called it nothing but a 'miserable subterfuge'.[1] Unless a creature can determine itself, it is not a moral being: whether it is causally determined, or floats about at random, or is subject to statistical laws, it is not a moral agent.

Kant is absolutely definite on this point. There is at least one respect in which man is, for him, absolutely unique in the universe: although causal laws may affect his body, they will not affect his inner self. It is central to Kant's thought that physical laws apply only to what he calls the world of phenomena or appearances, which is for him the external world, the only world dealt with by the sciences. 'If appearances were things in themselves,' he declared, 'freedom could not be saved';[2] and again, 'that my thinking self ... in its voluntary actions should be free and raised above natural necessity ... is among the foundation-stones of morality and religion'.[3] If there were no freedom, there would be no possibility of moral law.[4] Freedom is not merely the feeling of freedom. A clock might, if it could speak, claim that it runs on its own motive power, but this would be an illusion; it runs only because it has been wound up. If man were so made, freedom, and therefore morality, 'could not be saved'. But moral principles can be known a priori; they are certain: hence determinism must be false. Moral laws are not imposed upon us by some outside agency – not even by God himself – they are, as Rousseau had made clear, imposed by ourselves on ourselves, acting rationally and freely. That is why they are principles or rules, not natural laws: even while we submit to them, we remain free; for we need not have submitted; and we can break them, if we choose, at the price of acting irrationally. From this a great deal follows.

Man's unique property, what distinguishes him from every other entity in the universe as he knows it, is his self-government, his autonomy. Everything else is in the realm of heteronomy. Autonomy means giving laws to oneself – freedom from being coerced, from being determined, by something that one cannot control. Heteronomy is the opposite: obeying laws that issue from something outside oneself – for example, the material world, in

---

[1] ibid., p. 96, line 15.
[2] *Critique of Pure Reason*, A536/B564.
[3] ibid., A466/B494.
[4] KGS, vol. 5, p. 4, line 36; p. 97, line 5.

which causality reigns, the realm of the natural sciences; this includes the sphere of empirical psychology – whatever in our psychic life is governed by natural laws. The doctrine that man is an end in himself, and not a means to anything not himself, derives from this view: since he is the ultimate author of the rules to which he freely submits, to make him submit to something that does not proceed from his own rational nature is to degrade him – to treat him as a child, an animal or an object. To deprive a human being of his power of choice is to do him the greatest imaginable injury. This will be so, no matter how benevolent the intention with which it is done. Kant's doctrine is directed against all paternalism – in particular, against enlightened despotism, like that of his own king, Frederick the Great of Prussia – and against the utilitarian materialism of the leading French thinkers of the day.

In a short but remarkable essay called 'An Answer to the Question: "What is Enlightenment?"' [1] Kant declares that to be civilised is to be grown-up, that is to say, not to be content to abdicate one's responsibilities to others, not to permit oneself to be treated as a child, or barter away one's freedom for the sake of security and comfort. And elsewhere he says: 'a *paternalist government*', based on the benevolence of a ruler who treats his subjects 'as dependent children ... is the greatest conceivable *despotism*' and 'destroys all freedom'. [2] And again: 'The man who is dependent on another is no longer a man, he has lost his standing, he is nothing but the possession of another man.' [3] This is an echo of Rousseau, directed against the materialistic utilitarians who, like Helvétius or Holbach, maintained that in order to secure peace, happiness, harmony, virtue itself, it was necessary to institute a rational, legal and educational system, armed with appropriate rewards and punishments, which would condition men to avoid anti-social conduct, and cause them to behave in the manner desired by the enlightened educator or legislator – much in the way that one breeds and tames domestic animals. Ethics is the agriculture of the mind, said Holbach; Helvétius said he did not care if men were virtuous or vicious, provided they were intelligent – that is, knew what makes them happy and unhappy: the rulers can

---

[1] KGS, vol. 8, pp. 31–42.
[2] ibid., p. 290, line 35.
[3] KGS, vol. 20, p. 94, line 1.

create an arrangement of sticks and carrots that will generate the desired character and behaviour.

These men wished, above all, to stamp out ignorance, prejudice, superstition, which they thought to be the causes of cruelty, misery and injustice. They believed in the power of discovery and invention, in universal enlightenment. Yet even they might have recoiled from the modern versions of the methods of re-education they recommended: psychological techniques of conditioning human beings, from subliminal suggestion to threats or brainwashing or shock treatment. In this respect, the methods advocated by B. F. Skinner in *Beyond Freedom and Dignity* are fully in the spirit of Helvétius or La Mettrie: the purpose of them all is to produce a peaceful, well-adjusted, contented flock of human beings.

Kant was intensely concerned about precisely dignity and freedom. Hence his constant insistence that human personality literally means independence of the mechanisms not only of men, but of nature too. No act can be described in moral terms, indeed it can scarcely be described as an act at all, unless it is freely chosen by me. To act and not be acted for or upon; to choose and not be chosen for; to be given the opportunity of choosing badly rather than not choosing at all; that is, for Kant, a fundamental human birthright. 'All other things must: man is the being that wills,' said Friedrich Schiller,[1] the poet and dramatist, who was a faithful disciple of Kant: even God cannot take away this power from us, without destroying us as human beings. 'Beings who have received the gift of freedom are not content with the enjoyment of comfort granted by others.'[2] This saying is the key to Kant's entire ethical outlook. That is why Kant, who doubtless disliked other vices too – cruelty or cowardice or lack of principle – nevertheless reserved his harshest words for what we now call exploitation: the use of men as means, not as ends in themselves; that particular form of inequality whereby you make other men – by persuasion or coercion, or something in between – pursue courses the goals of which you know, but they do not. The whole terminology of exploitation, degradation, humiliation, dehumanisation and, as against this, the ideals of social or economic or individual emancipation of workers or women or artists or oppressed groups or nationalities – the entire language of liberal and socialist ideology, in the last two centuries,

[1] *Schillers Werke*, vol. 21 (Weimar, 1963), p. 38, line 8.
[2] loc. cit. (p. 232 above, note 1).

stems from this passionate plea for self-determination, insistence on the development of moral freedom, even if it leads to suffering and martyrdom.

With this, the entire modern attitude to nature and the natural order was changed. The central tradition, at any rate in Western thought, both in its classical Graeco-Roman form and in many, though not all, of its Christian and Moslem forms, incorporates the belief that there is a world structure in which man has a definite place established by God or nature. It is only when, through blindness of some kind, man does not know what this place is that he loses his way, goes wrong, becomes vicious and causes misery to himself and others. According to some thinkers the world is a great natural hierarchy, a pyramid, with God at its apex, and, at descending levels, the realms of angels and men and the higher animals, and finally the amoeba, plants, and the lowest orders of inanimate nature. According to others, the world is a great organism, in which every element is a function of every other; or, again, it is a marvellous system of mathematically expressible harmonies, as Pythagoras and many subsequent thinkers and mystics have supposed; or else an orchestra with a score for each player; or after Descartes and Galileo a marvellous machine, or a factory with cogs and wheels and pulleys. These images are found among eighteenth-century materialists, influenced by the triumphs of Newtonian science; and, after them, among a good many anti-vitalist thinkers, until our own day. What is common to all these systems is the notion that everything has its appointed place; everything follows unbreakable laws; man is no exception. Deluded through their own ignorance or folly, or deliberately deceived by unscrupulous men seeking power or some other unfair advantage, or as a result of variously changing conditions, techno-logical or geographical, racial or climatic or institutional or what-ever, men are caused to stray from the path of reason or nature, to neglect the illumination that God (or nature) alone provides. The problem, then, is to get men to understand nature, with themselves as parts of the natural world – say, by destroying the social conditions in which their ideas are necessarily perverted, and substituting some other system in which they will know the truth, and live in its light, and so be enabled to be happy and harmonious for ever after. But if Kant is right, and the forces of nature, if we surrender to them, reduce us to mere turnspits (as, for him, things and animals are), then the very notion of nature is revolutionised.

Nature is no longer what it was for the French Enlightenment – the beautiful model which, with the help of science, we shall understand and accept, and ourselves fit into frictionlessly. For Kant, nature is either neutral stuff that we must mould to our own purposes as free, choosing creatures; or something more sinister and ambivalent: a power which, even while it provokes us to valuable emulation and progress, by setting us against one another, also threatens our freedom, and is therefore to be kept at bay, to be resisted, if we are to rise to our full human stature as free, self-determined moral beings.

This is indeed a dramatic break. No doubt the roots of this view go back to the Christian doctrine of grace as against nature; to the Hebraic notions of life as a sacrifice, if need be, to God's commandments, irrespective of whether it will bring us rewards – happiness or fulfilment of our natural desires; back to Protestantism with its stress on the voice within, irrespective of what the external world is like. It may be traced to the political consequences of the Reformation in Europe, which destroyed the vision of one great spiritual society governed by a single set of universal principles that rule over inanimate nature, the animal kingdom and man alike; of the union of reason and faith, of which Church and State, Pope and Emperor, were, or should be, expressions. Sociologically, it is perhaps a consequence of the accumulating resentment of men in German-speaking lands against, as it seemed to them, the contemptuous domination of French culture and French power, in every field of public endeavour – particularly after the havoc and humiliation of the Thirty Years War. But there was one region which even the proud French had no access to, that of the spirit, the true inner life – the free, autonomous human spirit, which they, the Germans, had preserved inviolate, the spirit that seeks its own path to fulfilment, and will not sell itself for material benefits. How have all those powers and dominions, all those glittering prizes, been won? Were they not gained at the price of spiritual death – enslavement to an inhuman, soulless, machine-like political, social, cultural system, all those arrogant French officials with whose aid the renegade Francophile King Frederick in Berlin is trying to crush all that is spontaneous and original in Prussian lands? This protest against secular progress and the victories of science, which could be heard among pious Germans, especially in economically backward East Prussia, and in Rousseau, too, after his own fashion, in the mid-eighteenth century, this outcry against the intellect now echoes round the world.

Kant was, of course, in no sense a romantic enthusiast who appealed to the untrammelled will against reason and order. Far from it. He hated undisciplined, passionate, dishevelled attitudes of this kind, hated them as deeply as any thinker of the Enlightenment. At the centre of his entire teaching is the doctrine that men are endowed with reason, and that this faculty enables any man, in the moral as well as the theoretical sphere, to arrive at answers about what is to be done, how life is to be lived – answers that are valid for all other rational creatures in the same circumstances, wherever and whenever and however they live. Only upon this rock of universal reason – mutual respect for the common rational humanity in all men – can any harmonious arrangement, peace, democracy, justice, human rights and liberties, rest securely. Some such assumptions are common to Locke and Rousseau, Jefferson and Hegel, and indeed most of the champions of liberal democracy, socialism, idealistic anarchism, communism, every form of belief in peaceful world organisation, until our own day; at least, this is so in theory, even if not, as we know to our terrible cost, in practice. Nevertheless, there is another strain, too, in Kant, which comes from his Lutheran, pietist, anti-Enlightenment upbringing: the immense stress on independence, inner-directedness, self-determination.

Pietism, the ancestor of Methodism, arose in German lands during the seventeenth and eighteenth centuries, a time of humiliation and political impotence for the Germans in their divided land, ruled over by over three hundred petty princes, not too many of whom were either competent or well-intentioned. The more sensitive among their subjects reacted to this much as the Stoics did to the conquest of the Greek city-states by Alexander: they retreated into their own inner life. The tyrant threatens to take away my property – I will train myself not to want property. The tyrant wishes to rob me of my home, my family, my personal liberty – very well; I shall learn to do without them. Then what can he do to me? I am the captain of my soul; this, my inner life, no outside force can touch. Yet nothing else matters. By contracting the vulnerable area, I can make myself free of nature and of man, as early Christians did who escaped to the Theban desert or remote monastic cells from pagan persecution or the temptations of the world, the flesh and the devil. This is, of course, in the end, a

sublime form of sour grapes; what I cannot have, I pronounce to
be of no value. If I cannot have what I want, I shall want only what
I can have. Political impotence means spiritual freedom: material
defeat means moral victory. Since I cannot control the consequences of my acts, only that which I can control – my motives, my
purposes, the purity of my heart – that alone counts.

This note of austere self-insulation is very deep in Kant. In him
it takes quietist forms. But in his successors it becomes defiance,
resistance against anyone and anything that seeks to diminish or
degrade my inner kingdom, the sacred values by which I live, and
for which I am prepared to suffer and to die. This lies at the heart
of romanticism – the worship of the heroic martyr, the lonely
thinker or artist in a vulgar and philistine world, dominated by
values that are alien to him, alien because they are not born of the
inner spirit, but forced upon him by brute force or the commercial
market-place. Above all, one must remain true to one's inner
vision, one must never sell out, never compromise for the sake of
success or power or peace or even survival. This is indeed a
transformation of values. The traditional heroes of mankind had
once been those who were successful, those who knew the correct
answers, whether in theory or practice – sages, men who had
discovered the objective truth about what there is in the universe,
or about what one should do, about what is real, good, worth
making or admiring – priests and prophets, philosophers and
scientists, depending on one's view of how and where the truth is
to be found. Or, alternatively, they were men of action – founders
and preservers of States or Churches, conquerors, lawgivers,
leaders, doers and makers who dominate their fellow men, shape
their lives. In the place of these, the new hero was the man who
was ready to lay down his life for his convictions, for the inner
light, ready to be defeated rather than give in, who would not
calculate the odds against him, the exemplar of heroic – if need be,
tragic – integrity.

It takes but two steps to reach the romantic position from Kant's
impeccably enlightened rationalism. The first is to hold that, when
I act and live in the light of certain values, this is not because they
are made or discovered by the reason that is present in all fully
developed men, and therefore guaranteed by it, and universally
valid for all rational creatures. No: I do indeed live by such values,
not because they are universal, but because they are my own,
express my particular inner nature, the particular vision of the

universe that belongs to me; to deny them in the name of
something else would be to falsify all I see and feel and know. In
short, there is now some sense in which I can be said to create my
own values. I do not find them as objective constituents of the
universe which I must obey: I choose them freely myself, they are
my values because I am 'I', and have, when I am at my best, freely
chosen them.

This is, in effect, despite all his talk of universality and reason,
what Kant's unfaithful disciple Fichte, the true father of romanticism, came near to saying. 'I do not', he declared, 'accept anything
because I must, I believe it because I will.'[1] Or again, 'I am not
hungry because food is placed before me; it is food because I am
hungry for it.'[2] In other words, it is my hunger that makes
something a good for me – if I were not hungry it would not have
this attribute. Kant was certainly horrified by this direction of
Fichte's thought (Fichte's first book, ironically enough, was at
first attributed to Kant). But one can see how, out of Kant's
enormous stress on the value of autonomy, of determining my
own moral conduct, some such existentialist position could begin
to develop.

The second, and even more fatal, step is the new conception of
the chooser – of the choosing self. For Kant it is still the individual,
even though he attributes to the moral will a transcendent status
outside space and time – outside the lower realm of blind, causal
necessity. For Fichte this self becomes a timeless, transcendent
activity that is often identified with a world spirit, an absolute,
divine principle, at once transcendent and creative. But there is also
another development of the notion of the self in the pages of
Fichte, which becomes more prominent after the invasion of
German lands, first by French Revolutionary armies, then by
Napoleon, during the passionate revulsion and patriotic resistance
which this provoked in many lands in Europe east of the Rhine.
Herder had maintained that a man is shaped by the river of
tradition, custom, language, common feeling, into which he is
born; he is as he is in virtue of the impalpable relationships with
others, of his social milieu, which is itself the product of the
endless, dynamic interplay of historical forces. It is this constant
interaction that makes each age, each society, each tradition, each

[1] SW ii 256 (for 'SW' see p. 180 above, note 1).
[2] SW ii 264.

culture unique in character, different in unmistakable but unanalysable ways from other, equally organic, social, linguistic, cultural,
spiritual wholes. It was not long before Fichte, writing in the early
years of the nineteenth century, declared that the true self is not the
individual at all: it is the group, the nation. Soon he began to
identify it with the political State. The individual is but an element
in the State, and, if he cuts himself off from it, is a limb without a
body, a meaningless fragment that derives its significance only
from its association with – the place that it occupies in – the
system, the organism, the whole. This is the secular version of the
old Hebraic-Christian House of Israel, the mystical community of
the faithful who are parts one of another. Some tended to identify
it with a culture, some with a Church, some with a race or nation
or class. It is this collective self that generates the form of life lived
by individuals, and gives meaning and purpose to all its members;
it creates their values and the institutions in which these values are
embodied, and is thus the eternal, infinite spirit incarnate, an
authority from which there can be no appeal. Fichte, Görres,
Müller, Arndt are the fathers of German and, in due course,
European political nationalism. Peoples (and social classes) which
had been victims of oppression or aggression or humiliation lashed
back like a bent twig at their oppressors – the simile is, I believe,
Schiller's – and developed a defiant pride and a violent self-
consciousness which ultimately turned into burning nationalism
and chauvinism.


### III

Of course Kant would have repudiated this misbegotten by-product of his deeply rational and cosmopolitan philosophy; but the
seeds of it are there, not, indeed, in his political writings, but in his
more significant ethical works. For it was his ethical views, with
their uncompromising moral imperatives, that made the deepest
impact on human thought. In the first place idolisation of nation or
State derives, however illegitimately, from his doctrine of the
autonomous will, his repudiation of the objective hierarchy of
interrelated values, independent of human consciousness, which
had hitherto dominated Western thought in many guises – in the
Platonic vision of eternal real Forms, outside the world of change
and decay; in that of Natural Law, which, after Aristotle and the
Stoics, entered the Christian, and especially Thomist, conception of

God and nature, and man's relation to both; in the metaphysical conception of nature as a rational structure; in the objective naturalism of Locke and the Utilitarians and their successors in liberal and socialist movements. But, in the second place, there was in Kant's thought something deeper still, of which this doctrine of the will is, in some sense, an expression.

It was Kant more than Hume, who is usually charged with it, who cut off the world of nature from the world of goals, principles, values. So long as values were objective entities embedded in the nature of reality, the reasons for doing one thing rather than another – say, for obeying authority, or for fighting wars, or for sacrificing oneself or other men – were sought in the very nature of things, the objective *rerum natura*, the single, coherent structure, independent of men's wills or thoughts, all the elements of which could be explained in terms of their relations to the whole. But if truly moral conduct consists in aiming at certain specific goals for their own sakes, no matter what the consequences, no matter what may be the nature of the world – of the facts, events, things which philosophers or scientists seek to describe and explain – then the idea is born, or at least gains force (for it derives from Hebraic-Protestant sources), that life is, or should be, a reaching after, and, if need be, a sacrifice to, an end or ends that can be described as ultimate; ends that justify both themselves and everything else, ends on their own that need no explanation or justification in terms of any all-embracing system wider than themselves.

In Kant this is, of course, vastly modified by his constant insistence that categorical moral imperatives of this kind must be rational in character – universal maxims binding on all rational beings in a given situation. But the impact made on the European consciousness, perhaps through the ideas of Fichte and the romantics, was that not of the rational aspect of this doctrine (which was not new, familiar as it was in the teachings of both the Roman Catholic Church and the Enlightenment) but of the stern and vehement tone of the literally inexorable, absolute commandments – a voice that a man hears within him, for if he does not, then he is outside morality, blind and deaf to what matters most. It needed only the transformation of the notion of Kant's rational self into something wider and more impersonal, and the identification of this greater entity with an end in itself, the ultimate authority for all thought and action, to create a more terrifying form of

Hobbes's 'mortal God',[1] a new absolutism. Hence the worship offered in the nineteenth century by conservative thinkers to Burke's more empirically conceived, more flexible, politically accommodating vision (albeit the source of traditional authority) – the great society of the living, the dead and those yet unborn. Hence the deification of the stream of history in which I am but a drop and outside which I have no significance; or of Herder's historical spirit of my people, my *Volk*, of which I and my life are but passing expressions – in short, the expansion of the notion of the self into some quasi-metaphysical super-personality that engages all my loyalty, all my desire to merge my individual self in a great collective whole, to which I yearn to sacrifice myself and others, since it will, I feel, lift me to a height that my confined empirical self could never have risen to.

Once this morality of ultimate goals that I seek to fulfil simply because they are what they are, and not because of any relation they may have to some all-embracing system that includes and explains reality as a whole – once this replaces the older religious or scientific outlook, the path is open to a variety of such absolutist faiths. Some preached an absolute personal morality of duty, total repression of emotion in submission to the moral law. Others were prepared to sacrifice everything to aesthetic goals – the creation of works of art – art for its own sake, free of compromise with personal or social considerations, still less with moral obligations; and applied, with disastrous consequences, aesthetic models to social and political life. Yet others believed in the discovery and propagation of truth, truth for its own sake, no matter how socially disruptive or painful to individuals it might prove to be, scientific or social or moral truth with its tearing down of the masks of convention, its destruction of the myths by which societies sometimes live.

In the realm of politics, this took the form of the glorification of the true subject of social growth, whichever it was conceived as being – of the State, or the community, or the Church, or the culture, or the social class – but most of all of the nation, conceived as the true source and perfect realisation of social life. In the case of the relatively independent, socially developed, culturally progressive societies, this sense of the nation as a central source of moral

[1] *Leviathan*, chapter 17: p. 120 in Richard Tuck's edition (Cambridge, New York etc., 1991).

authority took a relatively mild form – for example, in England or Holland or Scandinavia and their cultural and political dependencies overseas. In lands where, as a result of economic backwardness or foreign domination, the upheavals at the turn of the eighteenth century released an immense current of cooped-up, indignant ambition and energy seeking to express themselves, to 'be and do something' (in Fichte's phrase),[1] to win a place in the sun, this took more fanatical and violent forms. Nationalism is, it seems to me, the sense – the consciousness – of nationhood in a pathological state of inflammation: the result of wounds inflicted by someone or something on the natural feelings of a society, or of artificial barriers to its normal development. This leads to the transformation of the notion of the individual's moral autonomy into the notion of the moral autonomy of the nation, of the individual will into the national will to which individuals must submit, with which they must identify themselves, of which they must be the active, unquestioning, enthusiastic agents. The doctrine of the free self with which Kant attempted to overcome what seemed to him the danger to moral freedom from acceptance of a mechanical, impersonal, determined universe, in which choice was illusory, became magnified, and indeed perverted, into the doctrine of quasi-personalised history as the carrier of the collective will, the will to growth, to power, to splendour, a vision half biological, half aesthetic, at the centre of which is the notion of the interest and the purpose of the nation or the nation State as a kind of creative, self-developing work of art. This is a simile which even the rationalistic Hegel uses: he sees the nation State as the creative force of the spirit – the world *Geist* – which cannot and must not be restrained in its victorious march by any limits or barriers. For everything is subordinate to the central creative principle, that is to say, to it, to itself.

I do not, of course, mean that it was simply ideas and theories which led to all this: ideas are not born of ideas only; there is no parthenogenesis in the history of thought. The Industrial Revolution and the French Revolution, and the disruption of European unity by the Reformation, and the backlash of Germany against France after the humiliations of the late sixteenth and the seventeenth century – all these were dominant factors in what occurred. But neither must the role of ideas be underemphasised. In the vast awakening of national consciousness among crushed minorities, in

[1] SW vi 383.

oppressed or backward classes and nations in their revolts against unjust rule, or humiliation, especially by foreign masters, in the revolts which took place in Latin America and Italy in the nineteenth century and in Africa and Asia in the twentieth, these powerful ideas – the autonomy of the will of a nation or a society, ends in themselves in their socialised forms (ideas that Kant launched originally only upon the quiet-seeming waters of ethical theory) – blended with the explosive doctrines of Herder and Rousseau, and formed a critical mass, which, in due course, led to terrible explosions. Yet nothing, I must repeat, could have been further from the thought of that peace-loving internationalist, that rational and enlightened thinker, with his profound concern for individual rights and freedom.

Still more remote from anything he contemplated are the pathological developments of nationalism in our own times – of that movement (the most powerful, by far, of our century – more so than ever today) the frightening influence of which no one in the nineteenth century, however percipient, had predicted. No one, as far as I know, had ever prophesied the rise of modern national narcissism: the self-adoration of peoples, of their conviction of their own immeasurable superiority to others and consequent right to domination over them. To see this, you have only to compare the concept of national liberty as preached, say, by democrats like Mazzini or Michelet with the notion of it as consisting in the ruthless elimination of all possible obstacles to it from within or without, that is, the idea of a holy war against all rivals for power – internal classes or associations, and external forces, namely other nations. The same is even more true of the terrifying brothers of nationalism – racism and religious fanaticism. It is a far cry even from Fichte's fervid *Addresses to the German Nation* to these ferocious movements – the most frightening and barbarous phenomena of our own time. Thus do ideas turn into their opposites: the language of peace into a weapon of war, appeals to reason into the worship of the limitless material power that is sometimes supposed to embody it, sometimes to deny and fight against its claims.

# RABINDRANATH TAGORE AND THE CONSCIOUSNESS OF NATIONALITY

I AM shamefully ignorant of Indian civilisation, even of what is most valuable and most important in it, and for this I hope that I shall be forgiven. I can plead in extenuation only that where one culture is geographically remote from another, and has been historically insulated from it, bridges are genuinely difficult to build and to cross; and what is deepest in a culture, the most direct and authentic voice in which it speaks to itself and to others, its art, is difficult to transpose into an alien medium. All those who have, like me, been educated in England, know that this is the case even with the classical literatures of Greece and Rome. They lie at the root of Western civilisation. They have been transmitted uninterruptedly from generation to generation since their very beginnings. Yet English translations of Homer or Aeschylus or Virgil, no matter how felicitous, do not begin to convey the genius of the original. I should like to go further. I should like to assert, perhaps a little too rashly, that no man has ever truly experienced the presence of genius in a translation of a piece of lyrical poetry. Descriptive prose which conveys states of mind or spirit, or ideas, or situations which are part of the common stock of human experience – these of course can, to a high degree, be conveyed even in translation. Men do not have to read Russian to recognise the genius of Tolstoy, or Hebrew and Greek to be deeply affected by the Bible. This is to some extent true of dramatic literature, as well as epics and ballads – of story-tellers whose prose or poetry draws upon universal human knowledge of character and action. No one can doubt that the influence of Shakespeare in translation upon Frenchmen, Germans, Russians has been enormous. Molière, Schiller, Ibsen, poets as they were, can be carried over on to an alien canvas. But even there, where the poetry is in the words more deeply than in the images or the action – in Racine, Corneille and, I suspect, Calderón, as well as in the modern masters of poetic drama, Yeats, Hofmannsthal, Eliot, Lorca, Claudel – translations do not convey enough. We admire the renderings if we know the original, and think how remarkable the skill, the ingenuity, the sensibility of the translator; but I suspect that few can be truly moved by a translation unless it is itself an independent poetical creation. But then the power of the transformed work comes, as a rule, at least as much from the imagination and the genius of the translator, and this is another matter. Such transubstantiations are commendable, sometimes magnificent, but they are new creations, not bridges, not that self-effacing medium of a totally faithful rendering whereby a truly dedicated translator acts and lives – as an actor does – in the character and the life of the original. This is above all the case with pure, lyrical, deeply personal poetry. Translation, in the sense in which it is applicable to prose or verse which tells a story, here seems to me almost unattainable. The poetry is in the words, and the words belong to one particular language, spring from and convey one unique style of life and feeling, and speak directly only to those who are capable of thinking and feeling in that tongue, whether it is their native tongue or not: 'poetry is what is lost in translation' – these words, attributed to the American poet Robert Frost,[1] seem to me a precise statement of the truth.

These reflections were intended in the first place as a plea in extenuation of my own shortcomings in knowing too little of Indian literature, which, even in its prose and its epics and philosophical classics, always seems, through the dark glass of the translator, poetical, and indeed lyrical, in character; but they bring me also to the heart of the topic which I should like to discuss, namely Tagore, Tagore and the consciousness of nationality. For although there are many elements, and factors, and signs, and criteria of nationhood, yet one of the most powerful, perhaps the most powerful, of all of these is surely language. It may be counteracted by combinations of other factors, historical, social and geographical, but it is very strong. The more developed, mature and self-conscious a man becomes, the more he thinks and even feels in words, the less in sensuous images. The late Lord Keynes, the eminent economist, was once asked whether he thought in words or images: 'I think in thoughts,' he said. This was

[1] In Louis Untermeyer, *Robert Frost: A Backward Look* (Washington, 1964), p. 18.

a characteristically amusing reply, but it was not true, and not meant to be taken seriously, perhaps; indeed it was meaningless. We think in words or in images; we are told that children, primitive peoples, artists, and perhaps women too, think in images more than words. But once we begin to communicate coherently, conventional symbols dominate our lives: and these are mostly words. Tagore, who was a great master of words, seems to me to have spoken about language, and its connection with social and political life, with acute insight, and what he said has great interest for us today.

I do not wish to praise or attack nationalism. Nationalism is responsible for magnificent achievements and appalling crimes; it is certainly not the only destructive factor abroad today – ideology, religious or political, and the pursuit of power by individuals and interests that are not national, have been, and are still, just as revolutionary, brutal and violent. Nevertheless nationalism seems to me to be the strongest force in the world today. In Europe, where it first grew to overwhelming strength – one of the many forces released by the great French Revolution – it started in alliance with other forces: democracy, liberalism, socialism. But wherever they fell out among themselves, nationalism invariably won, and enslaved its rivals, and reduced them to relative impotence. German romanticism, French socialism, English liberalism, European democracy were compromised and distorted by it. They proved powerless against the torrent of nationalist pride and greed which culminated in the conflict of 1914. Those who discounted its strength, whether Norman Angell or Lenin, or the ideologists of dynastic empires or of world capitalist combines, and especially those who thought that they could harness it to their own purposes, failed to predict events, and their adherents were punished accordingly. Communism, for instance, certainly became a great force, but except in alliance with national sentiment it cannot advance. This seems to me the case in China; in the parts of Asia once governed by France or Holland; in Africa, in Cuba. When Marxism comes into conflict with national sentiment – we can all think of examples in recent history – it suffers as an outlook and a movement, whatever the alliance with nationalism may add to its material power and success.

One may wish to condemn nationalism outright as an irrational and enslaving force, as, for example, both Marxists and Catholics, enlightened internationalists and guilt-stricken ex-imperialists, and naturally enough its many victims, of all classes and races and religions, have condemned it. But it seems to me even more important to understand its roots. Nationalism springs, as often as not, from a wounded or outraged sense of human dignity, the desire for recognition. This desire is surely one of the greatest forces that move human history. It may take hideous forms, but is not in itself either unnatural or repulsive as a feeling.

It seems to me that the craving for recognition has grown to be more powerful than any other force abroad today. This protean entity takes many overlapping and interacting forms: individual and collective, moral, social and political. Nevertheless, it preserves its identity in all its incarnations. Small States demand to be recognised as sovereign entities with their own past and present and future, and struggle for equality with the great States, and claim the right to survive, grow, be free, be allowed to say their word. The poor wish to be recognised as full human beings – as equals – by the rich, Jews by Christians, the dark-skinned by the fair, women by men, the weak by the strong. Within modern centralised States minorities work and fight for power and status: this is felt acutely, perhaps most acutely, in affluent societies. There class-consciousness is one of the most influential forms into which the demand for recognition pours itself. In my own country, for example, it is perhaps the deepest root of our social discontents. The quiet economic revolution that has occurred, both in Britain and in many parts of Europe, has cured many economic ills, raised the standard of living, increased the opportunities for economic advancement and political power over an area and to a height not known before. In the less unjust orders of our time it is no longer economic insecurity or political impotence that oppresses the imaginations of many young people in the West today, but a sense of the ambivalence of their social status – doubts about where they belong, and where they wish or deserve to belong. In short, they suffer from a sense of insufficient recognition.

Such people may be prosperous, take an interest in their work, realise that the Welfare State protects their basic interests, yet they do not feel recognised. Recognised by whom? By the 'top people', by the ruling class. In a society governed by an oligarchy – say by a hereditary aristocracy (there are scarcely any such in Europe now) – this can take the form of a straight political struggle for power by one social class against another. In England, and in many other Western countries, the situation is a good deal more complex:

there the unrecognised or under-recognised are conscious of the existence of a group of persons in their society who, without necessarily being in political control, nevertheless set the tone: socially or culturally or intellectually. These persons may belong to conflicting political parties; what they have in common is the self-confidence born of an assured position as arbiters of the general way in which life should be lived, of the way in which one should think, write, speak, look, educate, engage in argument, treat other human beings, and, in general, conduct public and private life. Even when they rebel against some given political or social institution or orthodoxy, they do so in the right tone of voice, they speak by right and not on sufferance, as members of a natural élite. No doubt those who stand outside it tend to exaggerate the power or the close-knit texture of the élite; yet, in unequal societies, men commonly know who stands in the way of their advancement. The élite exists. In England it is still to some degree hereditary and tied to the public schools, to the old universities, to the humanities, and it possesses a sense of solidarity which those who wish to be accepted by it envy and admire. They may, as is usual in such cases, affect to despise it, and describe it as useless, decadent, reactionary, a doomed class, condemned to disappearance before the forces of history, but at the same time they envy it and seek its approval even while they feel the very notion of status to be an unworthy category by which to classify human beings, and feel angry with their own inescapable, and resentful, consciousness of their own social positions.

The excluded are not necessarily poor or politically powerless. C. P. Snow's concept of 'two cultures' seems to me fallacious; but what lends it plausibility is the fact that a good many natural scientists in Anglo-Saxon countries feel kept out of a world which they imagine to be living more enviable lives than their own. Even though it is recognised and asserted at all levels that it is they, the scientists, who are objectively more important, influential, original, far more crucial to the future of their societies than the humanist élite and the bureaucrats brought up in it, this gives them little comfort; for they know who truly dominates the scene. This paradoxical situation seems to occur whenever one process that vitally affects the development of a society falls out of step with some other equally central process or cluster of processes. Injustice, oppression, misery do not seem, at any rate in recent history, to be sufficient to create conditions for revolt or drastic change.

Men will suffer for centuries in societies whose structure is made
stable by the accumulation and retention of all necessary power in
the hands of some one class. Ferment begins only when this order
breaks down for some reason (the Marxist hypothesis of the
influence of technological invention is illuminating) and a 'contradiction' arises, that is, the development of one factor – say the
possession of political authority or control by a ruling group – is
no longer united to some other equally needed attribute, say
economic position or capacity for administration. Then the equilibrium of the system is disturbed, and conflicts are set up, with
corresponding opportunities to alter the distribution of power for
those who seek to upset the status quo.

In our world the crisis is caused by the fact that individual talent
and success, economic power and ability, and sometimes even
political influence, have fallen too far out of step with the all-
important factor of the craving for social status. Lack of adequate
status, humiliation of the parents, and the sense of injury and
indignation of the children drives men to social and political
extremism. It may take social or aesthetic, not political, forms: it
was the main force behind such phenomena as 'angry young men',
'beatniks', the addicts of 'hip' in America, and, to a perceptible
degree, what Anthony Crosland called the Aldermaston Movement in England, which, inspired as it clearly was by sincere
political and social idealism, was also driven by a class discontent
and acute status-consciousness on the part of its members.

This is not a novel phenomenon in the Western world. It is by
now a truism that among the causes of the French Revolution is the
wide disproportion between the economic power of the French
middle class in the eighteenth century and its lack of social and
political recognition. The revolutionaries of the nineteenth and
twentieth centuries were, as often as not, sons of capable and self-
made men, who had been socially excluded or rejected, or found
themselves in an embarrassing or false position in the social
hierarchy of their time. This was conspicuously true of Russia too.
Among the sources of strength of the Russian revolutionary
movement was the combination of moral and political indignation,
directed against a corrupt and oppressive regime, with a quest for
status by men whose resources and education entitled them to play
a part that they were rigidly denied by the State. The great
entrepreneurs of the rapidly growing trade and industry of the

Russian Empire – men of exceptional ability, imagination, ambition – could grow rich and economically powerful, but were, by and large, kept out of positions of honour and responsibility by the Court and the still aristocratically based regime. Pride and moral sentiment can, and do, outweigh material self-interest: the sons, brought up on liberal sentiments imported from the West, tended to sympathise with, and often threw themselves with passion into, the revolutionary movement, which was openly directed against, not merely the political, but also the economic order for which their capitalist fathers had fought so successfully. This happened in Central Europe and in the Balkans – young men with sufficient resources to obtain a far better education, especially abroad, than the majority of their countrymen were turned by the humiliating inferiority of the families' social status towards extreme opinions and courses. I suspect this must have happened too to the sons of the rich bourgeoisie kept down by the Pashas of Turkey and Egypt and Syria and Iraq.

This dissatisfaction is, as a rule, directed against an identifiable élite, pillars of the establishment – the Pashas, as it were – or it may break out against the very dissentients themselves, the Franklin Roosevelts, the Stafford Crippses, the Bertrand Russells and many a revolutionary Girondin or radical of aristocratic origin in France or Russia or America, men who, no matter how radical their views, are felt to belong to the ruling class, and possess its confidence, its manners and its tastes.

But the roots of discontent lie deeper, in loneliness, in a sense of isolation, in the destruction of that solidarity which only homogeneous close-knit societies give to their members. Ruskin and Morris, and before them Fourier and Marx and Proudhon, have long ago taught us to see that an increasing degree of industrialisation and mechanisation leads to the disintegration of society, to degradation of the deepest human values – affection, loyalty, fraternity, a sense of common purpose – all in the name of progress, identified with order, efficiency, discipline, production. We are all too familiar with the results: the steady dehumanisation of men and their conversion into proletariats – masses – 'human material', machine- and cannon-fodder. This, in time, breeds its own antidotes: the awakening in the most self-conscious and most sensitive among the victims, or even among the accomplices of this process, if they have any strength of will, of revolutionary indignation, fed by an immense desire to restore what they

visualise as the broken social unity and harmony and equality
(whether it ever existed or not); and, at the same time, of the kind
of uncalculating love and respect between men on which all true
human relationships rest.

This demand to be treated as human and as equal is at the base of
both the social and the national revolutions of our time: it
represents the modern form of the cry for recognition – violent,
dangerous, but valuable and just. Recognition is demanded by
individuals, by groups, by classes, by nations, by States, by vast
conglomerations of mankind united by a common feeling of
grievance against those who (they rightly or wrongly suppose)
have wounded or humiliated them, have denied them the minimum
demanded by human dignity, have caused, or tried to cause, them
to fall in their own estimation in a manner that they cannot
tolerate. The nationalism of the last two hundred years is shot
through with this feeling. Nationalism is the direct product of
wounds inflicted on a sense of common nationhood, or common
race or culture. Most commonly it takes one of two equally
aggressive forms. The first of these is awareness of shortcomings, a
conviction of backwardness or inadequacy, and an anxiety to learn
from the superior culture or nation, so as to emulate it and reach
equality, to obtain recognition by peaceful means, or to extort it by
violent ones. This is the ambition of new men and new States, to
catch up with, and overtake, to acquire whatever the modern age
requires – industrial might, political unification, technological and
cultural knowledge – until 'they' can no longer afford to look
down their long noses at 'us'.

Alternatively, it sometimes takes the form of resentful isolationism – a desire to leave the unequal contest, and concentrate on
one's own virtues, which one discovers to be vastly superior to the
vaunted qualities of the admired or fashionable rival. This is a
natural form for wounded pride to take, whether in the case of
individuals or nations. The rationalisation of this feeling is painfully familiar. Our own past, our own heritage contain far finer and
richer things than the gimcrack goods of the foreigner – to run
after the foreigner is in any case undignified, and treason to our
own past; we can recover our spiritual and material health only by
returning to the ancient springs which once upon a time, perhaps
in some dim, scarcely discernible past, had made us powerful,
admired and envied.

Students of the history of Russia are acquainted with the

celebrated debate between Westerners and Slavophils in that country in the nineteenth century, a paradigm case. The former pleaded for science, secularism, the march of reason, enlightenment, freedom, all the fruits of civilisation, of which the richest flowering was to be found in the West. The latter denounced the West for its chilly inhumanity, its dry, narrow, legalistic, calculating philistinism, its oscillation between blind (Catholic) authoritarianism and individualistic (Protestant) atomisation, the 'jungle' of capitalist competition, its social injustice, and, above all, the lack of love in the relations of human beings amongst themselves; they called for a return to the 'organic', 'integral' society of the uncontaminated Russian past, when there was no bureaucracy, no deep gulf between the classes created by Peter the Great's break with tradition; they invoked the deep sense of fraternity that had once united the Slav tribes, when men were parts of one another, and did not clamour for rights – for a right is nothing but a frontier and a wall between human beings, something that excludes and extrudes, something that men bound by natural human feeling, like the members of a family, do not need in order to live together in peace and dignity and pursuit of the common good. The obvious point I wish to stress is that the Westerners and the Slavophils represented two sides of the same coin – the demand for recognition. Nor did this die in 1917.

The same pattern of thought and feeling runs through the German romantics – the writers and thinkers who bound their spell on their fellow citizens and created the idea of the nation as a great collective entity that expresses the *Volksseele*. They substituted intuitive, 'synthetic' insight and poetical sensibility for scientific analysis, calculation, 'Cartesian' rationalism and individualism, for the 'arithmetical democracy', the dead mechanical life of the decaying West – that is, the French, by whom they had been crushed and decimated in the seventeenth century, and humiliated culturally in the eighteenth. Even in independent, proud and prosperous England this mood grows powerful and articulate in the idealisation of tradition and disparagement of rationalism by Burke and Coleridge, or the neo-medievalism of those who wished to return to pre-industrial Merrie England and to the old religion, or to renew it in the shape of a Tory democracy, or a Christian socialism which would restore the broken unity of social and spiritual life. It is to be found almost everywhere in Europe. This is still a form of the quest for recognition – of what we truly are and can be, of our mission and value in history – recognition if not by other nations then at any rate by our own kith and kin. There is always something of a sour-grapes attitude about such attempts to withdraw into oneself for inner strength: if 'they' will not recognise 'us', 'we' do not need 'them'; more than that, we despise them, we think they are doomed, they are the 'rotting West'; indeed, the very things they think vices in us, our primitiveness, our childishness, our lack of the virtues that they prize – sophistication, or political sense, or a modern outlook – are not deficiencies at all, but spiritual and moral virtues which they are too blind even to conceive.

Something like this seems to me to lie at the back of the resentful attitude of those new nations which have exchanged the yoke of foreign rule for the despotism of an individual or a class or group in their own society, and admire the triumphant display of naked power, at its most arbitrary and oppressive, even where social and economic needs do not call for authoritarian control. Liberals rightly deplore and denounce such developments. Yet it is necessary to try to understand them. To understand is not necessarily to forgive: but neither may one point a finger of scorn before one has understood the fact that citizens of ex-colonial territories may prefer harsh treatment by their own kinsmen to even the most enlightened rule by outsiders. This is not a strange or a disreputable feeling. The consciousness that although all oppression is hateful, yet to be ordered about by a man of my own community or nation, or class or culture or religion, humiliates me less than if it is done by strangers, no matter how considerate and disinterested, no matter how far removed from all bullying or exploitation or patronage – that sentiment is surely intelligible enough.

Yet the desire for self-government, for recognition, for social and moral equality, is often not capable of being satisfied by the attaining of political independence. For it may happen that the foreign culture has made a deep impress upon my own, and even when, in some respects, it has made inroads upon it, distorted it, and partially enslaved my own civilisation, yet once I have tasted it, I cannot expel it from my system without great damage, cannot reject or blind myself to what is true or good or delightful or noble merely because it comes from the wrong quarter. Once I have glimpsed such things I cannot forget them; and if, out of pride or desire for independence, I try to purge all memory of them from my system, this can be done only at a high and damaging cost to myself, by a great self-narrowing, by forcing obsolete armour upon my limbs, a deliberate reimposition of provincial standards, with the certain dangers of intolerance, stunting of growth, aggressive xenophobia, deliberate suppression of what only yesterday I knew to be the truth – charges justly urged against chauvinism and isolationism. That is a problem for all new establishments seeking to set up in freedom from their old masters, yet not to forget altogether those lessons which the masters taught them. The masters, as Karl Marx correctly maintained in the case of England and India, may not have had altruistic motives: they may have taught not in the interests of the pupil but in their own; but nevertheless, if Marx is right, they did drive their Indian subjects, it may be at times with brutality, through the unavoidable stages of material and intellectual development, in far less time and with far greater effect than these populations could have achieved for themselves.

I have wandered far afield from Tagore, with whom I started; and I should like to return to him, for these reflections, such as they are, come from reading essays and addresses by him. I know far too little about the history of Anglo-Indian relations; what I say may therefore be false or irrelevant or foolish. But it seemed to me as I read Tagore, particularly about the tasks of education and unification in India, that the problems that faced him were not, as I say, altogether unlike those that troubled critics and reformers in nineteenth-century Russia and Germany, and in other countries too – the United States in the twentieth century, and, I feel sure, Latin America as well. For all these were cultures that, as a result of long years of foreign domination, found themselves (whatever their stage of development) in an ambivalent position. For, on the one hand, foreign models expose a society to the danger of breeding apes and parrots, and killing native gifts, or at any rate distorting their proper path of development in the service of alien gods. On the other hand, the poison, if it is a poison, will have sunk too deep. The Germans could not be expected to forget the Greek and Latin classics, Roman law, the writers of the French *grand siècle*, which were the very foundation of their education. The Russian experience is even more instructive. Peter the Great inflicted on his people a deep traumatic shock. He knocked down walls, blew open doors and windows, founded the beginnings of an educated class, a class that from its very birth, because of its un-Russian habits and outlook, its use of a foreign language – French – was divided from the main body of the people, which continued to live in medieval poverty, ignorance, simplicity, and looked on the educated as semi-aliens.

The wound went very deep: the problem of how it was to be healed preoccupied every public-spirited, educated man in Russia for two centuries. The clearer-sighted among them realised that the effects of cultural invasion by the French or the Germans could not be solved by ignoring it, or by expelling the invaders – setting the clock back – for Russia lived in the world, and to barricade all entrances and exits, to build a Chinese wall, would not long keep out political and economic forces pressing in upon it from outside, and responding to similar forces inevitably stirring within it. Some bold reactionaries preached precisely this: if you stop secular education, arrest so-called progress, and freeze Russia as it now is, the fatal Western bacilli may perish, or at least work more slowly. But this method, the attitude of the Stoic sage – every crack stopped up against the external world – has never yet succeeded. Nor is an ancient culture sufficient to keep a modern people going. The new must be grafted on the old; that is the only alternative to petrifaction, or the miserable aping of some ill-understood foreign original. A nation cannot be treated as an exotic plant for long if it is to grow: it can grow only in the open air, in the public world that is common to all; one cannot be forced to feed exclusively on what is gone and dead, in a carefully preserved artificial light, and achieve anything but a stunted growth.

A not dissimilar problem seems to me, from what I have read in Tagore, to have faced India towards the end of the last century; and he never showed his wisdom more clearly than in choosing the difficult middle path, drifting neither to the Scylla of radical modernism, nor to the Charybdis of proud and gloomy tradition-alism. (I know that some have thought Tagore to have yielded too much to the West. I confess that I did not find this so in those of his works that I could read in English. He seems to me to have kept to the centre.) Not to give way at a critical point to the temptation of exaggeration – some dramatically extremist doctrine which rivets the eyes of one's own countrymen and the world, and brings followers and undying fame and a sense of glory and personal fulfilment – not to yield to this, but to seek to find the truth in the face of scorn and threats from both sides – left and right, Westernisers and traditionalists – that seems to me the rarest form of heroism.

On one side England, on the other the marvellous Indian past. Tagore was very well aware that English literature was a menace as well as a boon. In an essay entitled 'The Vicissitudes of Education' he said that those who forget India and identify themselves with the English that they learn at school are like 'Savage chiefs ... when they put on European clothes and decorate themselves with cheap European glass beads'.[1] This occurs where, as Tolstoy said very sharply and brilliantly in his educational tracts, education has no relation to the life of the pupils themselves, but only to some other life, remote, beyond the seas. The inner neuroses which such conflicts must have created were not confined to India. Certainly some phenomena in American life may perhaps – though I am not sure – be directly traceable to the fact that children of immigrants from non-Anglo-Saxon countries were (and are) brought up on Shakespeare and Dickens and Thackeray, or Hawthorne or Mark Twain or Melville: and indeed, what else was there for them to read? These excellent books told them about forms of life that could have been lived by ancestors of men of Anglo-Saxon, or perhaps Dutch or German or Scandinavian, stock, but not remotely resembling the lives of their grandfathers in Russian or Bohemian or Greek towns and villages, or the Jewish Pale of Settlement, or the hamlets of Sicily or Syria, or the African wild. Tagore says that when this situation occurs, the discrepancy between education and life becomes acute, and then they 'mock and revile each other like two characters in a farce';[2] and for this reason he called for a revival of the Bengali language, a natural medium for at any rate some of his countrymen, not a borrowed suit of clothes, however grand, however comfortable. Yet at the same time he realised that it was neither possible nor desirable to do what some evidently wished to do, to shut the door on English, to cleanse oneself of the Western disease, to return to the past, to the primitive simplicity of an age without machines, and reject the evil gifts of the West – industrialisation and all the degradation and destruction of natural human values that it brought.

He knew that the relation of India with England, for all its benefits, was nevertheless a morbid one: the English had come first as traders, then as masters, and, despite exceptional men who

---

[1] Rabindranath Tagore, *Towards Universal Man* (London, 1961), p. 45. All quotations from Tagore are taken from this collection; subsequent references are by page number alone.

[2] p. 46.

served India in a pure spirit and wore themselves out in her service (and he pays noble tribute to such men), the relation of master and subject distorted the nature of both, and neither found it easy to recognise the other as a human being, to like or to dislike him as he pleased, as an equal, a *semblable*. Indeed it was this phenomenon that was marvellously described in his phenomenology by Hegel, and a hundred years later, in a very different fashion, by E. M. Forster. Nevertheless, Tagore understood the British character and British achievement, and he admired them. He judged England and Europe without passion; his appraisal seems to me calm, acute and just. What the British had brought must not be cancelled or thrown away. Nevertheless, one cannot create in a medium that embodies, and is the vehicle of, an alien experience: such a language must cramp the stranger, and have the effect of a strait-jacket upon his thought and imagination, and force it to develop in unnatural directions – sometimes (as in the case of a Conrad or an Apollinaire) into brilliant virtuosity, at other times in painfully grotesque ways. The first requirement for freedom – independence, awareness of oneself as an equal citizen of the world – is to be able to speak in one's own voice; better nonsense in one's own voice than wise things distilled from the experience of others. 'What the British have set up may be grand but they do not belong to us ... It will never do if we seek to use somebody else's eyes because we have lost our own,'[1] said Tagore in his Presidential Address to Congress in 1908. English is the window open to the great world; to shut it would be – I take this to be Tagore's belief – a crime against India. But a window is not a door: to do nothing but watch through windows is absurd. The British 'are behaving as if we do not exist ... as if we are huge ciphers'[2] – even Morley is guilty of this.

How are Indians to direct themselves instead of being dependent on the placings of others? Only by acquiring strength. I quote from Tagore again: 'The only real gift is the gift of strength; all other offerings are vain.'[3] Like Thucydides in the Melian dialogue, like Machiavelli, like all the great realists he grasped that ignorance and Utopian escapism, fed by sentimental evasion of the truth, can sometimes be as ruinous as cynicism and brutality. To illustrate

[1] p. 121.
[2] p. 117.
[3] p. 123.

this he tells the story of the kid and the Lord. The kid, constantly set upon by beasts stronger than itself, said in despair to the Lord, ' "Lord, how is it that all creatures seek to devour me?" The Lord replied, "What can I do, my child? When I look at you, I myself am so tempted." '[1] Tagore draws from this marvellous and devastating fable the moral that one must be strong, for without strength there will be no equality, no justice. The equality of all States, great and small, is a piece of idealistic cant. Justice to the weak, given human beings as they are, is rare because it is difficult; and to change human beings so that they will not be as they are is Utopian. One must seek to improve mankind by available means, not by demanding of them unattainable virtue which only the saints can emulate.

Men seek recognition; rightly. They will not obtain it until they are strong. They must obtain strength by co-operation and organisation, and expect no gratitude. There are other paths to power, but Tagore rejects them: Nietzschean amoralism and violence are self-defeating, for these breed counter-violence. On this he agreed with Mahatma Gandhi and Tolstoy; but he did not accept Tolstoy's angry simplifications, his self-isolating, anarchist attitude, nor the Mahatma's essentially (on this I am subject to correction) unpolitical, unsecular ends. Organisation for Tagore means, even when he is thinking in purely cultural terms, the acquisition of Western techniques; moreover it needs the building of bridges between the educated and the masses, for unless this is done there will be élitism, oligarchy, oppression, and in the end, as always, that great and angry cry from the masses for recognition, which precedes the disruption of the social texture and the revolutionary upheavals, which may be unavoidable and right where things have gone too far, but bring justice at appalling cost.

No. Strength must be sought rigorously, even ruthlessly, but by peaceful means. The English 'hurt our self-respect'.[2] They do so because we are paupers: when we are strong, they will be brothers. Till then, they will despise us and not fraternise. Only unto him who hath shall be given. Begging will achieve nothing except further loss of the sense of our own worth. So long as India is weak she will be bullied and ignored and humiliated. This is the note – we have heard it more than once in this century – that heralds the

[1] ibid.
[2] p. 137.

dawn of the awakening social self-consciousness of a class or a nation or a continent. Only those who respect themselves will be respected by others. Therefore we must emancipate ourselves, for nobody else will help us. Indeed, if they help us too much, we shall, to that extent, remain unfree. The English say that they have given us justice. This may be so, but what we ask for, what all men ask for, above everything else, is humanity, and 'to get mere justice . . . is like asking for bread and receiving a stone. The stone may be rare and precious, but it does not appease hunger.'[1] It will not be appeased until we awaken and set our own house in order. Internationalism is a noble ideal, but it can be achieved only when each link in the chain, that is, every nation, is strong enough to bear the required tension.

It is one of Tagore's greatest merits, and a sign of that direct vision and understanding of the real world with which poets are too seldom credited, that he understood this. He understood it at a time when there was much shallow internationalism in the air. Races, communities, nations were constantly urged to abolish their frontiers, destroy their distinctive attributes, cease from mutual strife, and combine into one great universal society. This was well enough as an ultimate ideal: it would fit a world where peoples were of approximately equal strength and status; but so long as vast inequalities existed, these sermons addressed to the weak – who are still seeking recognition, or even elementary justice, or the means of survival – had they been listened to, would merely (like the doctrines of free trade and disarmament) have achieved for them the unity which the kid achieved with the tiger when it was swallowed by it. Unity must be unity of equals, or at least of the not too unequal. Freedom for the pike is death to the carp. Those who are scattered, weak, humiliated, oppressed must first be collected, strengthened, liberated, given opportunity to grow and develop at least to some degree by their own natural resources, on their own soil, in their own languages, with unborrowed memories, and not wholly in perpetual debt, cultural or economic, to some outside benefactor.

This is the eternally valid element in nationalism, the true and only case for self-determination – the forging of the national links without which there is no great chain of all mankind. On either side of this stand the two great powerful and attractive fallacies: on

[1] ibid.

one side the hungry wolves, in the clothing of sincere internationalists, preaching to the sheep the evils of petty and destructive
small-power chauvinism; on the other the sick longing on the part
of the sheep to be swallowed by the wolves, to give up the unequal
struggle, to merge themselves in what they fondly imagine to be a
wider unity, and lose their identity and their past and their human
claims – the desire to declare themselves bankrupt, and be struck
off the roll, and lay down the burden of freedom and responsibility.

Tagore stood fast on the narrow causeway, and did not betray
his vision of the difficult truth. He condemned romantic over-
attachment to the past, what he called the tying of India to the past
'like a sacrificial goat tethered to a post',[1] and he accused men who
displayed it – they seemed to him reactionary – of not knowing
what true political freedom was, pointing out that it is from
English thinkers and English books that the very notion of
political liberty was derived. But against cosmopolitanism he
maintained that the English stood on their own feet, and so must
Indians. In 1917 he once more denounced the danger of 'leaving
everything to the unalterable will of the Master',[2] be he brahmin
or Englishman. He said, in effect, that India must get rid of the
English but must cling to the truths by which the English have
lived. India may be stabbed in the back by her own people in the
course of this – by terrorists or by appeasers. This, he thought,
would not be effective enough. Indians are numerous enough, he
maintained, the land is big enough, to enable them to afford to
press for their goals by peaceful pressure; and if they go on and on,
all the millions of them, they will win in the end. And so it turned
out to be.

It is, as I tried to say earlier, easier to exaggerate, to lean to an
extreme. Perhaps only those who exaggerate are remembered in the
history either of action or of thought. Plato and even Aristotle, the
writers of the Gospels, Machiavelli, Hobbes, Rousseau, Kant,
Hegel, Marx all exaggerated. It is easier to preach passionately to a
country that it should adopt some vast, revolutionary ideology,
and centralise and simplify and subordinate everything to a single
goal or a single man or a single party. It is not difficult to call for a
return to the past, to tell men to turn their backs on foreign devils,

[1] p. 186.
[2] p. 193.

to live solely on one's own resources, proud, independent, unconcerned. India has heard such voices. Tagore understood this, paid tribute to it, and resisted it. He seems to me, during his long and marvellously fruitful life, absorbed in concerns more creative than social or political activity, to have aimed to make only what was beautiful, and to say only what was true. This entailed self-discipline, and exceptional patience and integrity. In setting down his social and cultural and above all educational ideas, he tried to tell the complex truth without over-simplification, and to that extent was perhaps listened to the less. There is a remarkable saying by the American philosopher C. I. Lewis which I have always treasured. He said, 'There is no a priori reason for thinking that, when we discover the truth, it will prove interesting.' Nevertheless it is surely better for words to be true than interesting. I can understand well that a country, and especially a great country with a rich past, and perhaps an even richer future, can justly feel proud of one of the rarest of all gifts of nature, a poet of genius, who, even in moments of acute crisis, when he spoke to and for his countrymen, and they craved not for mere reason, but for signs and miracles, did not yield; but unswervingly told them only what he saw, only the truth.

# INDEX

*Compiled by Douglas Matthews*